IMAGE OF LOVE

SAM,

I PRAY THIS BOOK IS ENCOURAGING

TO YOUR FAITH AS YOU ARE INCREASINGLY

CONFORMED INTO THE IMAGE OF LOVE !

Jeffry W. Saunder.

GR 02

Jeffrey W. Sauers Jr.
Website: jeffreysauers.com
Contact the Author: imageoflovebook@jeffreysauers.com
Permission Requests: GRPpermissions@jeffreysauers.com

Cover design by Thomas McCormick
Editor: Christy Callahan, Professional Publishing Services

Printed in the United States of America
First Printing: February 2021

Published by Glory Revealed Publishing

ISBN 978-0-578-70280-3 (print)
ISBN 978-0-578-70281-0 (e-book)
Library of Congress Control Number: 2020924897

DISCLAIMER The contents of this book are the personal opinions of Jeffrey W. Sauers, Jr. and are not representative of the views of the U.S. Marine Corps, the DoD, or the U.S. Government.

To my family, friends, and fellow image bearers who know King Jesus and wait in joyful hope for his return.

IMAGE OF LOVE

Experiencing God's purpose for your life through the image in which you were created

J. W. SAUERS, JR.

Glory Revealed Publishing

Contents

Acknowledgments

First and foremost, I would like to thank my Lord and Savior, Jesus Christ. This book is but a shadow of the work of the Holy Spirit in my life, whether presented through me or the other members of Christ's church who are referenced. Through consistent prayer, as well as the perspectives offered by my spiritual mentor Colonel Chet Arnold (USMC Ret.), the Lord has blessed me with the fortitude, understanding, and appreciation of the work God has done in my own life over my five short years walking with him. I am forever grateful for the everlasting hope of Christ!

Thank you to my beautiful bride, Holly, whom I courted, was engaged to, and married, all within the process of writing this book. Your encouragement, insight, and patience have been invaluable and a true demonstration of Christ in you. I love you, my dear.

Thank you to my father, Jeff, and mother, Suzette, for the gift of life. You have truly demonstrated the love of God in your steadfast commitment in marriage and the way in which you raised your children. This book would not have been possible without the sacrificial love you have poured into my life. Thank you to my sister, Michelle, and my brother, Michael, for your unwavering love and support.

I am eternally grateful for the strong men and women of faith who have walked with me through difficult times and led me closer and closer to our Lord, Savior, and heart's delight—Jesus Christ.

Some of these incredible people include Mary Alice Corame, Steven and Joyce Pope, Luke and Kyle Dailey, Jessica Pope, Brother Don Alger, Jabari Thomas, Brian McGrath, Christopher Robinson, Jacob Sanborn, Mitch and Esther Hackleman, Rod and Noreen Carver, Jamie and Jody Vandiver, Chet and Michelle Arnold, Ricardo Wassmer, Spencer Michelson, Joseph Tom, Christopher Day, and many others. You are a true example of what Christ intends for his church. God bless all of you.

Thank you to all who gave their time and energy making this book a possibility including, but not limited to Chet Arnold, Christy Callahan, John Romero, Jacob Dominy, Mary Lou Coffman, and Michael Hopkins-Gross. Thank you to Thomas McCormick for the beautiful cover artwork.

Finally, thank you to you, the reader. The fact that you hold this book in your hands, either digitally or in print, is a testament of your hunger for Christ, and you truly inspire me to continue to sit at the feet of the King and learn from him. Many of the lessons I present in this book were taught to me by members of the church like yourself. I believe God has called me to share these lessons with you so we may all come to a better understanding of him. I am eternally grateful for everything the Lord and his people have taught me, and my prayer is that you find the lessons useful.

Foreword

My wife, Michelle, and I serve as the Officers' Christian Fellowship Field Staff Representatives in Pensacola, FL. As such, we have the privilege of meeting and coming alongside some of the finest young men and women in our nation. They come from the service academies and a variety of civilian education institutions and arrive here in Pensacola ready to jump into Naval Flight School training. It is here we met Jeff.

Jeff is one of those young men who does not half step. It was clear when we first met that he was serious about life, which meant not only was he working hard in flight school but he was working hard at pursuing God. Jeff is the reason we started using the excellent material found at conquerseries.com to work with folks struggling with pornography. As he mentions in the book, this was an issue for him, and he had no intentions of sitting around waiting for a solution!

His tenacity and his aggressive pursuit of truth are evident in this book. Jeff is not afraid to tackle some of the thorniest theological issues and attempt to wrestle them to the ground. He freely admits his lack of theological training, but he does an excellent job of dealing with some very complex issues. You may not agree with everything you read here, but you will be compelled to dig deeper into God's Word, which is exactly what Jeff has done and wants to motivate you to do as well.

It is a privilege to know Jeff and be a part of what God is doing in his life. Michelle and I were also privileged to spend time in premarital counseling with Jeff and his wife, Holly, and we look forward to continuing to be a part of their lives over the years. Second Chronicles 16:9 tells us "the eyes of the Lord roam throughout the earth, so that He may strongly support those whose heart is completely His" (NASB). Jeff and Holly have hearts that are completely His and you will see Jeff's heart in this book.

My prayer is that as you read this book you are strengthened in your faith and become ever more certain of your purpose here as God's image bearer. God bless you.

Chester "Chet" A. Arnold, Jr.
Colonel, USMC (Ret.)
Officers' Christian Fellowship
Field Staff Representative at Pensacola, FL

Preface

*God does all that he does to display his glory for the full
and lasting enjoyment of all who embrace Christ as their
highest treasure.*

John Piper

All too often Christian sermons and literature alike make mat-
ter-of-fact claims that a piece of theology or teaching is true
because "we are made in the image of God." Time and again this
doctrine of humanity's creation finds its way to the surface of biblical teaching, but it is seldom *the teaching* itself. For me, this is true
from an educational standpoint, but it is also continually reinforced
through my experience as a member of Christ's church. Whether I
am fellowshipping at a Bible study or conversing with a brother or
sister in Christ on spiritual truths, I often wonder why a doctrine
with such universal application is not at the forefront of Christian
understanding with regard to humanity and our purposes here on
Earth. Rather, the doctrine is most often supplemental to this understanding.

Precursory internet searches for literature solely focused on the
image of God left me empty-handed in my attempts to resolve this
issue. Sure, there are plenty of short writings and subsections of literature on the image of God, but I was hard-pressed to find a work

in which the sole purpose is to sharpen a Christian reader's understanding as to why the image of God is such a fundamental doctrine to the Christian faith and our worldview as believers.

As a result of fervent prayer, I was led to write this book detailing the importance and significance of the image of God as it relates to the purposes God has placed on humanity—more specifically, believers in Christ. Of course, this decision was not without its doubts. One of the biggest hurdles I had to overcome in the decision to author this book is the question, "Who am I to write on such things?" Ironically, the answer lies within the very doctrine that is the subject matter of this book—that I am an image bearer of God who has the same life purpose of any other image bearer of God. It is true that God often uses less than qualified individuals throughout Scripture to accomplish his will so that he may receive the glory. I would argue that I am a less than qualified individual to author this book. I hold no formal education in theology nor authority by the world's standards to use as a platform for this work. I am not in formal ministry, except that which I pursue through my life and career. I am a graduate of the United States Naval Academy with a Bachelor of Science in Oceanography, and I was an unbeliever during the entirety of my time in Annapolis, MD. In short, I am just a regular guy who loves the Lord.

If I were to sum up my spiritual journey with one story from the Bible, the parable of the prodigal son best suits it (Luke 15:11–32). Throughout my entire childhood and growing up as a young man, I chose to take the amazing gifts that God has blessed me with and use them for my own ends. In the circumstances of my life, I immersed myself as deeply as I could in the world, pursuing my glory, and I wanted nothing to do with the pursuit of God's glory. Eventually, there came a painful point when I had run out of my earthly inheritance. I was spiritually devoid of life, and I had but one choice in front of me—to humble myself before my heavenly Father.

Fortunately, he graciously accepted me with open arms. God chose to work in me and bring about radical transformation in my heart, mind, and spirit. The change is so radical that my friends back home with whom I have lost touch over the years may read this book out of respect for me and be in disbelief that my name is on the cover. I was a dead man walking when they last knew me five years ago, and I most definitely did not ponder faith with any measure of depth or thought. This book is the crescendo of God's testimony in my life up to this point, and it is all for his glory—a truly humbling example of God's image in me.

The change that both the resurrection power of Christ and the regenerative power of the Holy Spirit have brought to bear in my life is the foundation upon which I claim my credibility to write on the image of God. While it is not my intention to limit God's reach with this book, I originally decided to write it purely for the benefit of my friends, family, and anyone they share it with. I admire all those great theologians who have helped bring clarity to my faith, and my hope is that this book does the same for others.

Because I understand my fundamental limitations surrounding the teaching of theology, I have been careful to ensure that my work has been thoroughly reviewed for biblical accuracy. My greatest fear in educating people on the faith is that I might mislead my readers by teaching unsound doctrine (James 3:1). While God's Word is inerrant, my words are not. If anything has slipped past the multiple revisions this book has undergone, I offer my deepest apologies and implore you to reach out to me personally for correction—I am open to it and hope to receive it from you. You will notice that I have included many direct Scripture quotations so you may have an easier time reading and understanding the content. I have also included parenthetical Scripture references throughout the book. I implore you to look them up in your personal Bible as you come to them. Looking up the biblical references will greatly enhance your understanding of the material, the Scripture behind the claims that I make, and your overall appreciation for the image of God as it relates to who he is and who you are in his image.

I can promise you that there are benefits in reading the message that I have to share with you. As a captain in the United States Marine Corps that pilots AH-1Z attack helicopters, warfare is at the forefront of my mind on a daily basis—something that should be at the forefront of every believer's mind as we fight the spiritual war for our souls. I am blessed to have had many unique professional and personal experiences as a Christian that lives out his faith in an organization that is designed to manage violence and death on behalf of our nation. I hope that these intense experiences will provide you with engaging anecdotal evidence for the godly purposes that lie behind the image of God in my life, which are equally applicable to you as a fellow image bearer. If you do not already know, my prayer is that by the end of this book you will understand who God created you to be and understand the incredible value and importance that you have in God's kingdom (Jeremiah 29:11). I hope that you will be able to apply your new understanding of the image of the God of love to the specific circumstances and path in your life to have a fuller spiritual walk with our Lord and Savior, Jesus Christ. Please join me in prayer:

Heavenly Father of endless glory, thank you for every spiritual blessing that you have given us in Christ. Thank you for creating us in your image. Because of this great gift, you have given us the capacity to share in your eternal joy both now as we are increasingly conformed into your likeness, and forevermore in heaven. We admit that we have fallen short of your righteousness in every way, and we ask now for your forgiveness. We pray that in such forgiveness you empower us to wear the righteousness and humility of Christ in our day-to-day interactions with each other as we display your glorious image to the world. We ask that your kingdom come and that your will be done for our lives—that we know nothing more than Jesus Christ and him crucified. We ask that this book help us to understand your deep love for us as sons and daughters of the King and that it open the eyes of our hearts to better understand the purposes that you've had planned for us since eternity past. We love you, Lord, and look forward to the day that we stand face-to-face with you in your heavenly glory. Amen

Introduction

Human glory is not just found in what people were orig-
inally created to be—the image of dynamic God, spiritu-
ally functioning like him in the physical world. This glory
is displayed even more powerfully in what they are now
redeemed to be—the image of his Son, Jesus Christ.

Jeremy Pierre

Who are we and why are we here? Before you read any further, stop and think about whether you know the answer to this question. Many people spend their entire lives *searching* for the answer, but they never *live* with confidence that they know the answer. There is a big difference between searching for the answer and living according to it once it is found. Each of us has an innate longing for purpose, belonging, and accomplishment, and we will stop at nothing to satisfy these burning desires in our hearts. For people who are apart from Christ and deep in the world, these desires often manifest themselves through the tireless pursuit of things that hold no eternal significance, consistently falling short of quenching an unending thirst. The pursuit of wealth, success, fame, power, materialism, and legacy are made the highest callings for many, only to leave them feeling unfulfilled at the end of their lives. The believer in

Christ does not have these concerns. We never hold doubts as to why we were made, or what our ultimate purpose is. As Christians, we fully understand and are confident in the current state of the world and the direction in which we are headed. We have no need to chase meaningless idols or question the reasons for our existence. Or do we?

God is good, but in the present state of the world, life is tough. As Christians, we know that this temporal life on earth is the furthest we will ever be from the comforts and joys of heaven, and the closest we will ever be to the pain and misery of hell. So, what are we doing here? We live in a world that is the host to unimaginable suffering, and yet our eternity has been secured through our faith in Christ. When will it end? Crippling disease, malnourishment, oppression, and poverty are the unfortunate realities of everyday life for billions of people worldwide—many of whom are seemingly innocent and believe in the gospel of Christ. While we as a race have earned every bit of our suffering through our sin, the goodness of God demands a righteous justification for suffering to continue to abound for his redeemed people (Psalm 44:17–26).

Many of us may not suffer as much as others, but we all experience suffering to some degree because we are living in a broken world under the influence of evil in which we were not designed to live forever. In America, most of us do not have to spend our days worrying about where we will receive our next meal. However, the average person is not exactly spending all of their time pleasantly meditating on the joyful hope of heaven, because we still need to face the trials that come with living in this broken world. Whether we experience the harsh realities of the world on a big scale or small, the battleground of our everyday lives is bloody. Yet through it all, God is still good. Why do I have such confidence in that? How can any Christian have confidence in that? I believe it is because we understand that God has provided us with a *way* and a *purpose*. While both are important, the primary focus of this book is on the latter—our purpose.

Jesus Christ is the way maker for humanity. His blood that was shed on the cross and his subsequent resurrection from the dead bought for us what we could not buy for ourselves—salvation from our willful rebellion to God. This is our way to be reunited with God; it defines *whose we are* because we were bought at a price (1 Corinthians 6:20). Every Christian understands that, but does every Christian understand their purpose? Our purpose is the reason for our creation; it is that which defines us, drives us, and connects us. Our purpose is *who we are*. The Son of God had a purpose that was set before him by his Father in heaven. Many Christians mistakenly believe that the purpose of Christ's coming to earth was to save humanity. This is an incorrect and inexact view of God that leads only to an unbiblical understanding of God and ourselves. Instead, Christ came to glorify God. Saving humanity was only the means through which he accomplished that. As God himself, Christ can have no higher calling than to bring glory to his Father and to be glorified by his Father. He perfectly accomplished his purpose on earth, and the result was the salvation of the world. What an amazing feat of God that in bringing glory to himself, humanity is also brought to both freedom and life!

What does this mean for us as beings made in God's image? Does this mean we have God's purposes as well—to bring glory to God? How much different would our faith walks look if we *truly* understood that God did not come to save us, but to glorify himself? If we do not understand this, then we as Christians have an identity crisis. We understand *whose we are* by the work of Christ, but we do not understand *who we are*. Understanding whose we are puts us in a position of gratitude as we accept the gift of the cross, but it doesn't lead us to understand that Christ's purpose in life is also our purpose, because we were made in his image. We are called to the same radical abandonment to the gospel and dedication to achieving God's glory that Christ demonstrated throughout his life, death, and resurrection.

Our response as God's image bearers should not solely be gratitude for the work of Christ, but action as well (James 1:22; 1 Peter 1:15). As the Savior of the world, Christ had a mission to accomplish. Surely Christ demonstrated gratitude to God the Father. However, his purpose was not merely fulfilled by offering thanks to God, but rather in glorifying him with the entirety of his being. As followers of Christ we are called to do the same. Our purpose in this life is to bring glory to God because we were made in his image and likeness. Unfortunately, like those who are in the world, we often completely miss out on the purposes that God has for our lives because we do not understand the implications of being made in his image. We coast through our spiritual lives in "receive" mode, while our true calling is to be light and salt for a dark world by displaying God's glory in and through the image of Christ that each of us possess.

In fact, this was me for the first twenty-two years of my life. I missed out on my true purpose as God's image bearer as I sought to find purpose apart from him. Fortunately, the Lord has made my paths straight and I no longer question whether my life has purpose. I know for a fact that it does, because I have aligned it to God's purposes.

Words cannot perfectly convey the doctrine of the *imago Dei*. This book will only serve to get you headed in the right direction to evaluate your faith walk and understand the greater purpose you have as a Christian bearing the defining mark of God. If we do not understand what our true purpose is for the short amount of time we spend on this planet, then it will be very difficult to sift through the voices out there that will attempt to define our purpose for us. This might mean that we simply miss out on the good things that

God has planned for us because we spend our lives pursuing empty causes; but more importantly, it is impossible to fully understand who God is and possess a deep and abiding relationship with him if we believe lies about who we are as human beings. We were created to glorify him and to have an intimate knowledge of him. Fortunately for us, God left us an incredibly beautiful love letter defining that purpose and identity. In it are some of the most insightful depictions not only of the true destiny for our souls but also of the creative design he imprinted them with—his own image. As image bearers of God, we cannot afford to wait to live out our purpose in our spiritual walks. God has blessed us with his purposes, and he is in the people-saving and people-changing business, so let us go forward confidently and glorify him with our lives so that we may do the same!

I

Soul-Searching

*"You will seek me and find me when you seek me with all
your heart."*

Jeremiah 29:13

In a scene from the movie *Ghost*—one of the most memorable
from my childhood in the early 1990s—a banker, Sam Wheat, and
his lover, Molly Jensen, share a romantic evening in the comfort of
their home. With their hands interwoven, Sam (Patrick Swayze) and
Molly (Demi Moore) struggle to form a clay vase on a potter's wheel.
Despite the couple's total failure to create a beautiful masterpiece
together, they were deeply in love, and that is all that mattered. The
rest of the world could have faded away into nothingness and they
would have hardly taken notice. Their romance was euphoric. The
intense and passionate love between the two was matched in magnitude only by the abrupt and tragic murder of Sam in the following scene.

Unbeknownst to Molly in the wake of such a horrific tragedy, Sam remained on earth after his death, but as an invisible "ghost." Sam did not arbitrarily remain in this earthly purgatory though. His ghostly existence had a purpose. As the story unfolds, it becomes clear that Sam's coworker Carl (Tony Goldwyn) orchestrated Sam's murder through a nobody henchman because of his greed for Sam's wealth. However, Sam's murder was botched. Carl needed to finish his devious scheme to get the money, and the movie implies that Sam's purpose was to set things right for Molly and protect her from Carl. The means through which Sam accomplished his protective mission was Oda Mae Brown (Whoopi Goldberg), a local spiritual medium who possessed the unique gift of "hearing" spirits. Because of Oda Mae, Sam's invisible ghost, or "soul," was able to gain access to the physical world to make a difference and keep Molly safe.

At the culmination of an adventurous plot, the spiritual and physical worlds united for a moment. Sam and Molly were miraculously able to share one final gaze into each other's eyes before Sam could "follow the light" and walk off into what lies beyond this earthly realm. Of course, this happens only after Sam tied up the loose ends of this love story, subtly implying that making things right for Molly was the condition necessary for the clouds of "heaven" to open for him—that his efforts were satisfactory to gain admittance.

While I do enjoy the movie *Ghost* and the associated nostalgia from the countless Oda Mae Brown quotes, I cannot help notice how popular culture has shaped my subconscious beliefs on the spiritual world. As I look back on my faith walk, I often find myself needing to unlearn much of what I once believed about human spirituality. Because I unintentionally formed a spiritual worldview as an unbeliever, I must now intentionally unlearn and replace that incorrect worldview with the truth of God's Word as a believer. I imagine misguided spiritual understandings from popular culture are common for many believers in the twenty-first century.

Ghost is by no means a theological masterpiece, and Christianity is not necessarily the underlying belief system on which the producers based the storyline. Additionally, the plot did not seem to have a spiritual agenda; the movie was made purely for entertainment. However, I find it interesting that the entertainment value of the movie is rooted in the acceptance of common views on how the human spiritual identity operates. The movie resonates with viewers because to a certain extent they believe these assumptions to be true. We can believe in the disembodied spirits of the deceased that have *earned* their way into "paradise" with other disembodied beings. If viewers do not willingly suspend disbelief, the movie is nonsensical—a plot that cannot be understood or enjoyed, because there is no basis on which the viewer can be empathetic with Sam's plight.

I use the movie *Ghost* as an example because this is familiar to me, but the concept remains true in our society at large. Are these views on the human spiritual identity accurate? If they are correct, then through Sam, Hollywood has accurately portrayed the path that leads to everlasting life and we should all adopt this way of thinking. Sam achieved everlasting life because he accomplished his spiritual purpose of "doing good deeds," which was keeping him from heaven. Sam's actions made a difference and gained for him what all of us desire—everlasting life. Still, if these assumptions are true, then Hollywood has made Jesus out to be a liar in his claims about how one reaches everlasting life. The gravity of Christ's words and the rest of Scripture have been watered down to the point where we will start to believe that our actions make a difference in our personal salvation—that everlasting life is attainable for anyone who "lives a good life" and "does good deeds."

Consider these Scriptures:

Jesus answered, "I am the way and the truth and the life. No one comes to the Father except through me."

John 14:6

"Enter through the narrow gate. For wide is the gate and broad is that road that leads to destruction, and many enter through it. But small is the gate and narrow the road that leads to life, and only a few find it."

Matthew 7:13–14

For it is by grace you have been saved, through faith—and this is not from yourselves, it is the gift of God—not by works, so that no one can boast.

Ephesians 2:8–9

Conversely, if we have erred by believing these cultural claims on human spirituality, and Jesus' words convey truth, then as Christians we must be very careful to guard our hearts (Proverbs 4:23). Jesus says that "only a few find it," when he refers to attaining everlasting life. If we are not careful, we could be in danger of believing views that are contrary to Scripture as we grow in our understanding of our spiritual identity. Our self-image will guide the way we think, act, and react to the gospel of Christ. If we believe the wrong things about ourselves, we will live our lives pursuing the wrong things. As a consequence of incorrect understanding, both our personal salvation and our chance of making real and fruitful contributions to God's kingdom are at stake.

No one is born with a mature spiritual self-awareness. Because of our sin nature, we have all been alienated from God since birth (Romans 3:23), and consequently no one starts life with a correct understanding of God or self (Matthew 11:27). We must spend time soul-searching to learn who God is and who we are as his creation in a godless world that largely does not know him but has much to say about him and our own identity (John 14:15–21).

All the understanding we possess, spiritual or other, is limited by the information that we allow into our life to inform our worldview and sense of reality. Our worldview as Christians is incredibly important and is directly tied to how we understand ourselves to fit into God's universe. Misinformation could preclude believers in Christ from forming a consistent worldview, and an inconsistent worldview could preclude us from living out our spiritual calling and purpose. This misinformation includes information that we passively acquire from the world around us.

* * *

What Is a Christian "Worldview"?

Christian author Gregory Koukl describes a person's worldview as a puzzle set. As with every puzzle, there is a picture on the box that depicts the finished product. Without such a picture, the person assembling the puzzle is left to wander aimlessly into perfection with no end goal in sight. The complete and consistent "Christian worldview" is the picture on the box of this puzzle. Other religious or secular worldviews are different puzzle sets that consist of different-sized and different-colored puzzle pieces by which different pictures are formed. Pieces from these sets will not help us to complete a "Christian worldview" puzzle, because the picture will not make any sense and their pieces will not fit. The only way the Christian worldview puzzle can be completed is by using the pieces that are specifically meant for the Christian puzzle.[1] The Christian puzzle pieces are truths from God's Word and sound biblical teaching. They cannot come from the puzzle sets of our current societal worldviews surrounding spirituality—these will not fit our Christian puzzle and offer nothing but inconsistency.

To have a proper Christian worldview, we as Christians must have a proper understanding of who we are as God's created spiritual beings. Our understanding of ourselves provides the corner pieces to our worldview puzzle—the starting point in our soul-searching. For the same reason that starting a puzzle with the corner pieces makes completing a puzzle easier, beginning our discussion of the image of God is made easier by discussing our spiritual identity. As Christians, we come to a properly informed and consistent understanding of our spirituality only as our relationship with Christ deepens throughout our lives through abiding in the Spirit of God and studying his Word. This is how we can fill in the gaps in our own puzzles.

Ask yourself this question: "Can I quote more movies or more Bible verses?" If the answer is the former, that may be an indication of a worldview that is heavily influenced by popular culture rather than one based on God's Word. Popular culture seems to believe in a spiritual schema in which humans possess a disembodied soul that experiences the ultimate spiritual fulfillment and access to life after death through passionate love and goodwill to our fellow man. All you must do is scroll through Netflix or Facebook or pick up the first tabloid you notice in the checkout line at the grocery store to agree with this. Have we been duped into this incorrect thinking along with the rest of the world? The Bible has much to say about humanity's spiritual identity and purpose, and this line of thinking is contrary to what it says.

Passionate love and goodwill are surely good things when seen through the proper lens, but are they or any other purposes we can conceive (other than God's glory) the end state of humanity's spirituality? Are they *God's purpose* for creating us, or the *purpose we want* for ourselves? In *Ghost*, Sam's spiritual purpose seemed to be fulfilled when he went to heaven after his goodwill and love reached their climax on earth.

In God's Word, however, we learn that heaven operates according to God's rules. There is no amount of goodwill or passionate love that Sam, or any of us, can give that could earn us entry into heaven (Titus 3:5; Ephesians 2:8–9). Heaven is not a place where the souls of those who have lived good lives go after they have accomplished what they deem their purpose in life. Heaven is the place where only believers in Christ will go, but not because of anything we do. It is because Jesus Christ accomplished his purpose of bringing heaven to us. He took our sin upon himself when he endured the full wrath of God's divine justice on the cross, so that we may have the life that he has when we are with him one day soon in heaven.

However, heaven is not the far-off, unimaginable realm as one might think. Heaven is a real place we will one day inhabit and continue to live out our God-given spiritual purposes, but it is also a place we can experience to a degree in the here and now. To the believer in Christ, heaven was first experienced by us when God's presence in the form of the Holy Spirit made his dwelling within us at the moment of our salvation (Ephesians 1:13). To be in heaven is to be in God's glorious presence, except in a magnificently beautiful, sinless, and incorruptible kingdom where all peoples are living and operating in harmony under one ruler, Jesus Christ. We experience a degree of it in the here and now as we live holy lives on earth through the indwelling of God's Holy Spirit and as we exercise the original design for our souls that God has given us as ambassadors for Christ (2 Corinthians 5:20). This should prompt us as believers to desire nothing more than to be in heaven and to live accordingly (Philippians 1:23). If we embraced our eternal destiny with clear eyes and pure hearts, then our reaction at the end of the movie *Ghost* would more likely be, "Cool story, but I can't wait to see the sequel of Sam living out his true purpose in heaven, with the star of the movie being Jesus Christ!"

* * *

Objective Truth or Spiritual Mysticism?

What exactly is a soul? The word "soul" alone is often used in many different contexts, which leads to confusion regarding a proper definition. The word is often used to refer to things that nourish the spiritual and emotional sides of oneself. Certain foods or music are claimed to be edifying to the soul. One of the most popular series of self-help books in the past few decades is entitled Chicken Soup for the Soul. It has sold more than five-hundred million copies worldwide, and the author set a record in the *Guinness Book of World Records* for having the most titles on the *New York Times* Best-Seller List at the same time. Another common use for the word "soul" is to reference that special someone who was specifically created to be our unique "soulmate," and coincidentally grew up in a similar zip code in a world of nearly eight billion people.

What is the true definition of a soul, and do we understand the implications of our own spiritual identity? Our culture seems to understand the word "soul" to be nothing more than an expression of the natural feelings, inclinations, or romantic sides to a person. Is this true?

Before a "soul" can be accurately defined, we must recognize that a spiritual being cannot operate in a world that does not possess absolute spiritual truth. Absolute truth is defined as universal, inflexible, and unalterable facts about reality. When discussing spirituality and world religions, it is logically impossible for all religions to make such divergent claims on the reality of the universe and for all of them to be true at the same time. How can we have any confidence in defining who we are as spiritual beings without a singular truth for our souls to operate within, and why should we hold confidence that the Bible is this truth?

A common belief today is, "All paths to God are equally valid." This line of reasoning is logically impossible. Most world religions attempt to explain an absolute spiritual truth through various lenses, but their claims all lead to different destinations. Going to heaven to have everlasting life with the God of Christianity is doctrinally and definitively not the same as reaching Nirvana in the Hindu faith. If Hinduism purports a cycle of reincarnation until one reaches a state of enlightenment (referred to as Nirvana, or moksha) and Christianity claims the ultimate fate of a soul is heaven or hell on the basis of accepting Christ, it is unreasonable to believe that a spiritual world exists that could accommodate both beliefs as absolute truth.

As previously mentioned, the message of Christianity is that we are saved by grace alone through our faith in Christ. There is *nothing we can do* to earn our salvation; it is the free gift of God (Ephesians 2:8–9). Meanwhile, the Buddha claims that one can reach Nirvana only after they have *worked* off all their bad karma from their current and previous lives. Who is right? The two views cannot both be true at the same time. They are contradictory in their requirements and absolute in their consequences.

If any single faith is true, then all others must be equally untrue, or else their absolute claims on the reality of the universe cease to be true at all—they are relative. Yet truth in the purest sense of the word is not relative. It does not change depending on how someone feels about it or whether they choose to believe it or not. If I choose to not accept the law of gravity on earth as truth and jump off a ten-story building, gravity will still reign true—I would almost surely die. Spiritual truth works the same way. Therefore, all claims regarding humanity's spiritual identity must be only as reliable as their doctrine is truthful. This leads to a deeper issue in our understanding of the human spiritual identity. How can we know which theological claims are true and which are heresy?

The issue in the understanding of humanity as spiritual beings that operate in the physical world is that the beliefs of other religions besides Judeo-Christianity cannot be tested in the context in which their scriptures were written. What do I mean by this? Faith in any religious system must be accompanied by objective criteria for examining the reliability of its doctrine. Subjective experience is insufficient grounds for claiming the doctrine of a particular faith to be objective truth—this is called spiritual mysticism.

Interestingly, many world religions and cults have historical figures who were real people who walked the earth, such as the Buddha, Mohammed, Joseph Smith, and Jesus of Nazareth. The existence of these individuals is a truth that can be objectively backed up with historical documentation—one of many objective criteria to test the reliability of religious doctrine. It is reasonable for a person to accept the existence of these individuals, and if they deny that these people ever existed, then they must first deny the legitimate processes by which historical evidence is accepted as reliable and therefore also deny all historical accounts as reliable.

The same methods could be applied to reconciling the Christian Scriptures with science by comparing claims to observable scientific laws in the universe.[2] Even further, the same could be applied to experiencing the spiritual truths of Christian doctrine. The issue of objective truth arises when one person's subjective experience is claimed to be "truth" with no legitimate way for another person to come to that same conclusion other than believing that what they claim is true. However, the real difference between the founders of different faiths and the founder of Christianity is the fact that only Jesus claimed to be God. He did not interpret subjective spiritual revelation to provide his own understanding of humanity; he claimed that *he himself is the spiritual revelation* of the ultimate truth (John 14:6) and that *he is the God* who created the universe and everyone in it (John 1:3,10; 1 Corinthians 8:6; Colossians 1:16; Hebrews 1:2). His resurrection from the dead—proof of the veracity of the Christian message and the assurance that Jesus was telling the truth about himself—was corroborated not only by hundreds of witnesses at the time of its occurrence, but also by secular historians from that period such as Josephus and Tacitus, who had nothing to gain from documenting the events surrounding the life, death, and resurrection of Jesus, but much to lose in terms of their own credibility.[3]

Hinduism, Buddhism, Islam, other world religions, and cults such as Mormonism offer no such objective criteria to substantiate their claims as objective truth. They cannot test their doctrine through scientific, historical, or experiential means in the way Christianity can be tested. They can claim from historical evidence that the founders of their faith existed at a point in time, but that is the end of the road. How would one go about scientifically, historically, or experientially proving the doctrine of reincarnation? Objective truth must be rooted in that which is reasonably understandable and testable, or there is no reason to believe such "truths" even exist.

For this reason, I hold confidence in the God of Christianity to accurately define the human spiritual identity, and this book will use the Bible as the authority on the matter. As human beings who are made in the image of God, our spirituality is more than a ghost that awaits freedom from this carnal prison, and it is far greater than the world around us would have us believe. We are beautifully designed beings who possess physicality and spirituality that were not originally designed to be operated in isolation of each other; they cannot operate in isolation of each other. Without a firm understanding of the connection between our souls and bodies, we as Christians cannot begin to understand the implications of being made in God's image—for our ultimate purpose lies within the image and is expressed through the connection of them.

* * *

Practice Makes Purpose

I am extremely blessed in the career God has given me. As an attack helicopter pilot for the United States Marine Corps, I get to work with some of the brightest and most capable people in our nation. Flying attack aircraft has given me incredible experiences I never could have imagined possible. However, they come at a cost. Despite what Hollywood may portray in the movie *Top Gun*, the profession of military aviation is not just skinny jeans and beach volleyball. Sitting at a desk studying and planning for hours each day is a more accurate job description.

Each combat pilot must memorize an incredible amount of information and recall that information on a moment's notice. Our very survival depends on it! To even get an aircraft off the ground, we must have an in-depth knowledge of the fundamentals of aviation and aerodynamics. We must know every intricate detail about the hydraulic, oil, electrical, flight control, engine, powertrain, avionics, fuel, communication, navigation, and tactical systems of the aircraft to successfully diagnose problems when in flight. From these systems, Emergency Procedures (EPs) have been developed for actions that must be taken immediately in the event the aircraft decides it is done flying before the pilot is. These procedures are accomplished to land the aircraft safely or keep the aircraft in the air in the event landing is not an option, such as over the ocean or in a combat zone.

Once we have mastered those elements of flying, we have reached the starting point of the things we need to know to "fight" with the aircraft. We must know everything about each weapon system, its capabilities, and the tactics to employ them. We must know the threat they are employed against to assess their effectiveness, as well as the counter-tactics to not be shot down by such a threat. We must know how to fight in every possible mission set in which our aircraft could take part. The list goes on and on. Military aviation is a unique career because the fast pace at which situations change while flying necessitates that pilots truly know and understand their trade. The life-and-death consequences that result from anything short of complete preparation and attention to detail place a remarkable premium on technical expertise. As I have matured as an aviator, however, I realize that what matters most is not how much I know about aviation, but how much this knowledge has changed the way I think, act, and react to the fast-paced and dangerous environments in which a pilot operates.

Knowing the information is important, but the information itself is not what saves a pilot when he or she is placed in a precarious situation; it is the cognitive and qualitative capabilities that are produced from careful study, meditation, and training that save the pilots and aircrew. A good pilot is not one who flies well; they are one who thinks well. Knowing the systems within our aircraft or the capabilities of the enemy is useful only so long as a pilot can make sound decisions to save lives or accomplish the mission. Without the ability to make such decisions from an intentionally developed mind, there is no decisive victory on the battlefield. Good combat pilots have a well-developed "aviator worldview" that guides all their thinking and actions, whether they are planning a mission or in the middle of one.

Likewise, in our spiritual walks, our entire worldview needs to be something we have intentionally developed from careful study, meditation, and training in God's Word. Are we as Christians planting God's Word deep in our souls to inform our spiritual disposition to the world in the same way pilots must plant the information of their profession firmly in their minds to develop their ability to fly in combat?

God's purpose for our lives is our truest profession and calling as believers (Ephesians 4:1). We are operating in a fast-paced and ever-changing world in which we are at war with the spiritual forces of evil (Ephesians 6:12). We must be firmly rooted in God's eternal truths, which do not change. In this way, we remain grounded in God's will and calling for our lives as the world around us continues to abound in wickedness.

> Let the peace of Christ rule in your hearts, since as members of one body you were called to peace. And be thankful. Let the message of Christ *dwell among you richly* as you teach and admonish one another with all wisdom through psalms, hymns, and songs *from the Spirit*, singing to God with gratitude in your hearts.
>
> *Colossians 3:14, emphasis added*

I am grateful for the spiritual lessons God has taught me throughout my career. The requirements of my profession have enlightened me on the tough work required to transform the mind into something entirely new. While our sanctification as believers is primarily the work of the Holy Spirit, we have a role to play as well. The Spirit of God is our "instructor pilot" who guides us and teaches us in all things. However, it is we who must put in the effort. God has gifted all of us with the opportunity to be transformed into his likeness. We have the responsibility to use this gift fruitfully by persistently developing in ourselves the cognitive and qualitative attributes of his Son. If we fail to do so, then what are we doing here? We are wasting the precious years that God has given us to prepare for eternity in heaven and to make his name known by showing the world his image in us. If we have accepted the gift of eternal life provided through Christ, then we must be made new. If we have not accepted it, we will remain as we are—dead in our sin and spiritually immature image bearers of God.

Through consistent study and meditation on God's Word, our entire worldview is conformed to one that better approximates the worldview of Christ. We as believers should seek to see the world as Christ does if we desire to live out our true purpose in this life. As the Marine Corps has forged me into a pilot, the Holy Spirit works in and through us to transform our thinking as we are forged into Christlikeness.

> Do not conform to the pattern of this world, but be
> transformed by the renewing of your mind.
>
> *Romans 12:2*

Even two thousand years after the resurrection of Christ, science is beginning to catch up to the ancient, flawless, and eternal truths of God's Word (Proverbs 30:5) and also beginning to prove the power of the Holy Spirit in the renewal of our minds as presented by the apostle Paul in Romans. Renewing the mind is a lifelong process that was designed by God, and scientific discovery as of late has proven that the brain is fully malleable throughout the entirety of a person's life because of an ability called neuroplasticity.[4] This means that it is never too late to grow in Christ.

As a result of focused effort in learning a new skill or material, the brain continually creates and reorganizes synaptic connections, effectively creating an entirely new way of thinking or capability. This means that no matter a person's age, their mind possesses the ability to change. "Neurons that fire together, wire together," is a phrase describing neuroplasticity that was coined by the late Donald Hebb in 1949 upon which Hebb's Law was later developed.[5] In the same way that someone can create "muscle memory" for driving a car with a standard transmission, spending focused energy reading, studying, meditating, and praying over God's Word will create an entirely new way of life and thought for a Christian. Our minds will slowly begin to rewire themselves to think according to the truth of God's Word. As we do this day in and day out, we will begin to see ourselves in light of the greater plan God has for our life.

As indicated in Romans 12, the pattern of this world is to define our own purpose and identity and to use the world's wisdom to inform our worldview and understanding of ourselves. We are to plan our own paths in life and be "the captain of our souls," as the famous poem "Invictus" says. As Christians, we are called to ignore these patterns of the world and instead to experience a radical transformation in our lives through renewing the mind with the purifying and life-giving truth of God's Word and the help of his Holy Spirit.

Whether we are developing a new skill or changing our worldview by coming to a correct understanding of God, it takes hard work to renew the mind. However, the consequences of indifference and laziness only hurt our individual faith walks. For example, have you ever read stories in the New Testament where Jesus says or does things that do not make a lot of sense in the context of the situation? If you are like me and are not a Bible scholar, you know exactly what I am talking about—those stories that make you scratch your head because you have no idea why Jesus responds to situations in seemingly arbitrary ways. The truth of the matter is that nothing Jesus does is arbitrary. As both God and man, Jesus is the most calculated human who has ever walked the earth. Everything he does and says is intentional. It is his nature as God and man to be so precise. His worldview encompasses the totality of everything; he is the only completely informed person. Therefore, his words and actions can never be understood in a vacuum. As the one who is the truth (John 14:6), his words must be consistent with every other word in the Bible.

To Christians who are insensitive to God's Word because they are indifferent or have not continually immersed themselves in it, these stories are typically misunderstood. To Christians who have developed sensitivity through careful practice in reading God's Word, however, Jesus' words and actions make more sense in the context of the entire canon of Scripture, not solely in the context of the story we are reading. The Bible as a whole is the complete Word of God, and it is this completeness itself that enables us to understand God correctly. Every sentence is intricately and beautifully tied to and dependent on the others from Genesis to Revelation. The Old Testament makes Jesus intelligible when we read about him in the New Testament, and the New Testament makes the prophecies of the Old Testament intelligible when our eyes are opened to the truth that Jesus is the fulfillment of them.

Without the Old Testament, Christ has no platform through which to reveal himself. He has no mold in which he fits and can be consistent with to prove that he is the promised Messiah. God the Father used the Old Testament Scriptures to prepare the way for God the Son in the New Testament (1 Peter 1:10–11). Likewise, Jesus, as revealed by the New Testament, is logically required to make the Old Testament intelligible. Without Jesus, the Old Testament is only a bunch of prophecies and cliff-hangers that would forever be awaiting closure. In Christ, God is made known to humanity through the completeness of the Bible.

As the author of our faith, Christ possesses an understanding and worldview that is consistent with the *entirety of Scripture* (Genesis to Revelation), rather than the world's current understanding of God from one specific time and place. The people in Jesus' day only had half of the Bible! Understandably, his actions were contrary to the patterns of the world around him—he transcends all cyclical patterns of human understanding and is the likeness in which all peoples from every nation and generation are to be transformed. It is we who misunderstand God, not Christ—for Christ is God. Even though the people of biblical times did not have the full revelation of God, the condition of the human heart has not changed through the ages. As sinful human beings, we are blinded to God the Father's purposes because of our sin. Therefore, when his Son acts according to the true purposes of the Father and his actions do not meet our expectations, we are naturally confused. Only as our minds are transformed into the mind of Christ through the indwelling of the Holy Spirit and careful study of God's Word are we able to begin to understand him or his ways.

Like ourselves when we were spiritually immature, those around Jesus were also confused when he acted. The difference is that they lived in a time when oral tradition necessitated rote memorization of the Scriptures. Without the convenience of a printing press or the ubiquity of technology in which everyone owned a personal copy of the Holy Scriptures, they had no choice. They had to know the Scriptures and take care in preserving their integrity or lose them forever. Unlike us, the people who studied the Scriptures truly knew them; they had the *information*, but they lacked *understanding* because it was not planted deep into their souls with the help of the Holy Spirit. Their minds had not yet experienced the radical transformation that Christ intended for them. As Christians who have the Holy Spirit within us, we should not have this issue. It is better to plant a little bit of God's Word deep down into our souls with the help of the Holy Spirit than to know all of it at face value. We need only ask God with sincerity in prayer for him to work within us, and he is faithful to provide us with that which we seek (Matthew 7:7).

However, we cannot merely ask for understanding without doing our part. Understanding Scripture requires more than a surface-level reading of the entirety of God's Word. It requires a devotion even to the point of understanding the differences in way of life and thought. As a young believer, I often failed to disassociate the words of Christ from my limited worldview as a twenty-first-century American and connect them to the worldview of someone who possessed an incredible understanding of the bigger picture of God's plan. Christ had such a worldview. How many of us often fall prey to this common mistake when we read our Bibles? This is evident every time we ignore parts of the Bible because we think they do not apply to us in this day and age. The Bible is both living and timeless, and therefore always has applicability to life. The reason that we often miss truths that we could apply to our lives in the twenty-first century is because we fail to understand the cultural and temporal differences of the time. If we understood these, the lessons that Scripture teaches could be extracted and applied to life today.

Our Western perspective alone presents limitations to our understanding. We often approach reading our Bibles with the determination that we are going to "figure God out." That is what we do as Western thinkers—we remain skeptics until the evidence proves to us beyond a reasonable doubt of the truth of something. And yet, is the Bible literal or figurative for certain stories? The answer is *yes*. Is the Bible written for Easterners or Westerners? The answer is *yes*. Is the Bible a book focused on revealing to us a head knowledge of God, or a book focused on showing us the way to develop a relationship with him? The answer is *yes*. Do we enter relationships with other human beings in a purely academic way—evaluating each other's worth and weighing all the facts before we let someone into our hearts? Or is it a blend of both evaluation, trust, and personal change? The answer is *yes*. Let's not forget this as we pursue an understanding and relationship with the God of the universe.

The important thing to remember is that we have limitations when we approach the Bible. We must pray to God to reveal to us what is important for our understanding and adoration of him because knowing and glorifying him is ultimately what life is about. We must commit ourselves as believers to approaching the Bible with the understanding that the Word of God has infinite lessons to be learned and applied to our lives. The Bible is the revelation of the infinite God to humanity, so we should expect nothing less. If we are ever to understand God or ourselves, we must see Scripture as both a telescope and a mirror. We must use the Bible to bring the infinite God into focus as a telescope brings the vastness of outer space into focus. In doing so, we can see the finer details of God's nature with clarity. As we learn to better understand God, we can use the Bible as more than a telescope; we can use it as a mirror to our souls. In the same way that we use literal mirrors to point out superficial imperfections, the Bible is a mirror that points out deep imperfections of the soul as we compare ourselves to God's image. As we continue soul-searching in life, our goal should be to look in the mirror each day and see less of the world in ourselves, and more of Christ.

> And we all, who with unveiled faces contemplate the Lord's glory, are being transformed into his image with ever-increasing glory, which comes from the Lord, who is the Spirit.
>
> *2 Corinthians 3:18*

* * *

Who Am I?

In the most basic sense, who or what is a human being? As existential as this question is, it is immensely important regarding our response to the gospel of Christ. Without an accurate biblical understanding, our ability to live out our God-given purpose in this life will be severely hamstrung. As human beings, we were designed thoughtfully and intentionally (Psalm 139:13–14). However, where are we to look in the Bible for the definition of humanity and the intentions that God has for us? Put another way, what is the most complete description of a human in the Bible?

It does us no good to attempt to define ourselves in our current condition. In this fallen world, we are not complete. Due to our sin, we are neither humanity as originally designed by God, nor are we humans as intended by God for eternity in heaven. We are somewhere in between, and in our sinful state we are somewhat less than fully human. But fear not! Christ has won back our humanity, and we will once again possess it in heaven. Not only that, but we will possess even greater humanity than we had in the garden of Eden. While later chapters of this book will discuss more fully the implications of how the current state of the world is essential in possessing the full image of God, let us turn to the front of our Bibles to see what humanity was created to be.

> Then the Lord God *formed a man* from the dust of
> the ground and breathed into his nostrils the *breath*
> *of life* [*rûach*], and the man became a *living* [*nephesh*]
> being.
>
> *Genesis 2:7, emphasis added*

In the creation account, God forms a physical, lifeless body of a human. However, the man was not complete having only a physical body. He became a human being only after God breathed his *rûach* (Hebrew word transliterated as "breath of life" or "spirit") into him.[6] With this breath of life, man became a *nephesh* (Hebrew word commonly transliterated as "soul").[7] From this single verse in Genesis, we are provided with a few truths. The first is that a human's identity is robust. There is more to our identity than simply a body. However, I do not believe it is entirely useful to discuss how many "parts" make up a human when it comes to our spiritual purpose. While it is an interesting discussion, I hope not to divide my readers by stating my beliefs on understanding humans as a trichotomy (body, soul, and spirit), a dichotomy (body and soul), or a monism (the body and soul are the same). Regardless of doctrinal beliefs, Scripture is clear that humans possess both physicality and spirituality. Depending on the context in which they are used, they are sometimes mutually exclusive from the other while at other times they operate together.

It is more useful to examine how Scripture focuses on the unity of all aspects of humanity. The Hebrew word for "soul," *nephesh*, is a great example of this. Much like homonyms in the English language, the original manuscripts of the Bible used *nephesh* as a homonym. In our English translations, we do not notice how diverse this word is because *nephesh* translates into 27 different English words. The complexity of the word is lost in translation. Occurring 754 times in the Old Testament, nephesh is only translated as the English word "soul" 72 times.[8] The other 90 percent of the time that the word is used we are fully unaware that the original language of the Bible was trying to convey the broad meaning of the human identity. Consider the following verses:

> The Lord is my Shepherd, I lack nothing. He makes me lie down in green pastures, he leads me beside quiet waters, he refreshes my *soul* [*nephesh*].
> *Psalm 23:1–3, emphasis added*

> Save me, O God, for the waters have come up to my *neck* [*nephesh*].
> *Psalm 69:1, emphasis added*

> The mother of seven will grow faint and breathe her *last* [*nephesh*].
> *Jeremiah 15:9, emphasis added*

In David's famous Psalm 23, he exclaims that the Lord refreshes his soul in a purely spiritual sense. David is referring to the *immaterial* aspect of humanity that differentiates us from other creatures. However, in Psalm 69 David uses the same word in reference to his literal neck as a metaphor for the spiritual sea of trouble in which he is fighting to keep his head above water. The neck is the passageway through which we breathe, drink, and eat. Therefore, the neck is a vital part of the operation of our bodies. David abstracts his *physical* neck (*nephesh*) to his entire spiritual life in the way the English language abstracts the heart from the crucial organ that pumps our blood, to the symbol of love and affection. Without our neck, our physical bodies can do nothing. Additionally, in Jeremiah we see a story of a woman who is dying, and *nephesh* is used to refer to the literal *life* that leaves her with her last breath (*nephesh*). Three uses of the same Hebrew word, and all of them are used in different contexts. What does all this mean?

The second truth that we learn from the Genesis account of the creation of humanity is that we were created to operate as one complete being—body, soul, and life united as one. In the same way *nephesh* is one word that encompasses all parts of a human, so the human spiritual identity does as well. This is the complete picture of a human. The human "life" is not spirituality operating on its own program apart from the physical body. Conversely, the physical body is not to be ignored and mistreated simply because it is spiritually nourished (1 Corinthians 6:19–20). Rather, we should focus on what we are to do with all aspects of our humanity as stated in 2 Corinthians 7:1.

> Therefore, since we have these promises, dear friends, let us purify ourselves from everything that contaminates *body* and *spirit*, perfecting holiness out of reverence for God.
>
> *2 Corinthians 7:1, emphasis added*

Much like the unity of body and soul that humanity possessed from the garden of Eden, at the return of Christ we will possess incorruptible perfected bodies and souls that are eternally free from the devastating effects of sin. As we currently exist, this is not the case. Before we had faith in Christ, our souls were dead in our sin. If we have faith in Christ, Scripture declares us holy because we spiritually wear the righteousness of Christ (Colossians 3:12). As righteous as our souls are because of the work of Christ, we still have a problem. Our mortal bodies are bound to experience physical death. This is a reality of living in a broken world since humanity was cast out of the garden. In Christ, we are spiritually born again (John 3:3–7). We now presently await the redemption of our bodies as we are conformed more and more into the image of God. The current bodies that we possess are not compatible with heaven, so we must await their redemption.

> That the creation itself will be liberated from its bondage to decay and brought into the freedom and glory of the children of God. We know that the whole creation has been groaning as in the pains of childbirth right up to the present time. Not only so, but we ourselves, who have the first fruits of the Spirit, groan inwardly as we wait eagerly for our adoption to sonship, the redemption of our bodies.
>
> *Romans 8:21–23*

There is a purpose behind us having a soul that has been made right with God, while also remaining in this dying earthly body (2 Corinthians 4:16); this purpose was fashioned for us by God himself (5:1–10). God intentionally removed humanity from the garden, preventing them from eating from the Tree of Life so they might experience physical death (Genesis 3:22–23). In his mercy, God allows our bodies that are tainted with disease, disability, and fragility to die, rather than allowing us to live forever in them.

Later chapters will explore these truths. For now, all that is important to understand is that our purpose as God's greatest creation is best lived out when we possess a proper understanding of who we are as human beings. If we are going to understand the image of God at all, we must understand it from the perspective that when the image is complete in us, it will be the image of God on a perfect, complete human being—not a disembodied soul, in a dying body, or anything else but a perfected human that eternally lives and functions as we were designed. Randy Alcorn describes it best in his book *Heaven*:

> When God sent Jesus to die, it was for our bodies as well as our spirits. He came to redeem not just the "breath of life" (spirit) but also "the dust of the ground" (body). When we die, it isn't that our real self goes to the present heaven and our fake self goes to the grave; it's that part of us goes to the present heaven and part of us goes to the grave while we await our bodily resurrection. We will never be all that God intended for us to be until the body and the spirit are again joined in resurrection.[9]

Our spiritual purpose of glorifying God while on this earth is the starting point of this transition to perfection. The fullness of this transition will be realized in heaven, so we should focus our gaze on our true and eternal reward that we will enjoy and qualitatively be like forever—Jesus Christ. From this understanding, we can now move on from soul-searching to academically discuss what is meant when we hear that humanity was made in "the image of God."

QUESTIONS FOR REFLECTION AND DISCUSSION

What is the source of your understanding of your faith? Was it intentionally developed through careful study of God's Word, unintentionally by the world around you, or other?

What cultural biases do you have with respect to faith, and how have they affected your Christian worldview? Do you have any "puzzle pieces" that are not Christian in nature?

Do you believe in ultimate truth? If so, do you believe that the Bible is the source for ultimate truth? How does this belief manifest itself in your life? Do you approach every circumstance through the lens of Scripture?

In your life, are there any disciplines in which you put considerable time and effort? How have they shaped you into the person you are today? Does your mind think differently because of them? If so, do you consistently study, meditate, and pray over God's Word with the same vigor you put into other disciplines to renew your mind for Christ?

Before you read this chapter, what did you believe about the human soul? What was the original design of the human soul? What is the final design of the human soul? How do both of those differ from the current state of the human soul and what does this mean for us?

2

Imago Dei

Then God said, "Let us make mankind in our image, in our likeness, so that they may rule over the fish in the sea and the birds in the sky, over the livestock and all the wild animals, and over all the creatures that move along the ground." So God created mankind in his own image, in the image of God he created them; male and female he created them. God blessed them and said to them, "Be fruitful and increase in number; fill the earth and subdue it. Rule over the fish in the sea and the birds in the sky and over every living creature that moves on the ground."

Genesis 1:26–28

When I was a boy, I was fortunate enough to have attended the Masters Golf Tournament in Augusta, Georgia, with my father. At the time, I had no idea what a privilege this was for a child my age to attend, as tickets to this four-day event are the hardest to obtain in all sporting events, including the Superbowl. Attending the Masters at such a young age left me with some incredible experiences that I will never forget. The event left such an impression on me that I remember specific conversations I had with my father a decade and a half later. I recall asking him about the prize the winner would receive. The famous green jacket and a lifetime of invitations back to the tournament were awesome, but what surprised me was the relatively small pot of money the winner received in comparison to the salaries of other professional athletes. After all, if these were the hardest tickets in sports to get, shouldn't that be reflected in the size of the cash prize?

My father told me to pay attention to the apparel of the athletes. He alerted me to the fact that sponsorships from popular brand name companies are where most of the compensation in golf is earned. Sure enough, as Tiger Woods, Phil Mickelson, Gary Player, and the other big names in golf passed me by throughout this long spring weekend, I noticed that each was covered from head to toe in a single brand of clothing and gear. Whether it was Calloway, Nike, TaylorMade, or other famous brand logos on the clothing and gear of the players, each showed support for only one specific brand.

With millions of viewers worldwide, the Masters is an excellent opportunity for a business to display its logo to potential customers. Why is the brand logo for a company so incredibly important? What is a logo in the most basic sense? It is an image that represents the form or function of something greater. A logo is simple, yet it points to the greater reality of that which it is meant to represent. It is a company's way of connecting its underlying product to a potential customer. The logo is a visual summation of a company's brand that triggers a response in a person's psyche. With a well-liked brand comes trust, loyalty, good expectations, and positive experiences.

Like at the Masters Golf Tournament, companies often attach their logo to a champion they find worthy to endorse their brand.

Businesses do this to earn the trust of a potential customer through the merits of their champion, and they go to incredible lengths to ensure that their champion represents them alone. In turn, we as consumers who believe in the champion, buy into the brand, and further represent them when we use their products and wear their logos. We brand ourselves with all kinds of logos from many different brands. Through them we express ourselves, and our interests, and we relate to one another through them.

Do we realize that we have also been branded since before our birth for which someone has paid a significant price to place on us? Do we know that this logo necessitates our faithfulness because of the incredible price paid for us?

> Do you not know that your bodies are temples of the Holy Spirit, who is in you, whom you have received from God? You are not your own; you were bought at a price. Therefore honor God with your bodies.

1 Corinthians 6:19–20

The overarching theme of this book is that God is in the business of pursuing his glory, and his business has a logo that he uses to advertise his glory on earth—his image on humanity. God's champion is Christ Jesus, who perfectly bears the image (logo) of God (Hebrews 1:3). Because of the merits of Christ, we are fully able to wear and display God's logo to the world around us. However, this logo is not as simple as a "swoosh" that points to a sports clothing line (Nike), or a "partially eaten apple" (Apple) that marks our smartphones and laptops. God's logo is himself—the infinitely beautiful, complex, and mighty God. God's image on us is how he chooses to advertise himself to his creation and spread the message of his salvation provided through Christ.

As with most logos, the logos themselves typically have nothing spectacular about them. The significance is found in the underlying substance of what they represent. Although this is true for most logos, this is not true for humanity as a logo of God himself. Humanity is not a logo of God that possesses only *underlying* significance. We are a logo that bears many of the actual qualities of the Creator. Human beings are magnificent logos of God both inside and out. We are not an inanimate symbol of the living God but are living, breathing souls endowed with God's image. We are a physical logo of God, possessing functional bodies as well as higher mental and spiritual faculties. The fact that we are created in his image and likeness gives us God's infinite worth and purpose. Unlike any other beings, God gave us these abilities that he gave no other part of creation so that we may intimately know and commune with him.

Theologians have developed the theology of the biblical meaning of the "image of God" for millennia. Pope Emeritus of the Catholic Church, Benedict XVI, wrote: "Its nature as an image has to do with the fact that it goes beyond itself and manifests something that it is not. ... It is the dynamic that sets the human being in motion towards the totally Other. Hence it means the capacity for relationship; it is the human capacity for God."[1] Theory after theory has been debated, rejected, and expanded upon. Many of them still stand today, but with views that are open for further discussion. However, it is not difficult to imagine why this doctrine has been so thoroughly discussed throughout the ages.

Consider the beautiful depiction of the creation scene in Genesis that Michelangelo famously painted on the ceiling of the Sistine Chapel—"Creation of Adam." In this painting, God is portrayed as a patriarchal, white-bearded man who is carried by his angelic heavenly host and is reaching out to man with man mirroring God's gesture. While the painting is inaccurate, as God the Father is spirit and does not take physical form to be depicted as such (John 4:24), the painting displays man's form, his relational capacity with God, and that he has a remarkable likeness to God. This likeness is made evident not only in man's physical form, but also in the reddish cloak in which God and his angels are wrapped. The cloak takes the form and color of something oddly familiar to humanity—the human brain. This painting depicts the greater reality of humanity's creation that the key to relating to God resides within the six inches between our ears.

Surely our form and function as physical beings have a role in the image of God. This will be explored in detail below. However, humanity is unique among all creation concerning our higher mental, spiritual, and relational faculties. The innumerable complexities associated with the brain make it understandable as to why the *imago Dei* is such a difficult concept for us to grasp. Who can understand the depths of human consciousness?

Our brains weigh about three pounds and are composed of roughly one hundred billion nerve cells, with more than three trillion supporting cells. Each nerve cell possesses the ability to make more than ten thousand connections with the surrounding nerve cells, totaling more than a quadrillion connections, which can make more than one hundred trillion point operations per second.[2] This is the human consciousness created to relate to the infinite God, and every single person who has ever existed is unique. Surely it would take greater faith to believe that humanity is highly developed pond scum, as atheists would have us believe, rather than the result of intelligent design!

The theories that have been presented by theologians throughout the ages on what it means for human beings to possess the *imago Dei* generally fall into only a few categories. Rather than attempting to reinvent the wheel, I find that seminary professor Millard J. Erickson's textbook entitled *Christian Theology* presents three subcategories that will best aid us in our exploration of the image of God. These categories are the substantive, relational, and functional views on the image of God. To come to a complete appreciation of the image of God that we were given in our creation and will continue to develop throughout our life, we need to look at each subcategory with an open heart and test them against Scripture to verify their grounding in truth. My goal is not to claim that any single category discussed below is the complete truth, but to further the arguments presented in each with a broad and overarching perspective. I find that each view offers a bit of light and truth on the matter; therefore, all are worthy of our attention. Before we get to these views, let us briefly discuss the human capacity for God.

* * *

To Infinity and Beyond

In the earliest days of my walk with Christ, I was living in a small South Texas town and was blessed to have attended a church that was small enough that the senior pastor could regularly disciple me. As a young Christian man with a deep hunger for Christ, I absorbed my pastor's teachings like a sponge. Many of his words of wisdom have stuck with me, but one statement of his remains most profound. He told me, "As I learn more about God, I am made increasingly aware of the *ever-widening gap* of my current knowledge of God and what there actually is to know about him." Think about that. As our knowledge of God increases, the perceived distance between our current understanding of God and a complete understanding of him seems to grow. Does it really grow, however? Or has the infinite gap always been there, and we have yet to acknowledge its existence? Does this mean that we cannot know God if in our learning about him we are left with only more questions than answers? The depth of this statement intrigues me because it seems to point to two obvious truths.

The first truth is that we as humans have limitations as finite beings. As our limited understanding of God grows, we begin to appreciate how infinitely wonderful he is and how infinitely finite we are. It is not God that grows in greatness, because he does not change. Rather, it is we who shrink in greatness *in our minds* as we are overshadowed by the magnificence of the Lord Almighty.

The second truth is that there are certain infinite capacities that God has given to humanity—one of which is our ability to come to the knowledge of God. Just because God is infinitely great does not mean that we cannot know God. In fact, the very ability for us to grow in knowledge at all indicates the opposite. In the same way that married persons spend a lifetime learning about their spouses, we will spend eternity learning about God. As we grow more and more in the knowledge of God, we will always have more questions, but these questions will be met with answers, whether given to us now on this earth or later in heaven. As God's image bearers, we have been designed with the ability to pursue God. Revealing uncharted territory in our understanding and appreciation of God is a natural process that occurs as our minds are stretched and expanded so we may better comprehend God and ourselves in his image.

As alluded to in Pope Benedict XVI's quote, possessing God's image means we have the capacity to know God in us. However, fully knowing God is not an ability that humanity possesses. As finite beings, our understanding is limited to finite amounts of comprehension. To fully know and understand God, we would have to become infinite beings, and therefore become God. This is obviously an impossibility. Because we have a beginning in our creation, we can never fully comprehend that which has no beginning, or which was never created. God has always existed as the reality of everything, and this is a fact that we must accept as the starting point of faith in God (Isaiah 55:8–9; John 8:58). As we walk into a deeper understanding and love for God, we will always discover new aspects of him. This is part of God's beauty and majesty, that discovering new parts of him will never cease to amaze the human soul. Our capacity to know God is like a balloon that never pops, no matter how big it gets. The knowledge, relationship, and function of God in our life is the air, and our understanding and love for him is the balloon. The balloon grows bigger and bigger each day we seek him and his kingdom, but there is no limit or end to how big our "understanding balloon" will get.

If God is infinite and we are made in his image yet we are finite, then how do we begin to understand the limits of our "likeness" to God? As I have sifted through many theories on the doctrine of the *imago Dei*, I have concluded that simplicity is essential for one to build a foundational knowledge of it. My intent is for this concept to be approached similarly to the way one would approach sharing the gospel with a lost soul. Allow me to explain.

For the unbeliever, the Bible is not yet understood to be the final authority for truth. It would be silly for us to try and teach a person how to biblically resolve conflict, handle finances, or pursue Christian relationships before they understand the most basic of Christian truths. That would do no good for the eternal state of their soul, which is dead in its sin! They must first possess an understanding of their sin, the hopeless condition they are in without a savior, and that the Savior that came for them is the person of Jesus Christ. Instead of putting the cart before the horse, we keep their salvation as the top priority before moving on to all the implications and responses to salvation.

For the same reason that we do not begin to witness to an unbeliever with the ancillary topics of Christian living, it does us no good to discuss the specific ways we are made in the image of God before we can understand what the "image of God" actually means in the most basic sense. This seems obvious, but I have heard many sermons and have read many books that talk about specific ways in which we are "in the image of God" before I ever heard a sermon on what the image of God is in the context of a human being's entire life. This prompted me to write this book. The image of God is not a tiny piece of Christian doctrine; it is the foundation of the Christian worldview. Therefore, we must understand the doctrine properly before we discuss the many ways we are in God's image.

In the sources I have read for my understanding, many gifted thinkers present complex theories on the image of God, with multipoint theses attempting to cover the entirety of the concept. It is as if each theologian is attempting to redefine the concept with a "better" doctrine that covers all the bases of humanity's likeness to God. You will notice this in my descriptions below. I admire their work, and they have been incredibly useful to any Christian who seeks understanding, including myself. However, it seems to me that God was intentional in his Word to not go into excruciating detail about every single implication of the *imago Dei*. If God's Word does not point out every specific way in which we are made in the image of him, then why should we do so?

The simplicity that the words "image" and "likeness" hold regarding our experience as human beings is more complete in a broad and overarching sense than diving into specifics to pinpoint the exact meaning through any singular characteristics of humanity. Attempting to choose to believe only one specific aspect of the doctrine and expecting to have found the complete truth might mean that we will miss other wonderful truths that are part of our makeup in God's image. We may unintentionally disregard those attributes of God we have yet to experience because we assume that we have it all figured out. This is contrary to the very essence of our Christian walk. We will never cease learning, understanding, and growing in Christ for all of eternity. Essentially, I am encouraging you to consume this book as but one perspective on the image of God. As I write, I am 27 years old and with eternity ahead of me to learn and grow—I expect that we will never fully grasp his image in its entirety!

Any believer who has sought to truly know their Creator is intimately familiar with this. In my experience of walking with the Lord, I have come to many points where I discover new truths about a specific attribute of God. Because of the way I understand the image of God, I can see increasingly more of God's image in myself as I meditate on the truth of being made in his image and likeness. I have come to learn that there is no one simple implication of the doctrine that can be universally applied. The image of God is an overarching reality that involves every facet of our existence. This may raise some eyebrows, but when I say every facet, I mean it—even our sinful nature and all the evil that abounds from it contributes to the image. (We will not dwell on this now but will revisit this in chapters 5 and 8 of this book.)

Considering this, I think each of the three subcategories of views theologians of past and present argue contain pieces of divine truth. When Christ gave us the Great Commandment, he hit the heart of the matter concerning the response we should give to God as his image bearers:

> "Love the Lord your God with *all* your heart and with *all* your soul and with *all* your mind and with *all* your strength."
>
> *Mark 12:30, emphasis added*

As you read below the categories of views on God's image, try to relate this verse to each viewpoint. Try to see your heart and soul as the relational view, your mind as the substantive view, and your strength as the functional view. Regardless, we are to love God with *all* our being, because all our being was made in his image. Without a definitive understanding of the *imago Dei*, we will not have a framework to live our lives and apply this doctrine to each circumstance as we would have if we fully grasped the worth and purpose the God of the universe has placed on us as he knit us together in our mother's womb (Psalm 139:13).

* * *

The Substantive View

The substantive view of God is the most widely accepted view of God's image in humanity. Its purpose is to define a *specific* quality or characteristic that each of us, Christians and non-Christians alike, possess. Perhaps the most widely understood characteristic of the *imago Dei* is humanity's faculty of reason. Human beings have the greatest capacity for higher-level thought and ability to contemplate our existence in comparison to lesser beings. The degree to which this aspect of humanity has been emphasized in theology has varied over time as society changes.

For example, during the Enlightenment, rationality was highly stressed. However, in times such as the later part of the 20th century, theology developed a more visceral tone. As this thread of rationality has been pulled by theologians, they have even developed differences in the way in which the faculty of reason is defined. Examples of this include *Platonism* (abstract contemplation) or *Thomistic-Aristotelianism* (scientific thought).

Despite the changes in our fundamental understanding of the substantive qualities of humanity, has the image of God in us changed at all? I would argue that humans have not changed, but it would seem that the way we define ourselves from a theological standpoint has changed. Is our ability to reason to be stressed above all other qualities? Seminary professor Millard Erickson makes an interesting observation:

It is not surprising that reason has been singled out by theologians as the most significant aspect of human nature, for theologians are the segment of the church charged with intellectualizing their faith. Note that in so doing, however, not only have they isolated one aspect of human nature for consideration, but they have also concentrated their attention on only one facet of God's nature. This may result in a misapprehension. To be sure, omniscience and wisdom constitute a significant dimension of the nature of God, but they are by no means the very essence of divinity! [3]

At its heart, the substantive view isolates individual facets of the *imago Dei*. It claims a specific attribute of humanity is definitively how we are made in the image of God to the exclusion of all others. Other theologians have thought that the specific characteristic of humanity in God's image is his free will. God in his sovereign power possesses the freedom to do whatever he pleases and gives humanity that same type of freedom. This freedom is made obvious in that humanity ultimately used it to deny God and fall from grace in the garden of Eden.

Yet others have pointed to the ability of humans to understand and live by the standards of morality that are common to all men. As an American, this is evident from the core values of the Founding Fathers of the United States in the preamble to the Declaration of Independence. In it, they declare the unalienable rights endowed by our Creator. While not all the Founding Fathers believed in a government rooted in godly principles, many of them did. John Adams, one of the Founding Fathers who held these beliefs, once pointed out that the standards of morality for any government to operate are rooted in the morality given to us by God alone:

We have no government armed with power capable of contending with human passions unbridled by morality and religion. Avarice, ambition, revenge, or gallantry would break the strongest cords of our Constitution as a whale goes through a net. Our Constitution was made only for a moral and religious people. It is wholly inadequate to the government of any other.

John Adams

John Adams defined the timeless purpose of government by declaring that only God's standard of morality can be used for the governance of the people. They are the only standards that can be universally agreed upon because these standards come from a power (God) who transcends the divergent and sinful desires of evil people. When left to our sinful desires, morality is simply a matter of personal opinion; there is no standard on which foundational moral precepts are to be based. The truth is that morality can *only* come from God! As God's image bearers, there are standards of morality that resonate as true for all of us, because God designed us to be like him—that is, as beings who understand the intrinsic value of life that mirrors his in value. Each of us knows these to be true if we search the deepest reaches of our soul.

Aside from rationality, free will, and the morality that is common to all, other thinkers have developed an understanding that the words "image" and "likeness" from the creation account relate to two completely different aspects of the image of God. The second-century theologian Origen of Alexandria claimed that the "image" in humanity is something that we *have* in our very makeup, whereas the "likeness" is something that would be *given* to us by God at a later point in time. This idea was later expanded on by the theologian St. Irenaeus, who saw the "image" to be our free will and reason, and the "likeness" to be a sense of righteousness that we had in the garden of Eden that was lost when we fell into sin.

For this reason, St. Irenaeus argues that humanity still has the capacity for God, even after the fall of humanity, in that everyone possesses a natural endowment of rationality and free will to choose or deny God, but the likeness to God (the righteousness of humanity) was something that had to be bought back at a later point by Jesus Christ. Martin Luther later rejected the idea that they are distinct entities when he maintained the position that the words "image" and "likeness" were a common practice in the Hebrew language called parallelism. Luther maintained the position that they are synonymous, and that the full image of God remains intact as it relates to God's intentions for humanity, but that only fragments of the image are displayed in us.[4] Martin Luther's observations seem to be more scripturally based, in that there is no reason to believe that Scripture offers any meaningful differentiation between "image" and "likeness" similar to common word groupings that we have in English such as, "cease and desist," "intents and purposes," and "each and every."

Throughout history, some have also thought the words "image" and "likeness" mean that humanity possesses a physical likeness to God due to the literal interpretation of the Hebrew word *tselem*[5] (image), meaning "statue" or "form." This understanding is not the most popular of the substantive views of the *imago Dei*; however, it has persisted throughout the ages and the Mormons are the most prevalent advocates for it today.[6] I believe there is a good deal of truth to it; however, it is by no means comprehensive in its breadth. St. Irenaeus was probably one of the most prominent Christian theologians who clung to the material body as a manifestation of God's image, among other qualities. He states:

> But man [he] fashioned with [his] own hands, tak-
> ing of the purest and finest of earth, in measured
> wise mingling with the earth [his] own power; for

[he] gave his frame the outline of [his] own form, that the visible appearance too should be god-like—for it was as an image of God that man was fashioned and set on earth—and that he might come to life, [he] *breathed into his face the breath of life*, so that the man became like God in inspiration as well as in frame. [7]

This argument is credible. St. Irenaeus did not feel that reason and free will are the sole factors that make us in the image of God, but that our physical bodies bore his image as well. He believed that while God the Father and God the Holy Spirit are spiritual in essence and took part in creation, it was through the Son who put on flesh that humanity was created. St. Irenaeus therefore believed that our bodies are an image of God with regard to the Son. He believed that belief in a disembodied soul that awaits escape from a bodily prison is not consistent with the revelation of the Son of God, because it is through the physical body of Jesus that God's purposes were achieved.[8] This view harmonizes with the doctrine of the physical resurrection of Christ and the physical resurrection that will occur as described in the final resurrection. As beings in heaven, we will possess an incorruptible and beautiful physical body in the same way that Christ had in his resurrection and has currently in the present heaven. The fullness of God's glory dwells within the physical body of Christ and will also dwell within us when we are physically raised with new bodies that are fit for heaven.

Of all the substantive views that have been presented through the ages, it is evident that there are specific qualities that humanity possesses that resonate with the creative design that God imprinted on the human soul. The human capacity for God is indivisibly steeped within our being, whether this manifests itself as the ability to understand him through the Scriptures, obey him with our ability to freely choose his moral attributes, or be a physical representation of him through the image of his Son. We must, however, be careful not to negate qualities that God fashioned within us to mirror his glorious nature in an attempt to pinpoint the "most important" quality in likeness to God. To do this would diminish the importance of everything discussed below.

* * *

The Relational View

> "Teacher, which is the greatest commandment in the Law?" Jesus replied: "'Love the Lord your God with all your heart and with all your soul and with all your mind.' This is the first and greatest commandment. And the second is like it: 'Love your neighbor as yourself.'"
>
> *Matthew 22:36–39*

In this passage of Scripture, it is evident that Jesus is pointing to a critical dimension of the image of God. Of all of the guidelines that the Bible offers humanity about how we live a full life, the first and second greatest commandments given by Jesus perfectly sum up the intention for the rest of the guidelines of God, dealing specifically with relationships. Relationships with God and other humans are a crucial part of what makes us human in the first place. The relational view, as defined by modern theologians Emil Brunner and Karl Barth, views the image of God as *experiential* rather than found in the *makeup* of human beings as proposed in the substantive view.

Brunner believes there are two senses of the *imago Dei*, one being the *formal sense*, and the other being the *material sense*. What exactly does he mean by that? The formal sense of the *imago Dei* is not that humanity possesses a natural endowment of rationality existing all by itself as the substantive view would argue, but that such rationality is *expressed* as humanity being responsible and personal beings. Humans are rational *because* they are responsible to God. Brunner understands the formal sense to be that which cannot have been lost in the fall of humanity because the ability to sin is what defines our responsibility to God. The ability to sin is what contrasts us from other beings such as animals, which have no specific ability to commit offenses against God. They are just along for the ride, experiencing the pain and brokenness of the world that entered through the sin of humanity. Humans, on the other hand, have higher-level faculties *because* we must be accountable to God. Did God command the animals not to eat the fruit of the Tree of Knowledge of Good and Evil?

The material sense of the *imago Dei*, according to Brunner, is the actual relationship that humans have with God. It is the *response* whereby a person accepts God and communes with him because of the formal sense of responsibility to God. Brunner argues that the material sense ebbs and flows in its presence within humanity. When we are most connected to God relationally, we are reflecting the material sense of God's image the most. When we are deep in sin, the material sense of the image is difficult to see. The relationship from the material sense is not necessarily restricted solely to humanity's relationship with God. The first and greatest commandment deals with our relationship with God, but the second refers to our relationships with other humans. Relationships with other humans offer a platform to demonstrate the image of God in the material sense in that it shows our genuine humanity in Christ.[9]

In some of his earlier writings, Karl Barth had quite opposing views from Emil Brunner on the image of God, but eventually he came to write on the image in ways that expressed similar ideas to the relational view as discussed by Brunner.[10] Barth views the image as having a few components to it. First, he believed that the only way in which a human being can understand what the image of God in humanity was supposed to look like is by examining the life of Christ. It was Christ's life that most accurately demonstrated humanity as originally intended. He viewed the image as something God created to be an expression of the relationship within himself as a Godhead, and that humanity reflects this relationship. In the Trinity, there is a vertical aspect to God's relationship from the headship of roles of his three members, Father, Son, and Spirit, and a horizontal one through the Godhead's equality among themselves. This will be discussed in detail in chapter 3, but the point is that the Holy Spirit is subordinate to the Son who is subordinate to the Father, yet all are equally God who share equal worth to the others.

This concept manifests itself with humanity's vertical relationship to God and horizontal relationships with their fellow humans. Because of this, Barth viewed humanity's creation as male and female to be the critical component of how God expresses the horizontal relationship he has within himself as a Trinity through his image in humanity.[11] In the next chapter, we will also go into detail on the interpersonal relationships between the Godhead and how the image of God reflects this in humanity as male and female.

Ultimately, regardless of the mental capacity of humans, their physical makeup, or moral capacities, every person who has ever existed has experienced relationships of greater depth than can be found with other species on earth. There are similarities here and there, but it is through interconnectedness with one another and with God that humanity finds their ultimate relational fulfillment. These relationships are broken in our sin and reconciled in Christ. This need for interconnectedness is felt by unbelievers and believers alike; however, only the believer is capable of the type of oneness and ultimate joy God intends for humanity. The purpose for which we were created is described well in Christian author Timothy Keller's book *Prayer*:

> The Father, the Son, and the Holy Spirit are adoring one another, giving glorifying love to one another, and delighting in one another. We know of no joy higher than being loved and loving in return, but a triune God would know that love and joy in unimaginable, infinite dimensions. God is, therefore, infinitely, profoundly *happy*, filled with perfect joy—not some abstract tranquility but the fierce happiness of dynamic loving relationships. ... If God did not need to create other beings in order to know love and happiness, then why did [he] do so? Jonathan Edwards argues, in *A Dissertation Concerning the End for Which God Created the World*, that the only reason God would have for creating us was not to *get* the cosmic love and joy of relationship (because he already had that), but to *share* it. [12]

* * *

The Functional View

Often after completing a late afternoon training mission when flying West from the California desert, I will opt to fly out by San Diego and hook a right up the coast towards Camp Pendleton, which is located a few miles inland in Oceanside, California. As we fly up the coast at one to two hundred feet above the water, I always appreciate the view. When most people come to the West Coast, they long to stand on the golden sands of the beaches and watch a beautiful sunset over the water as they look out as far as the eye can see over the vast Pacific Ocean. From my vantage point, however, as I fly north up the coast I look to my right and can see everything that the sun is setting on—hundreds of surfers waving up to us as we fly by, people playing with their dogs on the beach, the extensive and beautiful Mediterranean-style estates covering the coast, and the mountains beyond it.

Seeing Southern California from the air is quite impressive, and it relates to the functional view of the *imago Dei*. It reinforces a few truths of the purpose for which humanity was created. The first is that the human soul seeks paradise. The superficial appeal of Southern California is that it is the paradise of America, and the perceived joy and rest people believe it will bring them is why so many flock to it to live or visit for a vacation. The second truth is that all people spend their lives seeking after a piece of paradise to rule over in their life. In an area as crowded as California, this is plainly evident.

When I fly up the coast, I can see thousands upon thousands of extremely nice homes that line the cliffs overlooking the serenity of the Pacific Ocean. They are packed closely together, but nevertheless each owner is willing to pay the exorbitant cost of California real estate to own their little piece of paradise. I often wonder why so many are willing to abandon financial prudence as it relates to home buying. I have lived in other areas of the country where much bigger and nicer homes can be bought for much less money. The difference is the location, and California is undeniably a beautiful place. We all have a burning desire that exists deep in our souls to rule over the beautiful things of God's creation. We believe that when we have a little bit of paradise in our life we will be "home" and at peace. The beautiful reality is that this desire is God-given. God wants us to seek such paradise to rule over—that is what we were designed for! That peace we so desire will include ruling over paradise, but it is not in this present world broken by sin. This desire was given to us so that we may long for heaven with every fiber of our souls.

Is it coincidental, or is it the truth of our existence backed up by our experience that we were designed to rule? Ruling over God's beautiful creation was the basic command of God in the creation account in Genesis. God called humanity to have dominion over all the earth and its creatures. He said this both immediately before and after he describes humanity as created in his image. However, there was no brokenness from sin in the world. Much like the first chapter of the Bible, the last chapter in Revelation says: "There will be no more night. They will not need the light of a lamp or the light of the sun, for the Lord God will give them light. And *they will reign forever and ever*" (22:5, emphasis added).

Humanity was made to rule alongside God, and the functional view of the *imago Dei* claims that the image of God in us is not that we possess substantive qualities or relational capacity as the basis for the image, but that it is the role we are designed to fulfill. The view recognizes that because God is Lord, humanity was designed for lordship as well. Theologian Norman Snaith points out that Psalm 8:5–8 draws almost exact parallels to the creation story with humanity being "made a little lower than the angels," and that they would be rulers over all creation, including the psalmist using the same sequence of animals that God used in the creation story. He wrote: "Biblically speaking, the phrase 'image of God' has nothing to do with morals or any sort of ideals; it refers only to man's dominion of the world and everything that is in it. It says nothing about the nature of God, but everything concerning the function of man."[13]

Interestingly, in the substantive view we look at St. Irenaeus' argument for the physical makeup of our bodies to be the image of

God. Aside from the works a Christian does through their physical body, we can demonstrate our function through creativity that we have as a result of physically being in the image of God. Being an all-powerful Creator, God created the universe from nothing with incredible precision and beauty. In the same way, humanity mirrors this ability to rule and create in a way that no other living being can do. Our industrious and artistic nature is an expression of the creative nature of God himself, and he has commanded us to express this by ruling over the physical world.

In his book *Thou Shall Prosper*, Rabbi Daniel Lapin points out that this is a unique part of humanity being made in God's image because it has two implications: first, that humans are creative as the Creator himself is, and second, that each human is as unique in their existence as God is in his existence. He notes that it is almost poetic that God put fingerprints, the symbol of the uniqueness of individual humans, on our hands which are the medium we use to create.[14] Undeniably, humanity was designed with functional aspects in God's image. However, how would we function as created without substantive or relational aspects to our image in God's likeness?

* * *

As U.S. Marines Like to Say, "Words Mean Things"

I recently had a conversation with a dear friend about the use of the word "evangelical" as a pejorative. I found it coincidental that I was approached by him with this conversation piece, as it fits very well with our discussion of the Bible's meaning of the image of God. In this conversation, my friend was referencing a news outlet that was using the term to defame the character of a politician currently in the spotlight of our nation. I would have taken that title as a compliment, but how it was used by the reporter insinuated that the politician in question was a fanatic who was infringing on the religious freedoms of the people. However, calling a Christian an "evangelical" is not derogatory. The word is defined as a person who is, "of, relating to, or being in agreement with the Christian gospel especially as it is presented in the four Gospels."[15] I cannot help but think that the news anchor could have done a better job at picking an insult than stating that the person is in fact a Christian in the purest sense of the word.

However, we live in an age where the English language is rapidly evolving. It is perfectly acceptable for languages to change over time. This is nothing new and is not the issue at hand. The issues are the implications our understanding of language has regarding spiritual disciplines.

From the conversation I had with my friend, I do not believe that the word "evangelical" has completely lost its meaning because of one news anchor incorrectly using it, but I do believe that over time the specific meaning of words will change if careless speech continues to occur, and we must be cognizant of this. Unfortunately, many words are used today that have lost their original meaning due to an increasing number of misuses.

Great examples of words that are currently losing their meaning are the words "male" and "female." While most people know them as they are originally defined, our culture would claim there is no longer a binary definition based on genetic assignment in the womb, but of the feelings that a person has where their physical organs do not match what they believe their psychological makeup to represent. From this, a person "can decide" on what sex they are based on their feelings. This is a lie that has grown louder and louder in our culture, to the point that if one were to speak out and claim that sexual assignment is binary and not fluid, they would be labeled as an intolerant bigot. God's Word in the Genesis account of creation decrees that he created humans as two separate and distinct sexes for a purpose and that it is an abomination for them to get their assigned role confused (Deuteronomy 22:5). We now live in a culture in which we cannot even use the words "male" and "female" as a statement of fact, but rather of personal opinion, ultimately distorting our knowledge of beings created in the image of a good and righteous God. While we are in a transitionary period in society, and there are still many people that are not buying Satan's lies, this could have serious implications for future believers over time.

One of my favorite Christian thinkers of modern times, C. S. Lewis (1898-1963), discusses this very concern for the importance of utilizing the correct meaning of words in the preface of one of his most famous pieces of Christian literature, *Mere Christianity*. He describes the word "gentleman" and how it was formerly a word that was a statement of fact denoting a man who owned land and wore a coat of arms. Eventually over time, humanity decreed that the qualities that a gentleman possessed, namely courage and honor, were a better use of the word "gentleman," based on it sounding loftier than a man possessing land and wearing a coat of arms. In this day and age, the word is now a term of praise used to denote the qualities of a man who holds the door for ladies, dresses appropriately for the occasion, and has refined tastes in specific areas of culture. Lewis compares the demise of the word "gentleman" to that which has happened to the word "Christian," which has many more implications:

> Now if once we allow people to start spiritualizing and refining, or as they may say 'deepening', the sense of the word *Christian*, it too will speedily become a useless word. In the first place, Christians themselves will never be able to apply it to

anyone. ... And obviously a word which we can never apply is not going to be a very useful word. As for the unbelievers, they will no doubt cheerfully use the word in a refined sense. It will become in their mouths simply a term of praise. In calling anyone a Christian they will mean that they think him a good man. But the way of using the word will be no enrichment of the language, for we already have the word good. [16]

In my research on many of the different views of the *imago Dei*, I have concluded that the differences in opinions stem from a misunderstanding of the language of the creation story. In general, our culture *dilutes the power* of certain words to the point where they have lost their original meaning by attempting to deepen their meaning. In the same way that Lewis compared the cultural "deepening" of the title of Christian to mean broad and subjective qualities of a person, many theologians of the past and present have sought to do precisely the same thing by extracting more exact meanings of the words "image" (Hebrew: *tselem*)[17] and "likeness" (Hebrew: *demût*)[18] than were originally intended. Many of them were not wrong in their observations that such qualities are part of our makeup in the image of God, but they were not complete in their analysis of them. They do not offer an all-encompassing explanation as the original words imply. In fact, more meaning of the "image of God" is found in less meaning of the words "image" and "likeness." In an attempt to pull out the lessons God intended when he inspired the creation account of Genesis, the meaning has been lost by digging too deeply into the words.

The words used in the creation account in Genesis 1:27 are the only words that can perfectly describe the full meaning of the "image of God." Is it important to understand our specific individual faculties, relational capacities, and functional purposes as bearers of God's image? Of course, but only if one can come back to the original language used in our creation story and accept that an individual facet of the *imago Dei* is only a single piece of the puzzle.

Strong's Concordance, an exhaustive index of every Hebrew and Greek word and their associated verses in the Old and New Testaments, sheds light on the true meaning of the original Hebrew words. In the first half of Genesis 1:27, transliterated from the original Hebrew, "*bara elohiym eth adam tselem*," God is telling us that we are in essence a shadow, or a representation, of him. We were filled with God's image in the way a sponge is filled with water. We are completely saturated with God's image. *Everything* about us was designed to be like God, not just reason, relational capacity, and the function of ruling over creation.

It is correct to say that there are substantive parts of the human soul that are made in the image of God. It is also correct to say that there are relational and functional parts of the human soul that are created in the image of God. The three views are not mutually exclusive according to seminary professor Wayne Grudem:

> When we realize that the Hebrew words for "image" and "likeness" simply informed the original readers that man was *like* God, and would in many ways *represent* God, much of the controversy over the meaning of "image of God" is seen to be a search for too narrow and too specific a meaning. ... Such an explanation is unnecessary, not only because the terms had clear meanings, but also because no such list could do justice to the subject: the text only needs to affirm that man is *like* God, and the rest of Scripture fills in more details to explain this. In fact, when we read the rest of Scrip-

ture, we realize that a full understanding of man's
likeness to God would require a full understanding of *who God is* in his being and in his actions
and a full understanding of *who man is* and what
he does. ... The expression refers to every way in
which man is like God. [19]

Humanity, being in the likeness of God in every way, leads us to
a fundamental reality of God's being that was not specifically dealt
with *in detail* in the three views presented in this chapter. As the
story of the Bible unfolds throughout history, humanity is given a
clearer and clearer picture of God as each person of the Godhead is
revealed, thereby giving us a clearer and clearer picture of humanity
in God's image.

The pre-Christ nation of Israel surely could not have properly
understood Christ as the Messiah promised to deliver them. Although there were many prophecies in the Scriptures regarding a
Messiah who would one day come to deliver the nation of Israel,
Scripture proves that they completely misunderstood God's true
identity. This is evident in that when God revealed himself through
the person of Jesus Christ, they killed his Son on accusations of being a blasphemer when he was the exact representation of the Father
(Hebrews 1:3).

In the same way that the Israelites missed the mark on Christ,
Christ's disciples who were witnesses to his life, death, and resurrection missed the mark on many of his teachings and promises
made in the Upper Room Discourse (John 13–17) regarding the Holy
Spirit. Through Christ, the disciples were given a clear picture of
God the Father that the Israelites did not have previously (John
14:9). However, they did not understand what had yet to be revealed
to them—the Holy Spirit. The Spirit is given to them at Pentecost,
and the disciples go from being absolute failures to becoming titans

of the Christian faith as they live out God's will, spread the message of the gospel, and pass his inspired Word down to us with incredible understanding in the form of the New Testament Scriptures.

There are many points in the biblical story where the limited revelation of God was followed by humanity's failure to respond in a way consistent with God's true nature. Could we possibly expect anything more? What this means is that our understanding of ourselves as God's image bearers is contingent on the *fully revealed* triune God. This full revelation occurred once the final member of the Trinity was given to humanity and inspired the New Testament writings. At each point that God chose to reveal more of himself, through the giving of the law to the Israelites, through the sending of his Son, followed by the sending of the Holy Spirit, the characters of the Bible were able to grow and act in accordance with their knowledge of God at that point in time. Once the complete nature of God was revealed as a Trinity, humanity could now come to an understanding of what the image discussed in Genesis fully entails. Remember, in Genesis 1:26, God said, "Let *us* make man in *our* own image." The next chapter will discuss one of the most difficult and wonderful doctrines of God we possess in our makeup—the image of the triune God.

QUESTIONS FOR REFLECTION AND DISCUSSION

What brands do you display to the world around you and to what degree would others say they define you? How do these logos compare in importance in your life to the logo of God's image?

When you first came to faith in God, what did you believe about him? How has your perception of God grown over the years? How has your increased understanding of God changed your understanding of humanity that is made in his image?

Which substantive qualities in your makeup as a human being do you believe resemble God the most? Can you think of any other qualities not mentioned in this chapter? When you think about these qualities as part of God's image, are you reminded of Jesus? How so?

How do your human relationships display God's image? What aspects of them help you to see God more clearly? What aspects of God's character as revealed in Scripture help you to see the shortcomings of your human relationships?

What piece of "paradise" do you rule over in your life? What is the base motivation for ruling over it—peace, security, pleasure, accomplishment, or something else? What does your earthly "paradise" promise to give you? Has it delivered these things thus far, or has it brought you to the conclusion that you were made to rule over another world?

Given that the revelation of God occurs through the written Word, why is it important to study the original meaning of words in the Bible? How can different translations of the Bible affect your understanding of Scripture? Do you know of any other Hebrew words that have lost their original meaning in their translation to English?

3

❦

The Image of the Triune God

As soon as Jesus was baptized, he went up out of the water. At that moment heaven was opened, and he saw the Spirit of God descending like a dove and alighting on him. And a voice from heaven said, "This is my Son, whom I love, with him I am well pleased."

Matthew 3:16–17

There is no easy way to understand the Trinity. In fact, *fully understanding* the Trinity is not the purpose of this chapter and not particularly important in our discussion of the image of God. From this side of heaven, we have an incomplete understanding of it, and this is solely due to our limited experience as human beings. So imagine for a moment the experience of seeing heaven for the very first time. What if, among all the other incredible surprises, heaven was filled with new colors that do not exist on the present earth? Try to imagine what they would look like. Can you do this, or does your mind keep reverting to colors you already know to exist?

Our attempt at fully understanding the Trinity is like our attempt at imagining a new color. What do I mean? Because of our vision, we qualitatively understand colors. We know what it means to see, what the colors blue, yellow, or red look like, and we know the beauty that color adds to the human experience. We understand what color is *like*, but our minds can only imagine the colors that we have seen—the wavelengths of energy in the visible spectrum to which the cones of the human eye are sensitive. The instant we try and imagine a new color, we realize that we cannot do such a thing. Our imaginations are limited to what is inside of our human experience for such an endeavor.

Likewise, our understanding of color and our inability to imagine a new one is like our attempts to intellectually grasp the nature of the Trinity. God's *nature* as a triune (three-in-one) God is uniquely outside of humanity's experience like the color that does not exist. This means that while we understand some things about the Trinity, there are certain aspects that remain a mystery. We can understand the three individual persons of the Godhead, because they have been revealed to us through the Bible. If we are in Christ, then we have experienced the members of the Godhead in a way similar to how we have experienced colors on this earth—our spiritual eyes have been opened for us to see God for who he is. However, when we wade into the realm of understanding *how* the Trinity exists, we find that complexity and mystery surround God's triune nature, which cannot be grasped. Like the color that does not exist, we have nothing in the realm of human experience to aid us in obtaining such an understanding. Should it not be expected of an infinite God that aspects of him remain a mystery to us?

The doctrine of the Trinity can be stated quite simply: There is one God who eternally exists as three persons—Father, Son, and

Holy Spirit. And yet, this abstract concept defies human comprehension. If we were to make the definition of the Trinity a mathematical equation, it would defy even the basic rules of arithmetic, claiming that 1 + 1 + 1 = 1. The doctrine can be further expanded into three individual statements to better understand what the above statement means.

1. The Father, Son, and Holy Spirit are three *unique* and *distinct* *persons*.
2. Each of these persons is *fully* God.
3. There is only *one* God.

The Trinity is not a doctrine that is explicitly defined in Scripture by the biblical authors, yet the totality of Scripture points to its truth as the doctrine of God's *essential* being—that he exists and can only exist as a triune God. The revelation of this in Scripture is accomplished through foreshadowing, implicit language, and deductive reasoning. From the second verse of Genesis through the end of Revelation, the Bible is steeped with Scriptures that testify to this truth. The texts unanimously corroborate that the Trinity is the most plausible and exact explanation of the complex nature of God. Regardless of the biblical authors' reasons for not overtly including the word "Trinity" in the Scriptures, a person does not necessarily need to perfectly understand this doctrine to relate to God. However, to relate to God *correctly*, it must at least be accepted as the truth.

God can only be worshiped for who he is, and not who we think or want him to be. Belief in a god that is anything other than triune is belief in a false god. If this doctrine is not accepted, then none of the Bible, Old Testament or New, can be trusted. If God is not triune, then contradictions arise throughout the Scriptures, and the rational God of the Bible suddenly becomes inconsistent. The doctrine of the Trinity is the only doctrine that describes God's nature consistently throughout biblical revelation.

As God's image bearers, we must understand that God's triune existence has a great deal of impact on our own existence. To be made in the likeness of a triune God means that there are definitive qualities of the Trinity that have been communicated to us through God's image. This chapter will focus on these implications rather than explain how God can exist as such a being. Much of this book deals with the inward likeness to God that we possess as human beings. This chapter deals with such personal application of God's image, but in the context of community—more specifically, the community that has existed since eternity past and will exist forevermore—the Trinity.

* * *

Revelation through Divine Inspiration

How is it that the Bible can unanimously support the doctrine of the Trinity without explicitly teaching it? The answer to this question lies in a theological concept called *divine inspiration*—that God is the motivating force who works through the minds of finite beings to fill Scripture with divine wisdom and truth (2 Peter 1:21). The Bible contains a multitude of texts that point to God's triune nature. It is beyond the scope of this chapter to explore each of them, but we will focus on one specific example that fits our discussion on how the Trinity is applicable to us as God's image bearers.

Moses, the author of the Pentateuch (Genesis, Exodus, Leviticus, Numbers, and Deuteronomy), wrote many things in the Scriptures that point to God's triune nature. Despite the biblical revelation of all three members of the Godhead being far from complete, Moses' words not only support the trinitarian doctrine but also make sense only in the context of it. Like the Pentateuch, the words of *all Scripture* were recorded through the minds of finite beings, and they convey truth and meaning that far surpass any one person's understanding (2 Timothy 3:16). Through divine inspiration, the Holy Spirit empowers the Word of God to be relevant and consistent throughout all the ages because God's wisdom is inerrant in its truth and not limited by the temporal existence or finite understanding of human beings (Psalm 18:30; 19:7–10; Isaiah 40:8; Hebrews 4:12). This is how Scripture can speak with authority and accuracy on events at which the authors were not specifically present, such as the divine discourse we read about in the book of Job or events that have yet to come to pass in the apocalyptic literature of Daniel and Revelation.

Because the words of Scripture were divinely inspired, the doctrine of the Trinity was implicitly revealed to us through the 66 books of the Bible. Consider the statistical probability of contradictions to arise on this doctrine in the development of Scripture. The odds are remarkably high for such contradictions to be found, and yet they do not exist. The Scriptures were written by forty authors, over 1,500 years, in three languages, and in geographically disparate locations. Most of the biblical authors had never met, let alone lived in the same time period, or reviewed each other's works before recording their portion of Scripture, and yet all of them unanimously support this doctrine. Although the Trinity is not an explicit teaching in the Bible, the words of each author were written as if they all understood God as a triune being, without the slightest hint of contradictory evidence. My question is, "Did they really understand the Trinity, or is this proof of God's hand in biblical revelation?"

God did not wait to reveal himself as a triune God until the final person of the Godhead, the Holy Spirit, was revealed to humanity.

This truth, which is woven throughout the entire canon of Scripture, was a truth that God made readily available for us to see from the beginning; however, we could not understand what such Scriptures pointed to until the Godhead was fully revealed. Think back to the "color" illustration. If one were to try to describe color to a person who was blind from birth, would that person understand the qualities of color? Certainly not, for they do not know what it means to see! Now, if that person's eyes were miraculously healed and they were to see color for the very first time, the words describing color, which they have heard their entire life, would now make perfect sense. Once we have "seen" Jesus and the Holy Spirit both in the Scriptures and in our experience, we can *properly* read the Scriptures that pointed to their existence as members of the Godhead all along. This applies both to humanity on a large scale, as God revealed them to the world through the biblical story and to each of us on a small scale, as we are individually given the Spirit when we accept Christ as our salvation. What was once outside human experience, God has brought inside so we can properly know, understand, and worship him for who he is.

A perfect example of such revelation of the Trinity from God's Word that was plainly revealed is humanity's creation in the image of God in Genesis. Although Moses recorded the words, he obviously was not present for humanity's creation. Yet what do these words detail about God's nature? In the creation story it is written, "Then God said, let *us* make man in *our* own image" (Genesis 1:26). The "us" and "our" of this verse indicate a multiplicity of persons that took part in the creation of man and that they are collectively the substance of the image being placed on humanity.

If we were to critique this verse from a language perspective, the Hebrew word used for God in this verse is "*Elohim*." This is the plural form of "God" in Hebrew, hence the English translation of God referring to himself as "us" in our Bibles. This has one of two implications. The first, and less likely of the two, is that this form of the word indicates God is putting an emphasis on his majesty rather than expressing a pluralistic nature, as many have argued. In many languages and cultures throughout history, there are examples of individual persons of royalty being referred to in the plural to emphasize their greatness and majesty to the audience. People with this understanding believe there is *one* God and that this God is *one*. This view is maintained by the Jewish belief in monotheism, which finds its roots in a biblical statement of their faith, the *Shema*: "Hear, O Israel: The Lord our God, the Lord is *one*" (Deuteronomy 6:4, emphasis added).

The second possibility is that God inspired the use of the word "Elohim" to literally present himself as "us" as he communicated to the divine audience within himself. In Scripture, God makes it clear that he alone is the one true God, so it does us no good to give any credence to an argument that multiple gods were present when these words were spoken. That would be completely inconsistent with the rest of Scripture. Because no other divine creators existed to hear the words used in the creation of man except God alone, only God could be the possible audience to the words in which he spoke. What good would it do to speak to himself in such a way if he were *only* the person of God the Father? God does not have dissociative identity disorder to speak to himself in such a confusing way. Based on the revelation of the entire canon of Scripture, it is more likely that there was an audience within himself to hear these words. Millard Erickson noted:

> What is significant, however, from the standpoint of logical analysis is the shift from the singular to plural in the first and third of these examples (referring to Genesis 1:26, Genesis 11:27, and Isaiah 6:8). Genesis 1:26 actually says, "Then God said

[singular], 'Let us make [plural] man in our [plural] image.'" The Scripture writer does not use a plural (of majesty) verb with 'Elohim, but God is quoted as using a plural verb with reference to himself. Similarly, Isaiah 6:8 reads: "Whom shall I send [singular]? And who will go for us [plural]?"'

Furthermore, from this creation account it is clear that those to whom God spoke must also possess the ability to partake in creation—a quality reserved only for the divine. The statement itself was an invitation for those listening to participate in humanity's creation with God the Father. Many Orthodox Jews reject the deity of Christ and the Holy Spirit on the grounds that the doctrine of the Trinity negates the teaching of the *Shema*. However, if this were the case, would it not be more beneficial for the *Shema* to say, "There is *one Lord*," rather than, "The *Lord is one*?" The Trinitarian view of God is not contradictory to monotheistic Jewish belief, as indicated by its language. The Trinitarian view of God is by definition monotheistic! The Lord is in fact *one*, and this statement seems to be emphasizing this fact. It seems to be written in such a way that it is inclusive of God the Son and God the Holy Spirit who were yet to be revealed. Those who believe in the Trinity fully agree that there is one God and that this God is one—*three*-in-*one*. The *Shema* is as true of a statement to Christians as it was for the nation Israel. The distinction lies in our belief that the oneness of God is made up of three divine persons. This is a difficult thing for our minds to comprehend, because we cannot come to accept it until we first admit that it makes no sense to us. However, limitations on a finite being's understanding do not preclude the reality of an infinite being's existence.

The story goes on to say: "So God created mankind in his own image, in the image of God he created them; male and female he created them" (Genesis 1:27). It is interesting that within the structure of the sentence itself lie three distinct statements, further emphasizing the plurality of God's nature. However, the last sentence is the key to God's pluralistic mark on humanity: Because humans are created in the image of God, they will possess diversity within the makeup of their humanity in a similar, but less complex way than God has within himself. This is not to say that God is of multiple genders as is humanity. God created humanity as an expression of himself, and we are not to project our humanity on God—that would surely diminish his infinite nature.

Of importance in this discussion is not gender—it is the qualitative difference in our humanity as male and female. Humanity possesses two *distinct persons* as male and female who have *unique roles* in the context of human relationships, while remaining the *same in essence* as human beings. This is a less complex, but similar existence to God as three *distinct persons* who have *unique roles* in the context of godly relationships, while remaining the *same in essence* as God. Males and females are all of one type of being—human beings. The Father, Son, and Holy Spirit are all one type of being—God. The three statements in Genesis are so closely tied in thought that God is defining his image to be beautifully represented in the very fact that he created *distinct* differences in humanity as male and female to resemble the *distinct* differences within himself as one being.

If God were an individual being with no distinction of persons as he exists within the Godhead, creating humanity as male and female would not be logically consistent with who he is. If he were an individual being, it would make more sense for him to create a genderless human that could reproduce and expand God's kingdom on its own. However, this is not what he chose to do, because God is not an individual within his being. Without such diversity in humanity, the crucial roles and relational intimacy God shares within himself would be lost on his creation. God desires human beings to be representations of himself that display his glory through loving and diverse communities. This is manifested best in that God's infinite nature is displayed in humanity as male and female.

This is further emphasized by God's declaration that all things are "good," with the exception of the one being that he created in his image. God declared the *state of man being alone* as "not good" (Genesis 2:18). This singular being was not complete by himself, because he did not yet resemble the community of persons that God has within himself as a Trinity. Without the woman, the man was unable to function relationally as God intended. Therefore, God declared the existence of a single human "not good." To reconcile this, he created a qualitatively different human whom he called "woman" to complete man's inward longing for an interpersonal and *equal* relationship with a person that is like him, but different. God accomplished this by creating her from the man's side so they would share the same human essence. The method of creating the woman is in direct contrast to how God created the original human—from the dust of the ground as a unique being in God's image. Instead, God created woman by taking a rib from the man's side. In doing so, humanity was given the ability to relate to another human being who possesses distinct differences but is of the same singular human essence as God is one in essence.

* * *

Equality in Being and Subordination in Roles

One of the unique aspects of being in an aviation unit in the United States Marine Corps is that pilots view rank differently than the rest of our warfighting brothers and sisters in the ground forces. There is a linear rank structure in the ground forces by which roles and re-sponsibilities are strictly delineated for superiors and subordinates of higher and lower ranks. This is not necessarily the case when fly-ing, because flying is a skill in which rank has no effect. The cock-pit of the AH-1Z gunship is designed to be crewed by two qualified pilots—both of whom are essential to accomplish tactical missions. There is no room in a combat aircraft for dead weight. I find often myself, a captain, paired to fly with another pilot who is also a cap-tain. When we are on the ground, we do not use formalities to ad-dress each other's rank, render each other salutes in passing, or take orders from each other. As far as the overarching organization of the Marine Corps is concerned, we are equals.

When we are flying together, however, this is not the case. One of us is assigned the role of aircraft commander and ultimately takes responsibility for the $32 million aircraft, the weapon systems on-board, at what and whom they are fired, and the life of the other pilot. The other pilot is assigned the role of copilot, and with that comes the responsibility of completing many essential tasks re-quired for mission success—such as the employment of weapons on-board or flying the aircraft. Regardless of how important the job of the copilot is, the final authority for all decisions and actions made within the cockpit lies with the aircraft commander. The copilot of the aircraft must understand that although they may be equal in rank to the aircraft commander, they must choose to subordinate their will to the will of the aircraft commander. The result of this willful subordination of equals is harmony and effectiveness in the cockpit. However, if both pilots were to act as aircraft commanders, who is ultimately in charge? How would one differentiate the air-craft commander from his or her copilot? There would be two pilots in the cockpit, yet no distinction or authority between them.

This situation illustrates how the members of the Trinity have eternally related to one another as completely equal, yet distinct individuals with essential roles to execute. Within the Godhead, each member of the Trinity is fully and equally God. If this is true, then how does one differentiate the Father from the Son from the Holy Spirit other than by name?

For three distinct persons within the Trinity to exist, there must be a *quality* that differentiates them as there is a *quality* that differentiates the pilots in a cockpit of which both are captains. In the Trinity, each member must individually be fully and equally God, or else the doctrine crumbles. We cannot say that the qualities that differentiate the members are complementary attributes of divinity, which will be discussed in the next chapter—omniscience (all-knowing), omnipresence (existing at all places at once), omnipotence (all-powerful), etc. If each member were to have differentiating divine qualities that complement the fullness of the Trinity's divinity, then the individual members of the Trinity cease to be fully God. They must *all* possess *all* the attributes of divinity for the doctrine to stand. Remember that the doctrine of the Trinity is $1 + 1 + 1 = 1$, not $1/3 + 1/3 + 1/3 = 1$.

However, if all three persons of the Godhead are the same concerning their divine attributes, then how can we differentiate them as *distinct* individuals? The distinction comes from their *roles*. In the roles the Father, Son, and Spirit fill within the order they created lie the distinction between them. Without the distinction of roles, the Trinity is simply a cockpit with three captains, all acting as aircraft commanders.

There is a dichotomy to the nature of the Trinity, which allows them to exist as distinct beings. Traditionally, these components have been defined as the *ontological Trinity* and the *economic Trinity*. "Ontology" is the study of the nature of being[2] or essence of something (in this case, the Trinity). The "economy" of the Trinity refers to the specific function, or role of the members. These words are a bit too fancy for my taste, so to make an already difficult concept easier to understand, I will refer to them as "being" (ontology) and "role" (economy) from this point forward.

Understanding each concept is essential for us to understand the Trinity correctly and ultimately to understand how human relationships harmonize best in the Trinity's image. Human beings possess the image of both equality and subordination of roles in their very makeup, and the correct application of them leads to harmonious interaction with one another. It emphasizes living out our calling to glorify God, because we are freed from the expectations that this broken world places on us as men and women, and we can accept the beauty of how we were fearfully and wonderfully made to function by God (Psalm 139:13–14).

One of the greatest Christian theologians of history, Augustine of Hippo (354–430 AD), used an interesting analogy regarding the *being* of the Trinity in his famous work, *De Trinitate* (On the Trinity). While there are no perfect analogies, this one does an adequate job of giving us a picture of how the Trinity displays itself within the context of human relationships. Augustine thought that our loving relationships with one another are a great representation that helps us to understand the Trinity, because the Trinity is the ultimate display of perfect loving relationships.

St. Augustine points out that because of the scriptural claim that "God is love" (1 John 4:8,16), those who bear the image of God, which is everyone, must also possess an image of this love. He thought this manifested itself in our love for one another. In the same way that there are three members of the Trinity, Augustine noted that there are also three components to loving relationships. There is a person who loves, a person who is beloved, and the love itself.[3] I find this analogy to point to an interesting and essential characteristic of the Trinity. In a loving relationship, who can say that one component is more important or valuable than the others? If one element is taken away, the loving relationship no longer exists. The necessity of each

component to exist in any loving relationship requires each component to share *equal value* to the others—so it is with the members of
the Trinity. God the Father exists, and can only exist, as the Trinity
because each member is equally important. Without a member, God
ceases to exist as God in the same way a loving relationship ceases
to exist in the absence of one component of the relationship. Therefore, to deny the deity of any member of the Trinity or to deny the
doctrine altogether is to deny the existence of the God of Christianity. God is who he is and cannot be anything other than himself,
which is triune.

One of the foundational truths of the Trinity is that each person
of the Godhead is fully and *equally* God. There is no distinction of
worth or value regarding any member. This is important to note, because deep down I think that most of us would agree we have a difficult time understanding all three of the members of the Godhead
as equals. From a doctrinal vacuum most people agree with this, but
experientially we tend to view the members of the Godhead in vary-
ing equality. For example, how often do we neglect the Holy Spirit
in our personal faith walks?

From our point of view, God the Father is the highest standard
to which the other members of the Godhead must measure up. The
entire conception of the Christian God starts from an understanding of God the Father. He was the first member to be revealed to
humanity, and he gives us the context in which we can understand
the other members. The first verse of the Bible introduces God the
Father to us, and the entire Old Testament interacts with him as
the basic conception of "God." The conflict of understanding *in our
minds* arises when the Son and Holy Spirit are brought into the fold,
placing them on a level of perfect equality with God the Father. We
understand God the Father as the sovereign God, and through the
gospel we are presented with the two other members of God's being
and must then learn to place them on level ground with the Father.

This is a difficult thing to do, but Scripture is clear that each member is fully and equally God—there should be no requirement in our minds for the others to "measure up" to the Father. God the Father does not consider them as lesser, and neither should we.

In what ways does Scripture make their equality clear to us? This is by no means a comprehensive list but let us first look at the equality in the divinity of Christ to the Father. In Scripture, Christ is referred to in ways that can only be attributed to God himself. The most obvious of these being that Jesus referred to himself as God (John 5:18; 10:33). Jesus is referred to as the *Word*. He is the personification of God's communication with humanity. In Christ, we can know God the Father, because Christ is God himself and is one with the Father (John 1:1, 14). Jesus is the *first* and the *last*, a title that God reserves for himself as the only eternal being both inside and outside of creation (Isaiah 44:6; Revelation 1:17–18; 2:8).

Jesus also claimed that the only way to get to heaven, *God's* dwelling place, is through him—that he is the one who holds the keys to eternal life for humanity. This is an ability possessed by God alone (John 14:6; Romans 10:13; 1 John 5:20). We pray to Jesus. Who can answer a prayer in faith but God alone (Acts 7:59–60)? Jesus is worshiped as God. In his birth, magi came from afar to worship him (Matthew 2:1–2). After his death and resurrection, Scripture records women falling at his feet to worship him (Matthew 28:8–9). Worship of anything or anyone other than God is considered idolatry, yet Jesus was worshiped, and he did not rebuke those who worshiped him. Through Christ, we also find and place our faith in him for salvation (John 3:16; Romans 10:8–9; and many others). Additionally, only a being with equal power to God himself could possess the power to satisfy the full wrath of God for the sins of the world. Christ not only took the full wrath of God on the cross, but he satisfied it so well that he walked out of his own grave three days later! Finally, in the Great Commission Jesus commands his apostles to "go and make disciples of all nations, baptizing them in the name of the Father and *of the Son* and of the Holy Spirit," placing his name and the name of the Holy Spirit on equal ground with that of God the Father.

So, what about the Holy Spirit? How do we reconcile the Holy Spirit as fully God from Scriptures? In addition to Christ testifying to this truth, the Holy Spirit was present and involved in the creation of the world—something only God could have taken part in, both from an ability perspective and simply because before creation there was nothing but God in existence (Genesis 1:1–2). The apostle Paul defined the believing human to be the temple of God, in which Scripture indicates that God's abiding presence on earth is manifested by the Holy Spirit that lives within the believer (1 Corinthians 3:16–17; 6:19).

Additionally, the Holy Spirit can be sinned against. Humanity can sin against each other, but ultimately *all* sin, whether against a fellow human or not, are sins committed against God. Because the Holy Spirit is equal to God the Father and the Son, offenses can be committed against him and cause him grief as it does the Father and Son (Acts 5:3–5; 2 Corinthians 3:17–18; Ephesians 4:30). Scripture suggests that the Holy Spirit also possesses many of the divine attributes of God the Father, such as omnipresence, omniscience, and omnipotence (Psalm 139:7–8; Isaiah 40:13; Luke 1:35).

In our hearts, do we really value the work of the Holy Spirit as highly as we value the work of the Father and the Son? Or do we sometimes unintentionally overlook the power of the Spirit? I know in my life I have unintentionally failed to appreciate the work of the Holy Spirit to that of God the Father and God the Son. This attitude of my own heart points to my incorrect valuation of equality within the Trinity. In the Scriptures, we do not see the Holy Spirit doing the high-impact events we see with God the Father and the Son. The mysterious nature of the Spirit may lead us to think that his work and existence in the Godhead are not as essential as the work of the other two. This is far from the truth, however. The Holy Spirit is often the being who supplies the divine power to make such events possible.

The difficulty in our understanding of equality within the Trinity lies in the fact that we view equality to be synonymous with position or *role*. Because the members of the Godhead possess different *roles*, we misunderstand their equality in *being*. Everything in the structure of our society indicates that a person's *role* equates to their value in comparison to others. Higher positions yield more value and lower positions yield lesser value. In business, the CEO has power, pay, and privilege that the general employee does not have. The rank structure of the military demonstrates the same principle. "Rank hath its privileges" is a common saying among military members because it is true in practice. In the Roman Catholic Church, the pope is considered to be infallible in the execution of his office when the general Catholic churchgoer is considered "more fallible" in their life as a Christian, despite both the pope and layman possessing the same sinful nature. The underlying issue is that humanity's valuation of equality and roles is defined from a life that is under the curse of sin—we have never known a world in which the most humble of positions possesses the glory and honor of the most exalted of positions as it will in heaven. Because of this, we have a difficult time accepting that the Son and Spirit share equal value with the Father, despite the Trinity possessing a *hierarchy of roles*.

The problem with this is that equality and position are not related to each other in that way as they are in our fallen world. God's dwelling place, heaven, projects itself on humanity—not the other way around. Our societal structure is a shadow of heaven, and our sin corrupts its original design—the truth is that the ground is level at the foot of the cross. God does not look upon us and adopt our values in his kingdom. We are meant to look to him and understand how we have gotten it wrong. When Peter asked Jesus what they would receive for having left everything to follow him, he responds:

> Jesus said to them, "Truly I tell you, at the renewal of all things, when the Son of Man sits on his glorious throne, you who have followed me will also sit on twelve thrones, judging the twelve tribes of Israel. And everyone who has left houses or brothers or sisters or father or mother or wife or children or fields for my sake will receive a hundred times as much and will inherit eternal life. *But many who are first will be last, and many who are last will be first.*
>
> *Matthew 19:28–30, emphasis added*

Jesus taught his disciples that the value system in heaven is much different from the value system on the present earth. Those who serve and sacrifice for the kingdom of God are the ones who are highest in the eyes of God, not those who seek only to build their own kingdom here on earth. Christ was teaching us that the world's way of evaluating equality and worth is too prone to error and is not how God evaluates them. Jesus points out that our value system is not only incorrect regarding *what* we value, but also that the very way we *determine value* is misguided. If we place our view on God that equality is hierarchical as are roles, we are wading into dangerous waters.

In the kingdom of God, equality and roles are not tied to one another. Jesus taught us this when he demonstrated it was not beneath the King of kings to wash the feet of his disciples (John 13:1–20). Jesus, who is the sum of all worth, humbled himself to emphasize this point. In heaven, the kingdom of God will be operating under the rules of God's nature rather than the rules of humanity's nature. If we are to understand our equality as human beings made in the image of God, we must first understand the equality God possesses within his being. Our response should be that the Trinity humbles us in our valuation of ourselves and others. Now let's move on to the *roles* of the Trinity.

> In the beginning, *God* created the heaven and the earth. Now the earth was formless and empty, darkness was over the surface of the deep, and the *Spirit of God* was hovering over the waters.
>
> *Genesis 1:1–2, emphasis added*

> In the beginning was the *Word*, and the *Word* was *with God*, and the *Word was God. He* was *with God* in the beginning. Through him all things were made; without him nothing was made that has been made. ... The Word became flesh and made his dwelling among us. We have seen his glory, the glory of the one and only Son, *who came from the Father*, full of grace and truth.
>
> *John 1:1–3, 14, emphasis added*

There are many ways in which the roles of the Trinity could be approached, but none stand out more obvious to me than the creation story, since all three members of the Trinity are intimately involved. In the creation of the world, it was God the Father that first spoke to initiate creation. As the Father, his role is to lead within the Godhead and own all authority for his will to be accomplished. If you are a leader in any capacity, you know this all too well. A leader in an organization has a vision, and those subordinate to them go forth to bring this vision into existence. The role of a leader is to provide the oversight that the subordinate members of a team do not provide. This is not because of inability of subordinate members, but because it is the organizational role of the leader to provide such oversight and vision to bring it to completion.

God the Father is the leader within the Godhead, as he speaks his eternal vision to the other members of his being. His leadership includes being the source and provider of all life and love. The Bible is clear that Jesus's great love flows from God the Father, who was moved to create the world and initiate the salvation of humanity by sending his Son so that all could share in such love (John 3:16; Romans 5:8; Ephesians 2:4–5). The love of God displayed on the cross was the ultimate vision that God the Father had for humanity—and it was Christ who perfectly brought this vision to reality.

Christ as the Son is the medium through which all creation was made, as indicated above in the opening to the Gospel of John. Everything that exists was created by Christ, for Christ, and through Christ. Additionally, everything in creation is at every moment being held together in existence by Christ (Colossians 1:17). God the Father initiated creation; Christ the Son accomplished creation. It is the nature of the Son to act in accordance with and accomplish the will of the Father. This nature is the universal model for earthly fatherhood and sonship. Jesus is the mediator of all the affairs of God, from creation, to redemption, to judgment, and to whatever else that God desires. Since before the beginning of the world, that has always been Christ's role in the Godhead. He is to accomplish the will of the Father. In the same way that an earthly son of royalty would be his father's military commander, emissary, or representative in political matters, Jesus' eternal role within the Godhead is to bring the Father's love to humanity by laying down his life for us that he might become the eternal King of his redeemed people and the judge for those who fail to accept his free gift of redemption (Matthew 7:9–11; 18:12–14; John 17:25–26).

The Holy Spirit's role as a member of the Godhead is to apply the work of the Son to humanity that was initiated by the Father. It is the nature of the Holy Spirit within the Godhead to *complete* the work that was initiated by the Father and procured by the Son. We easily understand what is meant by the Father initiating his plan and the Son procuring it, but *how* does the Holy Spirit apply it to us? The Holy Spirit applies the work of the Son by bringing the necessary intangibles of spiritual life to humanity, which Philip Ryken and Michael LeFebvre described in their book, *Our Triune God*:

> What greater gift could God possibly give us than the gift of himself, in the Person of his Spirit? In giving us the Spirit, God is giving us himself in all his saving grace. To have the Spirit is to know the truth of God's Word, because the Spirit who inspired the Word also opens our minds and hearts to understand it. To have the Spirit is to know forgiveness, because the Spirit convicts the conscience and leads us to repent of our sin. To have the Spirit is to have eternal life, because the Spirit convinces us of the truth of the gospel and enables us to believe in Jesus Christ. To have the Spirit is to have God's comfort in every trial we suffer, because when Jesus said that he would be with us always [Matthew 28:20], he was talking about the abiding presence of the Holy Spirit, who is the Comforter of God [John 14:16]. To have the Spirit is also to have grace for personal sanctification and power for Christian witness.[4]

Why are both the equality in being and subordination of roles so essential for us to understand human relationships as God's image bearers? As mentioned above with the example of St. Augustine's work *De Trinitate*, the lover, the beloved, and the love itself each possess an equally valuable component of a relationship. However, the roles required to exist in such loving relationships are extremely important if we are going to mirror the harmonious unity of the Trinity within our own relationships. The late Larry Burkett, a famous

Christian radio host and money expert put it, "Opposites attract. If two people just alike get married, one of you is unnecessary." We as human beings are all equally valuable in the eyes of God. We possess diversity in our makeup as God does, and with that comes roles that we must play. We were designed for these roles and function best when we fill them.

Each individual member of the Trinity has a necessary role for their existence, and each remains entirely equal in *being*. The image of the Triune God is a part of our makeup as human beings and is most fully reflected in our interactions with one another. The roles played by the members of the Godhead are all out of willful submission and love for the other members. This submission is not oppressive, nor is it mandatory, and yet it remains the eternal state of God's existence. Humanity should mirror this image in *every way we can conceive* within the constructs of human interaction whether this is in our marriages (Ephesians 5:21–31; Colossians 3:18–21), in the workplace (Colossians 3:23; Hebrews 13:17), within our government (Romans 13:1), in our communities (Ecclesiastes 4:9–12; Proverbs 27:17; Hebrews 10:24–25), or our interaction with God himself (Job 22:21; James 4:7; 1 Peter 5:6). We should commit ourselves to drink deeply of the knowledge of God's triune nature through his Word and make every effort to apply it to our lives.

* * *

Which Came First, the Chicken or the Egg?

Have you ever wondered *why* the titles of the first two persons in the Godhead are Father and Son? Do we understand what is meant by "fatherhood" and "sonship" as we examine God the Father and

God the Son in the context of the Trinity? I have often been intrigued as to why we call God a Father and refer to Jesus Christ as
his Son. From our perspective, there are qualitative differences in
the fathers and sons of earth to those of the Godhead—the most obvious being procreation, but also relational differences. So, which
occurred first regarding God's titles, their *form* or *function*? By form
I am referring to humanity's view of fatherhood and sonship—what
we see as fatherhood and sonship down here on earth. By function,
I mean the design of fatherhood and sonship that God has within
his being—the way God eternally operates as "Father" and "Son" and
the way these positions were intended to be functionally mirrored
by humanity.

We need to consider the fact that sin has distorted our understanding of God. Unfortunately, many of us do not understand God
correctly because we came first to the knowledge of man's titles of
father and son (form) before we came to the knowledge of God's relational roles of Father and Son (function). We grow up seeing the
world's definition of fatherhood and sonship and these worldviews
become deeply rooted in us. These worldviews are often incredibly
distorted, so in our hearts a war is waged between our experience
of fatherhood and sonship and the reality of God as *the Father* and
Christ as *the Son*.

I am truly fortunate to have grown up with a strong father figure
in my family. He made God the Father quite easy for me to understand when I finally came to saving faith in Christ. Unfortunately,
this is not the case for many people in our society. A 2018 survey
of American families shows that one in four children under the age
of eighteen is growing up in a house led by single mothers.[5] While
this is a testament to the strength, dedication, and faithful love of
mothers, unfortunately the absence of strong father figures in our
society has destroyed many people's understanding of the true purpose of fatherhood in the family—to be an earthly example of God

the Father. Many fathers in the world take on the "form" of a father but fail to "function" as one. This ultimately perpetuates the cycle of absent or weak fathers, because a generation is being raised of men who neither learned to be a son as Christ is a Son nor had a father as God is a Father.

Children who either grow up in the church or meet God as an adult with misguided views on the Trinitarian roles displayed in their own family unit continually hear that "God is a good *Father*." How confusing this must be for them! How could the love of God the Father resonate with someone who, in their minds, have only images of absent, abusive, or weak fathers? The framework in which they come to know God is distorted from the very start. Some people may have even had a father that was physically present in the home but shared no spiritual or relational intimacy with them. Does this sound at all like the way God the Father interacts with his Son? The language in which God the Father speaks about Christ the Son in his baptism or transfiguration indicates a deep satisfaction in his Son (Matthew 3:17; Mark 9:7). What about the way Jesus speaks of his intimate love for his Father many times in the Gospel accounts? Yet, many Christians, knowingly or not, place their unfortunate views of fatherhood on God's existence as Father.

Let's not forget the ones who came first—God the *Father* and Christ the *Son*. Human familial roles are meant to reflect the Trinitarian roles. With a sinful nature and human limitations, these relationships will never perfectly mirror those within the Godhead. While we remain under the curse, God's ultimate harmony of familial relationships will be masked in the human family (Psalm 27:10). We must remember this as we come to understand God so we can continue to work towards such harmony in our own families. The relationships we have on earth are meant to be the closest approximation of God as a "Father" and "Son" when lived out correctly. What I mean by this is that the *role* of a father is represented in God the Father and the *role* of a son is represented in God the Son, who together manifest the image of God in human families when lived out as originally intended. This is not solely limited by actual fatherhood and sonship but applies to all familial relationships—wives, children, etc.

The original design of the family was put in place by God to give us as humans an image of the nature of the relationships God has within himself as a pluralistic being. God the Father, Son, and Holy Spirit have had specific roles in their relationship for all of eternity. The Creator *preordained* that creation would mirror these roles for his glory and our enjoyment. If you are a member of a family, there is a relational role in the Trinity for you to look to for guidance on how to operate best. Let's look to God for examples of the perfect relationship and not to this broken world.

* * *

God, the Son of Man, and the Spirit of Truth

As discussed in the closing paragraphs of chapter 2, God was not always as fully revealed to humanity as he is now. God chose to reveal himself progressively over time through his sovereign plan of salvation provided in Christ Jesus. Why? This progressive revelation of God is important to understand, because on it hinges both God's ultimate plan and our ultimate purpose. In chapter 8 we will discuss the fall of humanity and why the fall was an inevitable necessity for us to possess the fully mature image of God. For now, let's focus on another important theme in Scripture—*sanctification* (the process of becoming more like God). Through the power of the Holy Spirit, we are conformed into the image of Christ as we share in the sufferings of Christ and become like him in his death (Romans 8:14–17; 28–30). This sanctification is, by definition, *change* in our very being—an attribute that is unique to humanity, but foreign to God. The reality of change is that it is a function of time. Because we are bound to time, we are bound to change. God does not change, but we are not God. Therefore, we must experience change to become more like God.

For us to fully understand our ultimate purpose on this earth, we must understand how God humbly chooses to work through his creation and reveal himself over time so that we may be sanctified in his image over time. God's special revelation to humanity in the Bible is the source for beginning to understand and relate to him, and from that we can then know how we are to understand ourselves, relate to one another, and live out our true callings.

The doctrine of the Trinity has caused heated debate and division throughout church history. As a Christian who lives in the twenty-first century and has the entire history of the church and millennia of theological debates and councils that make biblical doctrine seem like common knowledge, it is easy to forget that "hindsight is twenty-twenty." Could the nation of Israel in its infancy have rightly known God the Father for who he is as we currently understand him? Did Moses travel up to meet God on Mount Sinai (Exodus 19–34) and understand God's nature as a triune being? Maybe, but maybe not. Who were Christ and the Holy Spirit to Moses before the Israelites had received even the basic Law of God?

God's Law was the starting point for his chosen people to come to a knowledge of him. The biblical narrative is the story of how God provided a way for the veil between God and humanity to be rent in two (Matthew 27:51). This veil was placed between God and humanity when they were cast out of the garden of Eden. In Christ, there is no more separation between humanity and God. However, Christ's mission was accomplished in time, and the time in which this occurred was well after Moses walked the earth. Surely, the nation of Israel would have misunderstood God if he had laid out his entire plan to them at once without a robust history of God's interaction with Israel to reveal his character and accomplish his salvation in Christ!

In fact, at this point, the Israelites held mostly a paganist view of God. Their knowledge of God needed some serious overhaul to see God for who he truly is. While I am sure Moses was enlightened to much about God's nature during the forty days and nights he was on top of that mountain, in the end he came back down with only ten basic commands that embodied godly living. By the time he made it down the mountain to tell his friends about them, they had already forgotten the God who delivered them from the oppression of Egypt through plagues, the hardening of Pharaoh's heart, and the parting of the Red Sea. They were so forgetful and apathetic that despite them literally witnessing God's presence in the form of the storm cloud that had descended on the top of Mount Sanai, they decided to make a false image of their own to worship. The Israelites assumed God was something that could be fully grasped, understood, and controlled—like a golden calf.

This story is not unique to the early times in Israel's history. This story is the broken record of the Old Testament. Israel continually rebelled, continually fell into oppression, and continually received mercy and salvation from God. Each time they were delivered, and God's mighty deeds were recorded in Scripture, God used his actions to reveal to us who he is. This is Israel's history, but is this not our personal history as well? Do we not come to the knowledge of God through our own rebellion, repentance, and deliverance by God's mercy in Christ? It is humanity's sinful nature to seek our own way in life, and it is the Lord's nature to be relentless in his love and mercy in the pursuit of us. God used humanity's rebellion throughout history to reveal himself to us. This revelation did not stop at God the Father's interaction with Israel. The hardness of humanity's hearts is a condition that would not have changed on its own, no matter how long God persisted through Israel's failures. The same is true for people today without the salvation provided in Christ.

The revelation of God the Father was only the beginning. He intended it to pave the way for Jesus Christ to bring God's ultimate and final salvation to all of humanity—and in it we can properly know God and boldly approach him (Hebrews 4:16). While it was Jesus' death and resurrection that provided us a way to God, his ministry provided us with the needed revelation of God for our understanding of ourselves in his image. During his ministry, he took great lengths to point out how the hearts of God's people had grown so hard that many could no longer see or hear God's truth. This is evident in the nation of Israel's spiritual blindness. Jesus' perfect consistency in character with the Father should have made it plainly obvious for the Jews to see God the Father in Christ. Predictably, their religious pride precluded them from understanding what was revealed through Christ.

Christ decided to separate the wheat from the chaff by speaking in a way only the *humble of heart* could understand and the *hardened of heart* could not. When questioned about this, Jesus quotes a passage of Scripture any knowledgeable Jew would have known and accepted as truth because it came from a titan of the Jewish faith, Isaiah:

> The disciples came to him and asked, "Why do you speak to the people in parables?" He replied, "Because the knowledge of the secrets of the kingdom of heaven has been given to you, but not to them. Whoever has will be given more, and they will have an abundance. Whoever does not have, even what they have will be taken from them. This is why I speak to them in parables:

Though seeing, they do not see; though hearing, they do not hear or understand. In them is fulfilled the prophecy of Isaiah:

'You will be ever hearing but never understanding; you will be ever seeing but never perceiving. For this people's heart has become calloused; they hardly hear with their ears, and they have closed their eyes. Otherwise they might see with their eyes, hear with their ears, understand with their hearts and turn, and I would heal them.'

But blessed are your eyes because they see, and your ears because they hear. For truly I tell you, many prophets and righteous people longed to see what you see but did not see it, and to hear what you hear but did not hear it."

Matthew 13:10–17

God took special care in putting words of warning in the Scriptures for both those who would witness the revelation of himself before their very eyes, and for us who read about it millennia later. Unfortunately, instead of falling prostrate before the Son of God when the time came for him to be revealed in full, many had unbelieving hearts and *chose* not to understand his teaching.

Jesus was not making the truth of God a secret. He simply presented it in such a way that only those who have a hunger for truth could understand. The funny thing about truth is that to those who hate the truth, the truth often sounds a lot like hate. For this reason, Jesus remains the most controversial person to have ever walked the earth—for he is the purest, realest truth there is and his existence as the truth cuts deeply into a world that is ruled by the father of lies (Satan). Anyone whose heart is willing to accept the truth will accept Christ. We must all ask ourselves if our heart is hardened to the truth or humble enough to accept it.

God put that prophecy of Isaiah in place a long time before Christ walked the earth to prepare the way for the Son. As is evident in Christ's crucifixion, Isaiah's words held true that people still had ears to hear but did not understand. God was not surprised by this, however. Christ's death was a necessity for God's eternal plan to unfold. The salvation procured by Jesus on the cross was accomplished through people who truly did not understand the revelation of the final two members of the Trinity. For if they had truly understood, they would not have crucified the Lord of Glory (1 Corinthians 2:8), and yet his crucifixion was necessary. His lifeblood had to be poured out for the atonement of our sins. Without the Son's salvation, we could never understand the Son or ultimately be in his image. How would the Spirit execute his eternal role of applying the work of the Son if the Son never accomplished the work given to him from the Father? Chapter 8 will dive deeper into this as we look at the fall of humanity and subsequent salvation of the world as a necessity for us to be conformed into the image of the Son. For now, we will continue with God's progressive revelation of himself through the Son of Man—Jesus Christ.

One of Jesus' favorite titles for himself in the Synoptic Gospels is the "Son of Man." In fact, he used it to refer to himself exactly eighty times. What is the difference between the title, "Son of Man" and "Son of God"? Jesus very rarely stated directly that he is God's only begotten Son. Why? What would be the natural consequence of him making it so plain for everyone to hear him claim the title Son of God? Jesus' ministry was extremely well known. His teaching was completely countercultural and captivating to those around him. No one, even those in opposition to him, denied that he worked miracles through healing, controlling nature, and changing matter. They only tried to justify them as anything but the power of God

(Matthew 12:24; Mark 3:22; Luke 11:15). Most of his miracles were done in private, or at least in the company of only a few, and he often told people not to tell anyone about them (Matthew 17:1–13; Mark 7:36). When they were done in public, such as the feeding of the five thousand, we see his true motivations for referring to himself as the Son of Man: "Jesus, knowing that they intended to come and *make him king by force*, withdrew again to a mountain by himself" (John 6:15, emphasis added).

To a nation that was promised a Messiah to deliver them and four hundred years had passed since God had last spoken to them, this would have been a better time than ever for Jesus to claim the title of king. Many thousands of people had just witnessed his divine power. The consequence of claiming to be the Son of God at this point would be that God's purposes of best glorifying himself would have fallen short of his fullest possible glory. It was not yet time for God to reveal himself in that way. God's plan was not yet complete. Jesus came to be the King of kings in a redeemed world, not to be the king of a fallen world. He didn't come to be a just ruler who teaches people how to be better; he came to take away the very nature that makes us bad people in the first place—something that could only be accomplished through his death and resurrection. So instead of calling himself what he really is, the Son of God, Jesus chose to refer to himself as the "Son of Man." For those that truly had "ears to hear and eyes to see," meaning those who were open to the truth of the revelation of God, Jesus was implicitly revealing the truth of himself to them through this title.

In the Hebrew Bible (Old Testament) there is a concept of one who is to come like a "son of man" that was presented in the book of Daniel:

> I saw in the night visions, and behold, with the
> clouds of heaven there came one like a *son of man*,
> and he came to the Ancient of Days and was pre-

sented before him. And to him was given dominion and glory and a kingdom, that all peoples, nations, and languages should serve him; his dominion is an everlasting dominion, which shall not pass away, and his kingdom one that shall not be destroyed.

7:13–14, emphasis added

Most people today—myself included—are presented with the gospel of Jesus as the starting point of their faith. We often have no framework of the biblical story up to this point that makes the person of Christ intelligible in the context of Israel's history. This is something that takes a great deal of study of the Old Testament to understand, and because of this we often miss some key truths of God's identity. This was not so with the Jews. Unlike our culture, their faith was their way of life. They grew up under constant teaching of the Scriptures. Those who had "ears to hear" knew what Jesus was referring to when he referred to himself as "Son of Man." Those words would have hit their ears and immediately acted as a hyperlink to the prophecies of their faith that pointed to the Messiah.

The prophecies of the Old Testament were put in place to give those who had ears to hear undeniable proof that Jesus is the fulfillment of them (Matthew 27:54; Mark 15: 39; Luke 23:47). In fact, as Peter Stoner points out in his book *Science Speaks*, it is statistically undeniable that Jesus is the promised Messiah. There are more than three hundred prophecies in the Old Testament referring to the Messiah. Some of the most basic of these prophecies include being born in Bethlehem, being preceded by a messenger (John the Baptist), entering Jerusalem on a donkey, being betrayed by a friend who received thirty pieces of silver as payment, remaining silent before his accusers, and dying in the manner Romans used for criminals (crucifixion), in which his hands and feet were pierced.

Stoner points out that the odds of any man fulfilling these prophecies alone would be 1 in 10 to the 17th power (1 in

100,000,000,000,000,000,000). Essentially, it is so unlikely that it would take an act of God to fulfill only these seven. He continues his statistical analysis, stating that for a person to fulfill only forty-eight of the three hundred prophecies, the odds would be 1 in 10 to the 157th power. Statistical impossibility is generally accepted to be anything less likely than 1 in 10 to the 50th power. These odds are so infinitesimally small that Stoner related them to the entire state of Texas being covered with 10 to the 157th silver dollars (which would be two feet deep over 268,597 square miles), marking one of them, sending out a blindfolded person to walk in any direction across the state for any amount of time and to bend down and pick up the single marked coin.[6] Those are the odds of a person fulfilling only forty-eight prophecies. Has there ever been anything more unlikely than this? And yet Christ fulfilled all three hundred of the prophecies. Anyone who truly knew the Old Testament Scriptures would have seen the life of Christ and fallen prostrate before him in belief, and those whose hearts were open to the truth did. The application for us is that if we were not bathed in the Old Testament Scriptures growing up, we should respond as the Bereans did when Paul shared the gospel with them in Acts:

> Now the Berean Jews were of more noble character than those in Thessalonica, for they received the message with great eagerness and *examined the Scriptures* every day *to see* if what Paul said was true. *As a result, many of them believed*, as did also a number of prominent Greek women and many Greek men.
>
> *17:11–12, emphasis added*

The Jews in Jesus' day who were familiar with the Old Testament prophecies would have known exactly what Jesus was referring to with regard to the concept of the "Son of Man," and it was not a proclamation to the humanity of Christ. As seen in the Scripture from Daniel 7, this title is referring to the one to whom the "Ancient of Days" (God the Father) will present the dominion and glory of his kingdom, the one who is like a "son of man." This title implied a position of power and authority of a ruler who would one day come from God on the clouds of heaven and eternally rule all people. This is the name Jesus used to refer to himself! There is nothing humble about "son of man"—it is an incredibly bold claim of identity.

Perhaps the most obvious of Jesus' claim to this title of power and position is when he stood before the Sanhedrin on the night he was betrayed. In response to questioning from Caiaphas the High Priest asking if Jesus is the Messiah, he states:

> "I Am," [God's proclamation of identity to Moses—see Exodus 3:14] said Jesus. "And you will see the Son of Man sitting at the right hand of the Mighty One and coming on the clouds of heaven."
>
> *Mark 14:62*

At this point, Jesus' mission was reaching its climax as his imminent death on the cross stood before him. However, right before Christ's betrayal at the end of his earthly ministry, Jesus revealed to his disciples some of the most profound principles of the Christian faith, as well as revealing to them the final member of the Trinity. In a few short hours, he would accomplish what he was born to do—to die for the sins of humanity and subsequently take up his life again to be the proof of our faith in him.

It was a difficult pill for his disciples to swallow. They had left everything behind over the last three years to follow Jesus, and he was now saying that for him to accomplish his mission, he must be led away to die. I can only imagine how confused and scared they were as this reality sank in. Jesus left them with an interesting promise, however. In his Upper Room Discourse he states:

> "If you love me keep my commands. And I will ask the Father, and he will give you *another* advocate to help you and be with you forever—the *Spirit of Truth*.

The world cannot accept him, because it neither sees him nor knows him. But you know him, for he lives with you and *will be* in you. I will not leave you as orphans; I will come to you. Before long, the world will not see me anymore, but you will see me. Because I live, you also will live. On that day you will realize that I am in my Father, and you are in me, and *I am in you*. Whoever has my commands and keeps them is the one who loves me. The one who loves me will be loved by my Father, and I too will love them and show myself to them."

John 14:15–21, emphasis added

The Holy Spirit, also known as Spirit of Truth, was the promise of Christ's abiding presence after he left his disciples. The progressive revelation of God at this point is the most complete picture of our triune God until the return of Christ. While Jesus was with the disciples during his earthly ministry, he was filled with the Holy Spirit, but he was now getting ready to go away for a time, and the Holy Spirit would be departing with him (John 15:6; 16:7). Jesus promised his disciples that although he was leaving, they already knew the one whom he would send to them—the Spirit of Truth. They had seen the power of the Holy Spirit work in the life of Christ, and he promised that this same Spirit would soon be given to them to work in their lives as well.

Scripture makes it clear that the Holy Spirit is a separate person from Christ and God the Father. Jesus (one) claims he will ask God the Father (two) to send "another" (three) who will be with them after Jesus departs. There are three separate persons involved in this statement. How confusing this must have been for the disciples to hear! Jesus promises to them that he is going away, but that he is going to send "another" to live *in* them? And then once they have this "other" they will realize that "I am in my Father ... and you are in me

... and I am in you." *What are you saying here, Jesus? What are you revealing to us?* Jesus is affirming the doctrine of the Trinity.

He is saying that the two persons of God that have been revealed to the world at this point are both divine, separate, and *one* in essence by saying that "he is in his father." Jesus continues to say that they (the disciples) will be in him, which is ultimately a reference to his church as his bride (Ephesians 5:31–32)—a marriage that is to be fully consummated upon Christ's return (Genesis 2:24; Revelation 19:6–9). He then says, "I am in you." Only a few verses prior he said that it was the Spirit of Truth who will dwell in the disciples and that the Father and Son are "in" each other. By now saying, "I am in you" he must mean that the Holy Spirit in us is equal to Christ dwelling within us. This implies that the Holy Spirit is *also one* with the Son, therefore making the Holy Spirit *also one* with the Father because the Father and the Son are one with each other. Thus, while the disciples probably had no idea what Jesus was talking about at this point, Jesus affirmed the doctrine of the Trinity when he promised to send the Holy Spirit.

As promised, the Holy Spirit arrived at Pentecost and the apostles went forth into the world and proclaimed the good news of salvation to the ends of the earth as Jesus commanded in the Great Commission:

> Then Jesus came to them and said, "All authority in heaven and on earth has been given to me. Therefore go and make disciples of all nations, baptizing them in the name [not "names"] of the *Father and of the Son and of the Holy Spirit*, and teaching them to obey everything I have commanded you. And surely I am with you always, to the very end of the age."
>
> *Matthew 28:18–20, emphasis added*

John Piper once said, "The chief end of God is to enjoy glorifying himself."[7] Likewise, as stated by the Westminster Shorter Catechism's statement, "Man's chief end is to glorify God, and to enjoy him forever."[8] God is at the center of his universe and is the focus of all his affections, not humanity. As a righteous God, his concern of glorifying himself is inextricably tied to the love that he extends to humanity. God is the greatest sum of worth and beauty in all existence, and he freely gives himself to creation, so that he be glorified. Looking back through the history of God's people, we can see that this is the commonality that ties the revelation of the different parts of his being together. No matter whether it was the Israelites and their basic conception of God as they wandered through the wilderness, the twelve disciples as they struggled to understand how the Old Testament Scriptures all pointed to Jesus, or the church at Pentecost empowered by the Holy Spirit, God's purposes have always remained the same.

God's love led him to create relational beings to share in his joy and his glory, and he commands us to share in this love by being fruitful and spreading his glory because relishing in the work of God is the highest calling of humanity (Genesis 1:28). If the end goal for God of glorifying himself has never changed since the beginning of time, then our purpose as beings created in his image has never changed either. The basis for living out the image of the Trinity in our lives is not tied to our understanding of God but is tied to our participation as beings created in his image. This is significant because it teaches us about the nature of how God works in our lives. God's plan was not contingent on his people perfectly understanding him. God the Father used Israel to pave the way for his Son, the Son died to give us the Spirit, and the Spirit prepares us as the bride of Christ for eternity—all to God's ultimate glory. At each point in the world's history, God's purpose of glorifying himself was still achieved and will be forevermore. The real question for us is, will we work for his glory or against it?

QUESTIONS FOR REFLECTION AND DISCUSSION

What are six examples in Scripture that support the doctrine of the Trinity? Can you find three in the Old Testament and three in the New Testament?

How is God's image displayed by the fact that humanity was made in two genders? What characteristics of men and women complement each other to make up the fullness of humanity in a similar way to how the members of Trinity complement each other to make up the fullness of God?

What does the Bible teach about the equality of human beings given that we each bear the image of the Trinity? What does the Bible say about the roles in which we are to assume in our relationships? Considering your personal relationships, what are your roles? How does the nature of the Trinity's headship and willful subordination differ from the values of our society with regard to relationships?

How do the members of a family unit mirror the roles of the Trinity? Understanding that we are sinful people, have our family units distorted our understanding of this? In what ways have you projected your family's shortcomings on God or grown to be more Godlike within your family because of your understanding of the Trinity?

Having the complete Word of God, is his ultimate purpose clear to us? If we look back through the biblical narrative and forward into eternity, is God's ultimate plan contingent on any human being? What does this mean for us as his image bearers?

4

The Attributes of God's Image

And so we know and rely on the love God has for us.
God is love. Whoever lives in love lives in God, and God
in them.

1 John 4:16

The forecast called for sunny and eighty degrees on Saturday morning, which was the norm for a spring day in Pensacola, Florida. With no particular occasion to celebrate, my roommates and I decided to host an elaborate brunch for our friends in flight school. It turned out to be a lovely morning with incredible company, delicious food, and joyful conversation all around. I was ecstatic to see that an old friend of mine from college made an appearance. I remember a conversation that I had with him as we sat in the backyard by the pool and away from the other guests. As a relatively new believer, it seemed like a better time than any to share with him the newfound joy of my life, Jesus Christ.

"Hey bro, what are your beliefs on God?" I asked him optimistically. "I started going to church about a year ago while living in Texas and it has changed my life."

I was expecting indifference, but his response is one I will never forget. "Can God create a rock so heavy that he can't lift it?" he asked me, knowing I was utterly unprepared to give a reasonable defense.

"I guess not," I replied, realizing the tables had been turned, and it was now I who was on trial to defend God's existence. I sat there groping for words to recover this failed attempt at evangelism with a proud atheist who far surpassed me in intelligence and wit.

As I mulled the question over, he continued, "Think about it. You believe God is the all-powerful Creator. If God can create a rock that he cannot lift, then there are limits to his power. If he cannot create such a rock, then there are limits to his creative ability. You Christians don't believe in logic, and I refuse to believe in a God who is illogical."

How does a relatively new believer with no understanding of apologetics respond to that? While this conversation did not change my belief in my assured salvation and the personal proof of it in me, being the sanctification of the Spirit over the past year, it did get me thinking as to whether or not I understood God's attributes correctly. I was frustrated with my failed attempt to help a friend arrive at the saving knowledge of God, and so I prayed that God would equip me with the tools to give a proper defense for my faith in future conversations such as this (1 Peter 3:15). It is funny how God works with answering our prayers.

Less than one week after this conversation, I found myself reading the book *Tactics* by Gregory Koukl. His book is designed to arm Christians with the skills necessary to stand against attacks on our faith so that we may be on the offense for sharing the gospel rather than the defense. After all, we as Christians are on the side of truth. Should not the unbeliever hold the burden of proof to deny the existence of God? God has already deliberately made his existence transparent through all of creation, and so the believer does not have to prove this (Psalm 8:1–4; 19:1, Isaiah 6:3; Romans 1:20). Besides, unbelief is not actually an issue of God's existence; it is an issue of the unbeliever's existing hatred towards God, which stems from their love of self. If you are the "god" of your life, acknowledging the existence of the actual God usually requires substantial change in a person's life, and that scares them. I can say this in confidence because this was my personal story before Christ!

One of the main purposes of the book *Tactics* is to reinforce to the believer that it is not us, but Jesus who saves a person. Our jobs as Christ's humble servants is to merely "put an irritating rock" in the shoe of the unbeliever so that they can no longer ignore these self-evident truths. They must either live with the hopeless condition they are in apart from a savior or remove the irritating rock by acknowledging the eternally consequential question of God's identity and priority in their life. I thought it ironic that the "rock" I attempted to place in the shoe of my friend the week prior was based on a conversation about rocks. God surely has a sense of humor!

However, what was it that bugged me so deeply about my friend's question? It did not seem to be his unbelief that bothered me as much as it was that his question did not make any sense. Nothing about it seemed to fit within the logic of everything I had learned about God up to that point. Paul says in his letter to the church in Colossae: "See to it that no one takes you captive through *hollow* and *deceptive* philosophy, which depends on human tradition and the elemental spiritual forces of this world rather than on Christ" (Colossians 2:8, emphasis added).

In his humor, God led me to the subsection of Koukl's book, which is literally titled, "Can God Make a Rock so Big He Can't

Lift It?" It turns out that this question is a common paradox of atheistic reasoning. He proposes other questions such as, "Can God win an arm-wrestling match against himself?" or, "If God could beat himself up, who would win?" His point was that these questions are illogical because they are self-defeating.[1] They are internally inconsistent questions; the requirements of the questions invalidate themselves.

To pit one of God's attributes, such as omnipotence (unlimited power), against a component of the same attribute is illogical. Power to lift and power to create are different sides of the same coin when discussing an "all-powerful" being. It is abandonment of reason to ask if God's creative power could overpower his power of strength. My friend might as well have asked me if I could draw him a square circle. Even so, there are things that God is unable to do. While his argument was faulty, it can still be appealed with logic. For example, God cannot lie. The entire concept of sin is rooted in opposition to God's character. Humans who are made in God's image speak the truth sometimes, but we have the ability to lie. God, on the other hand, doesn't just speak the truth, he is the truth (John 14:6). The concept of truth, whether humans recognize it or not, starts and ends with God.

Fortunately, my friend's salvation is not dependent on my performance in that conversation we had by the pool, but on Jesus' perfect performance on the cross, should he one day choose to accept it. I now ask you to take a moment and pray for him, please. The prayer of a righteous person is powerful and effective (James 5:16).

Whether we are believers or not, I think that understanding the defining attributes of God stirs up a lot of confusion in us. When we get past the self-defeating arguments, we can rationally understand the basic attributes of God. We know that our Creator God is all-powerful, but if we are made in his image and likeness, then why aren't we? Where is the line drawn between how we are like

God and how we are not? Part of the difficulty in understanding ourselves being made in the image and likeness of God seems to be that there are so many obvious ways in which we are not like God. This makes the "image" hard to conceptualize because it is not exact. We know there are many ways in which God is greater than us, and because of this we tend to diminish the importance of all the many ways that we are like him. To understand God's image in humanity, it is useful to first note the attributes of God that we do not possess. Traditionally, the attributes that we do not possess are called the *incommunicable attributes* of God. As the definition implies, they were not communicated or given to us when we were created because to have them would require us to be God himself. When we understand the basic qualities that we do not possess, we will then be able to understand that there are infinite attributes of God that we *do* possess.

There is not enough paper in the universe to fully describe God's incommunicable attributes, nor do I possess the ability to fully comprehend them or effectively communicate them in this book. However, we can begin to grasp this concept when we understand our limitations as human beings. We know that these attributes are incommunicable because the being that possesses them (God) has obvious abilities that we do not. We are bound by the laws of our human existence. Our human existence provides us a glimpse as to how these attributes work, but it is faith in the eyewitness accounts of God's Word that allows us to accept them. So, what are they? The following is not a comprehensive list, but these six are sufficient to understand the general differences between God and us:

1. God is *immutable*, that is, he does not change. His character and will are fully mature and are not subject to change based on increasing experience, the acquisition of knowledge, or the

passing of time (Psalm 90:2; 102:27; Malachi 3:6; Hebrews 1:12; 13:8).

2. God is *omnipotent*, that is, all-powerful. There is nothing that is outside the realm of possibility for God to do (Genesis 18:14; Job 42:1–2; Matthew 19:26).

3. God is *omnipresent*, that is, he is in all places and in all dimensions at the same "time" (Psalm 139:7–12; Jeremiah 23:24; Matthew 18:20).[2]

4. God is *self-sufficient*, that is, he is completely independent from anyone or anything. There is nothing he lacks or needs. He is complete (Psalm 102:24–27; John 17:24; Acts 17:24–25).

5. God is *omniscient*, that is, all-knowing. He knows everything there is to be known and therefore does not possess the ability to learn because there is nothing to be learned that he does not already know. He does not forget, his memory does not fade, nor does he lack any understanding or wisdom (Job 38–39; Psalm 147:5; Matthew 6:8).

6. God is *eternal*. He has no beginning or end. Creation necessitates a beginning, and the beginning of creation infers the beginning of time. A creator is necessary for both creation and time to begin. As the Creator, God exists completely outside of time with no beginning or end to his existence (Genesis 1:1; Revelation 22:13).

Let's now examine the concept of eternity in greater detail. Believe it or not, eternity is of great concern to any believer because it shapes our entire worldview.

* * *

An Eternal Perspective

As Christians, our greatest hope in life is the *eternal* reign of Christ in heaven. From this hope, we should adopt a perspective that is focused on this state of existence. However, I believe that many of us as Christians have never really tried to accurately understand it. There is an important distinction that must be made to correctly understand eternity. Have you ever heard a person say something along the lines of, "In a million years when we are in heaven, will this really matter?" Is this question referencing everlasting life or eternity itself? It is a valid question in the right context, but the underlying principle of this question is *everlasting life*, which is what we will experience, not *eternity*, which God experiences. Placing a quantifiable amount of time on eternity defeats the very definition of it! A question such as this confuses our finite state of existence as everlasting beings with God's infinite state of existence as an eternal being. We have a beginning, but no end—this is what it means to be *everlasting*. God has no beginning or end—this is what it means to be *eternal*. Our understanding of eternity as an attribute of God is misguided if we fail to understand that God's existence as an eternal being is definitively not the same as our existence as everlasting beings.

How can one understand the concept of eternity, when the totality of a person's life is bound by such a brief period in time? Our life on earth is a vapor—here one moment and gone the next (Psalm 90:10; 144:4; James 4:14). To understand eternity, we must first understand time. If we do not understand time, then it is impossible to make the mental shift from understanding ourselves as beings who are bound to time to understanding God as free from it. Time is a constraint of all creation. It provides a framework within which the created order functions. There is a rhythm in creation, and it is that rhythm we measure to understand the passing of time. There was a beginning of time which was coincidental with the first of creation, and God has always existed apart from it.

In our attempts to understand God as independent of time, it is useful to think about our relationship with all the "beginnings" in our own lives. What has "begun" in your life? Maybe it was a marriage, the birth of a child, or the start of a new job. You existed prior to that beginning, and without you putting whatever it was into motion, it would not have begun. You were "outside" of that which began—you were not dependent on the thing that was put into motion, it was dependent on you. On a much larger scale this is how our universe, and specifically time, began with God. Like our existence, for a beginning to come into reality, there must be a creator that has existed since "before" that beginning. Using the word "before" when referencing the beginning of time does not exactly do the concept justice because the word "before" is a preposition that infers the sequence of time. There was no "before" time. The general concept is that the Creator is outside of time, whether one thinks of this as God preceding time or above it or around it.

Unlike us, God has no beginning or end because time is not a constraint of his existence—outside of time, God simply *is*. For God, there is only *existence* outside of time—no beginnings or ends. This is a very difficult concept to understand because we have never existed apart from time, and we never will (Isaiah 66:22–23; Luke 15:7; Ephesians 2:7; Revelation 5:9–12; 6:10–11; 8:1; 22:2).[3] The beginning of our consciousness was when we were born but that was not the beginning of time, and the day we die will not be the end of time. The bookends to our earthly life and everything that happens in between occurs on the linear progression of experiences which we call "time." Time is how we experience "*reality.*" It is difficult to imagine what the experience of being outside of time is like. What does "*reality*" look like for God if he has no beginning or end, but he *exists* outside of time? The closest earthly perspective that we have of this state of existence is what we call the *present moment*. God sees all of time—past, present, and future—in the same way that we see the vividness of the present moment. This is what it means to be eternal—to exist in the present with no progression of time.

"Truly, truly, I tell you," Jesus declared, "before Abraham was born, *I am!*"

John 8:58, emphasis added

The present moment is the closest representation I can understand to be outside of time because a figure of time cannot be put on it. Is a second the present moment? Or a tenth of a second? Or a hundredth of a second? Or a nanosecond? Each moment, when assigned an actual value of time, has a smaller portion of time that has faded into the past by the time the other portion of that moment has arrived at the present. This disqualifies any quantifiable amount of time as the present moment because the present moment is infinitely small. The present moment is by definition *timeless*. Quantifiable amounts of time are either the future, or the past. Yet, at each moment in time, we experience the reality of the present. In the same way that your senses are experiencing the present moment right now, God is experiencing all of time in this way. Let's now apply some of his other attributes to this concept in order to more fully appreciate it.

God is an eternal being with all the other incommunicable attributes simultaneously existing within him. In his omnipresence, in addition to experiencing all of time (past and future for us) as the present moment, he experiences all of time at all places and all dimensions. This gives him infinite perspective and clarity. Building on this, in God's omniscience, he experiences all of time as the present moment—in all places, dimensions, and with all knowledge and understanding. Without the ability to forget, the present moment of all time, in all dimensions, and all places does not fade into memory as a human experience would. The more incommunicable attributes of God's being you add to this, the more magnificent God's eternal perspective on time becomes.

To simplify the concept of eternity, here is an illustration. How does one read a book? Aside from those who like to spoil the ending by reading the last page, they start from the first page of the first chapter. As a person reads, they cannot jump to a random page in the middle of the story, because they have none of the requisite knowledge of the book's content prior to that point. A book progresses like time—from beginning to end. The reader of a book is like a human experiencing time. The reader must follow the book in the order it was written for it to make any sense. They are bound to the natural progression of information sentence by sentence and page by page just as we are bound to time second by second and day by day. A reader does not know what the next page holds in the same way that we have no idea what tomorrow holds (Proverbs 27:1). The reader of a book can remember what they have read in the past or anticipate what they will read in the future pages, but they can only read in the present. So, it is with our experience of time—we can only experience it in the present.

However, the author of a book has a much different experience than the reader. As the author of this book, I do not interact with my book as my readers interact with it. I am not bound by the natural progression of information the reader must go through for the story to make sense to me. The entirety of this book, representing the totality of time in this illustration, is my creation. I know the content and context of every page, regardless of what page I might choose to start reading, because as the author I created the entire work. I see it all from beginning to end, or end to beginning, or upside down and inside out. I have a bird's-eye view on the entire book. Likewise, God has a similar view on time. He sees it all and knows it all from his eternal perspective and God's-eye view. As the author of time, he is not bound to it as humanity is.

Imagine, for a moment, that our existence on earth is part of an elaborate story in a book. We are the characters of this book and are currently in the middle of an intense and complicated plot, which is human life. As it stands, we go about our daily lives making decisions, experiencing life, and being acted on by life. In our own consciousness we are free to continue to live and make consequential choices every single day. As with all characters in a story, we have a purpose. The author of any book would never waste pages on things that do not contribute to the overall plot. Likewise, every character and every sentence in this story of human life has a purpose and contributes to its grand climax. Now imagine for a moment that the grand climax of this story was for the characters in the story to gain a consciousness and intense familiarity with their author. This is a peculiar thing.

How does a character in a story come to know the existence of their author or that they are even in a story? Apart from the author making it known to them, they do not. There is no way for this to happen because their existence is limited to being entirely inside the story—a completely different reality than the author who sits outside of the story and writes it. Now imagine that the author of this story decides that the best way to accomplish his grand climax of revealing himself to his characters is by writing himself into the story. In doing this, he may interact with his characters now that he has entered their domain. Through this unfathomable and unprecedented turn of events, the characters have now gained consciousness of their author and an understanding of their purpose within the overarching story through their interaction with him.

Because we have met the author of our story, we now realize that there is something greater to our own existence than merely what is before our eyes. We realize that although it cannot always be seen, there is someone greater out there that is not bound to the progression of the story as we are—that this author knows where our story is headed because he wrote the ending. The author of this story does not stop at alerting his characters to his existence. He also wrote a detailed book within his book for his characters to read. This book was written to tell his characters where they are headed and how the story ends—to give them a direction and a destiny for their life. It was written for them so that they can make a consequential choice about their author. The author ultimately desires friendship with all of his characters, and he came to offer those who desire to be his friends an opportunity to be in a better story—a sequel where they get to be in a grander story in which the author is the main character.

Some of the characters decide that they want to be in this better story, while others decide that they do not. The author has made clear to all his characters on how the current story will end, and he even knows who will and will not decide to be in the better story. After all, it is his story—he is the author! However, he knows that true friends are only so because they want to be friends, and not because friendship is forced upon them by the stroke of a pen. At the same time, just because the author—the one writing the story of each character—makes this decision does not change the fact that it is the characters themselves who are making this decision in their own consciousness. In their minds they know they can choose to go left or to go right. After all, before the author made himself known to them by writing himself into the story, they had no idea there was even an author. Now, how absurd does it sound that some of the characters in this story are willing to deny the one who writes their future pages? Whether they know it or not, the book they are in is already complete. They need only recognize that the author has given them the choice to be in the better story. They are not changing their future with this choice; the author has already written it—they need only change their hearts *to understand* which sequel they will be in.[4]

But do not forget this one thing, dear friends: With the Lord a day is like a thousand years, and a thousand years are like a day.

2 Peter 3:8

To us as humans, time moves on one second after the next. By the time we are reflecting on the present moment it is already in the past. Time is an unstoppable reality of our existence. To God, the *entirety of time* is the present moment, it always was the present moment, and always will be the present moment. He sees it all from his "bird's-eye view" of the present moment as the author of time. A thousand years of human history could be experienced by God in the experiential significance of a day, and a day could be stretched out over a thousand years. How do you think the day Jesus was crucified felt to God? The experiential significance of that day was probably stretched out like an accordion throughout eternity.

We as human beings read about the death of Christ in the Bible as a historical event in the past, but God, in his view of time, sees it as the present. He is at this very moment experiencing his Son's death as if it were as real as this moment in your life. To God, Christ is currently hanging on the cross atoning for our sins as you are currently reading this book. Think about that. Yet, Christ's resurrection and ascension into heaven are also historical events that we read about in the past. If it is in our past that Christ rose from the grave and ascended into heaven, does that also mean that Jesus is currently seated at the right hand of God watching himself be crucified in time? Does that mean that Christ the Son is also currently returning for his people, since the future is the present to God? Does that also mean that in God's consciousness, Christ is currently interacting with our future selves in "the better story" that is heaven? It certainly does! I find this mind-blowing, and we will return to how this is possible in chapter 7.

Here is an excerpt from C. S. Lewis on time:

> If you picture Time as a straight line along which
> we have to travel, then you must picture God as
> the whole page on which the line is drawn. We
> come to the parts of the line one by one: we have
> to leave A behind before we get to B, and cannot
> reach C until we leave B behind. God, from above
> or outside or all around, contains the whole line,
> and sees it all. [5]

From the illustration above, the Bible is God's book about the reality of the world in which we live. He knows what the actual end of time will be like and has written it down for us and handed it to us so that we may have confidence in our ultimate destiny. While I would not advise ruining the plot of an earthly author's book by reading the last page, you should check out the last book of the Bible if you haven't done so already. Spoiler alert—Jesus wins, Satan loses, and heaven and hell are real.

Although we do not have the perspective of God with his incommunicable attributes, we should take extreme comfort in them. Because God is eternal, he already knows the outcome of the story of humanity: Jesus defeats sin and death. God's people spend eternity with him in heaven while the remainder of those who have denied his Son will spend eternity in hell. Eternity is an *ever-present* state of existence for God, and a *never-ending* state of existence for humanity. Trusting in God's view of time from his eternal perspective is not placing a bet on the better team with the better point spread in hopes that they win. Instead, we are betting on the team that has already won (Revelation 12:10–12), and for some unfathomable reason that should leave us slack-jawed in amazement, God is still accepting bets after telling us he is the victor.

> "Remember the former things, those of long ago; I
> am God, and there is no other; I am God, and there

is none like me. I make known the end from the beginning, from ancient times, what is still to come. I
say, 'My purpose will stand, and I will do all that I
please.'"

Isaiah 46:9–10

Now that we have spent some time discussing the attributes of
God that we do not possess, we will now discuss those that we do.

* * *

Four Communicable Attributes of God

Much like the incommunicable attributes of God that describe
God's infinite nature, it is important to note that there are infinite
ways in which we are like God. God's communicable attributes are
infinite in number, and we are in his image. My goal is to highlight
only a few of them, reconciling them with Scripture to provide you
with a framework so that you may investigate your own life to dis-
cern what it is about you that mirrors God's image. While the attributes discussed below are common to all humans, each of us are
unique in many ways, as God is unique in many ways. We will now
look at four attributes: God's love, goodness, generosity, and peace.

God Is Love

Weddings are one of the most joyous and exciting celebrations that
exist. They are focused around one thing—love. I always enjoy a
wedding ceremony with substance to the sermon. Weddings are a
nice time to reflect on the meaning of *true love* as you hear the lofty
words of the officiant and gaze upon a glowing bride beside her
groom.

I recently attended a secular wedding of a friend, and as I listened to the words of the officiant, I could not help but notice a misguided, and all too common, view of love being preached. To paraphrase as best as I can remember, the officiant said: "Love is an intoxicating feeling and an uncontrollable emotion that must be constantly expressed throughout one's life when it presents itself."

As I listened to this mini-sermon on "love," I could not help but ruminate on how different the love of the world is from the love of God. Unfortunately, the truth about love was twisted ever so slightly in this ceremony. It sounded good enough to captivate the audience of a wedding but missed the mark entirely on the truth of love. If it is true that love is an uncontrollable emotion, then what happens *when* (not if) this emotion and the intoxicating feeling of it fades within marriage?

Gary Chapman, the author of the famous book on how people express love, *The Five Love Languages*, notes that clinical research on human relationships indicates that the intoxicating feeling of love in marriage almost always wears off within eighteen to twenty-four months of marriage.[6] When this occurs are the two no longer "in love"? Should they get a divorce? What should they do if this feeling of love arises with someone other than their spouse—should it then be "constantly expressed when it presents itself"? The underlying societal assumption seems to be that love is only expressed when one feels it in the first place—that the only real definition of love is *eros* (erotic love), *philia* (affectionate love), or *storge* (familial love).

The emotional feelings associated with erotic, passionate love are not invalid components to love. They have a specific place and purpose in our makeup as God's image bearers. They were meant to move us closer to God and to each other, but they are not the sole forms or even primary forms of love that God shows within his character. I would argue that Christ felt no affectionate emotions towards humanity as he suffered from hematohidrosis[7] in the garden of Gethsemane, or as his body endured the excruciating agony of the cross as he slowly died from hypovolemic shock, asphyxiation, exhaustion, and acute heart failure.[8] Despite the brutal death that Christ suffered, we know that he willingly endured it out of "love."

When asked to describe God, people often say, "God is love." What do we mean by that? We say that "God is love," which is a true statement and direct quote from the Bible, but if our understanding of love is incorrect than we also incorrectly understand God. The apostle John wrote:

> Dear friends, let us love one another, for *love comes from God.* Everyone who loves has been born of God and knows God. Whoever does not love does not know God, because *God is love.* This is how God showed his love among us: He sent his one and only Son into the world that we might live through him. *This is love: not that we loved God, but that he loved us and sent his Son* as an atoning sacrifice for our sins.
>
> *1 John 4:7–9, emphasis added*

Self-giving, self-sacrificing love has existed at the very core of God's unchanging nature for all of eternity. In this Scripture, John claims that a person's demonstration of love is a demonstration of their knowledge of God, because God is love. Anyone who does not demonstrate love cannot claim to know God because love is not something you know—it is something you do. We cannot say, "I know God and therefore I know love." Knowing God always involves action, and that action is love. The action of love in likeness to the way that God demonstrates love is our knowledge of God.

Therefore, love is not a feeling as many would believe—emotions are a feeling. Love is a choice followed by action. The word "emotion" itself means "to move" or "to stir up." They are surely part of our makeup as God's image bearers because God also has emotions (Exodus 20:5; Psalm 37:13; Ezekiel 5:13; Matthew 20:34; John 11:35).

However, emotions are the motivating force behind love, not the substance of it.

In the famous story of Jesus feeding the four thousand in Mark 8, Jesus had been preaching for three straight days in the wilderness to these thousands of people, and he was moved with emotion for them because they would have passed out on their return journey barring food. It was Christ's emotion of compassion that moved him to the *choice* and *action* of love. Emotions have their place in our makeup and love of others, but they are by no means a requirement for such love to be demonstrated. Jesus' decision to go to the cross is the perfect example of this. As image bearers with the capacity to love as God loves, we should remember this in all of our relationships.

Knowing love is one thing, but the other side of this coin is that one can only *truly* love someone if they know God. How can this be? The apostle John is clear that the love that God is within his being is the only accurate definition of love and this love can only be known by us if we know God. Any "love" that is not motivated by our love for God is not truly love. It may have similarities to love, but it is not love as defined by God, which is the only accurate definition. Love is defined best when John says, "This is love: not that we loved God, but that he loved us and sent his Son as an atoning sacrifice for our sins" (1 John 4:10).

When left to our own sinful devices, we do not love according to God's definition. The only reason that we are even capable of love is because God first loved us (v. 19) through the sending of his Son. From this we can best understand how we were designed to love God and others properly.

"God is love" as a statement is nothing short of amazing! Love is the foundation of everything that flows from understanding God and consequently ourselves in his image. We will discuss goodness, generosity, and the peace of God below, but these are only a few of the infinite facets of his love.

Everything that God does is motivated by his love of himself—the Trinity is the perfect expression of this. Because of the Trinitarian roles of Sender, Savior, and Sanctifier (Father, Son, Spirit) discussed in chapter 3, God gives of himself to us in love. Because God the Father loves the Son internally to the Trinity, he desires to glorify him above *all things*. God does not only love himself; he also has a deep love for the world (John 3:16). Therefore, in his love for his Son and his love for the world, he sent the Son to die for us that the Son may be both glorified above all things in his death and resurrection *and* that we also be redeemed to life (see John 10:14–18, below).

What unfathomable love! For God the Father to glorify the Son in his role of self-sacrificial love, God must also love humanity so much that our salvation was worth the infinite cost of his Son's life. While the cost for us was great, God's love is greater because it is his all-encompassing and defining attribute. The world does not know this kind of love because of how radical it is (Matthew 5:43–45; 1 Corinthians 13:4–7), but through loving one another from a knowledge and experience of God's love for us, the world will know it (John 13:34–35). When we love one another according to God's standard of love, we best display the image of God to the world around us.

Jesus said,

> "I am the good shepherd; I know my sheep [*personal love*]—and my sheep know me—just as the Father knows me and I know the Father and I lay down my life for the sheep [*sacrificially selfless love*]. I have other sheep that are not of this sheep pen. I must bring them also [*all-inclusive love*]. They too will listen to my voice, and there shall be one flock and one shepherd. *The reason my Father loves me is that I lay down my life—only to take it up again.* No one takes

it from me, but I lay it down on my own accord. I have authority to lay it down and authority to take it up again [*dependable love*]. This command I received from my Father."

John 10:14–18, emphasis added

The love of God is at its core *sacrificially selfless* in that the cost of its demonstration possessed greater value than the entire universe. God selflessly gave up his Son. The Son gave up his royalty, glory, and fellowship with the Father and Holy Spirit to come down and take on our shame, sin, suffering, and rightful punishment. This love is *all-inclusive* in its breadth. It does not seek out only the beautiful, the rich, or the famous, but rather seeks out everyone and anyone who will accept it. In fact, God's love by definition seeks out his enemies—the entirely unlovable! We are all God's enemies (or at least *were* his enemies and have since been won over by his love).

God's love is also *dependable* no matter the circumstances (John 10:28–30; Romans 8:38–39). Most importantly, God's love is *personal*. He seeks an individual, unique relationship with every one of us because he made each of us as individual and unique beings in his image. As we navigate this life, let us always remember that we love, not because we love God, but because he first loved us.

God is Good, All the Time

Primary Flight Training at Naval Air Station Corpus Christi, Texas, was undoubtedly a very trying time in my life. As with many things in one's past, it is easy to look back and wonder why they were so difficult when we consider our present circumstances. How forgetful the human mind is when it comes to unpleasantry! Primary Flight Training is the seven-month crucible that every young Navy, Coast Guard, and Marine Corps student pilot must survive to prove themselves worthy as a military aviator. During this phase of training, every student pilot flies the T-6B Texan II—a single engine,

1,100 shaft horsepower, turboprop aircraft with tandem ejection seats and a glass cockpit consisting of 3 multifunctional displays. At a top speed of 316 knots (364 mph), flying this 6-million-dollar aircraft in the early stages of a pilot's aviation career feels like being a teenager again, and your parents just handed you the keys to an Italian supercar.

Additionally, a student pilot's final grades at the end of this phase of flight training determines the type of aircraft that they will fly for the remainder of their military career. Each day in flight school is a test, and every detail of a student's flying, knowledge, and demeanor is meticulously recorded to be compared among the other students for aircraft selection. The end goal for every student pilot is to earn the coveted Wings of Gold and designation as a naval aviator at the conclusion of flight training.

It was a Friday morning in South Texas, and I was scheduled to fly with an instructor I had never flown with before. This was my very first check ride, and it would have been an understatement to say, "I was a little nervous."[9] I had been flying every day that week in preparation and spent many nights of the preceding two months buried in the books. As usual, the brief time for my flight was at 5:15 in the morning. It was on this night that my body decided to catch up on some much-needed rest.

"Dude, you in there?" my roommate and a student pilot in a sister squadron said in a determined voice as he knocked on my door.

"Yeah, what's up?" I replied, as my eyes drifted heavily towards my digital alarm clock and read, "07:06 AM."

My pupils dilated and heart rate climbed. At that moment, it felt as if pure cortisol pumped through my veins. I panicked as I thought of how I was going to explain to my instructor that I had slept through the brief for my first check ride! This is unacceptable behavior of a Marine Corps officer to say the least. I frantically picked up my phone to call him and let him know that I would be there as soon as possible. I had six missed calls from the squadron duty officer. At this point, my career and childhood dreams seemed to be in the hands of one man who would have the authority and just cause to write the infamous "pink sheet" that could be a death sentence to a student pilot's dream of becoming a naval aviator.

When he answered the phone, I immediately said, "Good morning, sir. This is Second Lieutenant Sauers. I am aware that I am extremely late for our brief this morning. I overslept due to exhaustion and will be into work in no less than twenty minutes."

"Listen, we will talk about it when you get in. In the meantime, do not speed to get into work. I want you to arrive safely," he replied.

"Roger that, sir. I am very sorry for wasting your time. I will see you shortly."

What do you think I did at that point? If you are thinking that I woke up, stretched, and smelled the morning coffee then you would be wrong. I proceeded to break every traffic law in the state of Texas to minimize the damage that would be done to my career. I arrived to work faster in a car than I could have in the airplane I was supposed to be flying at that moment. I walked into the Ready Room drenched in sweat, out of breath, and prepared to take whatever verbal abuse that awaited me. My instructor was standing across the room facing away from me as he stared intently at a plaque on the wall that commemorated the heroic naval aviators of the past who sacrificed all for our nation.

"Have a seat, Lieutenant Sauers." He gestured to the leather couch next to him. "We're going to take the day off from flying today. You are extremely stressed, and it will be unsafe for us to fly together. I need you to be operating at one hundred percent when we are in the air. It would be a lie to tell you, 'I was never so tired on my combat deployments that I slept through a brief.' That is why we have our wingmen, though, to have our back when we make mistakes."

He continued, "What we are going to do instead of fly is brief the material that you are required to know for today's event so that you are extra prepared for tomorrow when you try this again. I will not be writing you a pink sheet, because I can tell by your demeanor that you won't be making a habit of this in your future aviation career. Now, go get yourself some breakfast and a cup of coffee and come back here for us to talk."

What incredible mercy! Every authority figure I had known in the military up to that point had showed me nothing but justice and judgement, the first two of the fourteen Marine Corps Leadership Traits. In that moment, the feeling of relief for not getting what I deserved (a permanent record of the incident in my training jacket and potential removal from the flight program) was overwhelming. I received a second chance. I hoped that the mercy I received that morning was something that I could show to my future Marines when they screwed up big time. It was a great example of the mercy that God shows to us when he no longer counts our sins against us.

What happened next on this hot South Texas morning was what seared this experience into memory. I returned from breakfast and proceeded to brief the required knowledge to my instructor. Much like the earthly consequences of our sins, I was not absolved from all the consequences of my actions from this morning.

After about an hour of briefing in excruciating detail, we were finished, and I had started to pack my bags to prepare for the next day when my instructor says to me, "So, I already gave our original aircraft to another flight crew on the standby list to fly today. However, another aircraft has been freed up from a student who is sick this morning. You seem in better spirits. How do you feel about going to fly?"

"Most definitely, sir! I feel ready to go, and I obviously got plenty of sleep last night," I said in a joking and self-deprecating way, attempting to make light of my obvious failures.

When we got to the aircraft, we started it up, took off, and flew out to the shoreline of the Gulf Coast, where I would perform all the maneuvers required for my check ride. My flying was unbelievable. I performed each maneuver with a precision that I had not been able to do up to this point. The evaluation portion of the flight was over in thirty minutes.

With plenty of gas to spare, my instructor says, "It's Friday, how about we have some fun to end the week?"

We proceeded to fly towards a bulbous group of clouds that hung perfectly in the middle of our assigned block of airspace from ten thousand to twenty thousand feet above sea level. As we flew over the top of them, my instructor rolls the aircraft upside down and pulls back on the stick, causing the aircraft to accelerate and barrel straight towards the earth at three hundred knots (345 mph). As we neared the bottom of the clouds, we pulled close to seven G-forces (seven times the force of gravity) to complete the loop. We continued to surf the clouds of the South Texas sky for the next forty-five minutes as he demonstrated and allowed me to perform aerobatic maneuvers for the very first time. Once we hit our "bingo fuel," the fuel state required to make it to a fuel source before the engine starves, we came in for landing and debriefed the flight.

"You performed very well today, Lieutenant Sauers. Don't let one mistake define who you are as a pilot. Congratulations, you passed your check ride! I hope to fly with you again sometime soon. Have a great weekend!"

As a new believer, this was the morning I learned what the grace of God truly meant—being given what you do not deserve. I was not only given a second chance through the mercy of my instructor, but I was graciously given a "pass" on my flight, the highest grades I had ever received, and a near out-of-body experience as I performed precision aerobatics for the first time. To this day, that is one of my most cherished memories of flying.

Are we to let our transgressions define who we are, or are the radical blessings of God's grace sufficient for us (2 Corinthians 12:9)?

The Lord is *gracious and compassionate*, slow to anger
and rich in love. The Lord is *good* to all; he has compassion on all he has made.

Psalm 145:8, emphasis added

I share this story to demonstrate that humans have the *capacity* to be "good" people as God's image bearers. However, what does it mean to be *good*? Are mercy and grace the only components of goodness?

In the story from my flight training, I thought my instructor to be a good person when he pardoned my honest mistake. I felt he was even more of a good person when he took it a step further and rewarded me despite my shortcomings. However, what if he chose to respond in the opposite manner, with justice and wrath? Would he have been any less *good* for it? There were rules that were very clearly outlined for the flight program, and I broke them. Justice would have been to give me a "pink sheet," and such wrath would have been justified.

The truth is that goodness cannot be defined by human beings. There must be a moral standard outside of humanity on which we can base what it means to be good. If this were not so, against what standard is goodness itself measured? Who is to say that one person's standard of good and evil is more correct than another's? We have all seen what the world looks like when people try and decide what goodness looks like in their own eyes. All one must do is look at the political climate of the nation in which we live, and it will be evident as to how vastly different people's beliefs are on what it means to be good as new lines are drawn in ever-shifting sands.

In *The Abolition of Man*, C. S. Lewis observes that in humanity's attempt to emancipate ourselves from the moral constructions of traditional "goodness," we are willfully unraveling as a species to the point that we no longer have the right to consider ourselves human. He wrote:

> To some it will appear that I am inventing a factitious difficulty for my Conditioners. Other, more simple-minded, critics may ask, 'Why should you suppose they will be such bad men?' But I am not supposing them to be bad men. They are, rather, not men (in the old sense) at all. They are, if you like, men who have sacrificed their own share in traditional humanity in order to devote themselves to the task of deciding what 'Humanity' shall henceforth mean. 'Good' and 'Bad,' applied to them, are words without content: for it is from them that the content of these words is henceforward to be derived. ... My point is that those who stand outside all judgements of value cannot have any ground for preferring one of their own impulses to another except the emotional strength of that impulse. ... I am very doubtful whether history shows us one example of a man who, having stepped outside traditional morality and attained power, has used that power benevolently. I am inclined to think that the Conditioners will hate the conditioned.[10]

The issue is that the objective standards of *goodness* can only come from a being that can hold everyone accountable to that standard. Ultimately, it is not humanity that we will answer to in the final judgement. We will answer to God, and he has made it clear that there is a moral standard of goodness, and that standard is him. Therefore, our opinions on goodness are really of no consequence.

Praise God that they are not because each of us would otherwise be left to our own personal flavor of goodness as we intentionally unravel to the tune of our evil desires with the hope that God considers them "good enough."

Because we are all sinners, there is nothing that humanity can conceive and there is nothing that we can do to develop a consistent standard of good and evil. These are timeless truths given to us by God alone, and they are written on our souls in the form of God's image. However, in our sin we continually try and develop a new morality apart from God in pursuit of what we deem a "better" standard of goodness. We believe that as we progress as a race, there are better ways than God's ways to be "good" people. However, there is nothing new under the sun—apart from God, no one is good, and no one can be good (Psalm 14:1–3; Ecclesiastes 7:20). We are fools to think otherwise.

A perfect example of this attempt at redefining goodness is the relaxation of laws over the last few decades regarding the expression of human sexuality. From promiscuous clothing to extramarital sex to homosexuality to gender confusion to abortion to pornography, the United States on a national level has completely changed its beliefs and mores over the last century on what is considered unacceptable, obscene, and lewd. Humanity itself has not changed at all, but for some reason we have convinced ourselves that we are now more enlightened to what is "good" and "right" in this area of morality. Is society getting any better with this new morality despite the continual rise in many unwanted consequences such as depression, anxiety, child sexual abuse, divorce rates, rape, STDs, unwanted pregnancy that leads to abortion, and medical conditions that are linked to sexual beliefs about ourselves?[11][12]

The definition of what it means to be good can come from God alone. Deep down we know this to be true. The very character of God is righteous, and we possess the image of this righteousness on our souls, however faint or marred by our sin it may seem. We know the goodness of God because it resonates deeply with us when we experience it and our souls long to express it. I believe there are four parts to God's goodness that are useful in coming to a gospel-oriented understanding of goodness—wrath, justice, mercy, and grace. Surely, there are many additional ways that God is good. Understanding these four will serve only as a baseline for us to continue to understand the goodness of God that is given to us in our image.

These four components are wired into us as human beings with the first two being polar opposites of the latter two, and yet they are balanced together perfectly in Christ. They allow us to function as members of an interconnected society and are constantly contending to find balance in our hearts. For example, if a fellow named John was to accidentally back his car into a gal named Nancy in the Saturday morning chaos of a crowded grocery store parking lot, he would think it "good" of Nancy to show him mercy and forgiveness rather than initiate a legal battle for justice and compensation. However, Nancy might be injured. Since she was the victim of John's actions, she may want justice. What is the "good" thing to do? Is she wrong for wanting justice, or is she wrong for extending mercy?

We know that both mercy and justice are good things when applied appropriately. The components of goodness by themselves have incredible power to bring about pain or healing and are constantly warring within us to find a proper balance. Where are we to find such perfect balance? It is God himself who is perfectly balanced in all components of goodness, and it is in Christ that we see it most clearly expressed in humanity. However, before we can understand how the scales are balanced in God's goodness, we must first understand sin correctly.

> To fear the Lord is to hate evil; I hate pride and arrogance, evil behavior and perverse speech.
>
> *Proverbs 8:13*

To sin against God is to commit an act that is outside God's moral standard of righteousness. As the Scripture above indicates, God hates such behavior. Sin is offensive to God and he will not and cannot be around it lest it impugn on his own righteousness. The original act of sin was committed first by Satan in the heavenly realms, and then through the fall of humanity in the garden of Eden. This original sin changed the very nature of humanity's freedom from guilt and condemnation, to a nature that is completely soiled by it. Since the fall, all of humanity has inherited this nature that opposes God in thought, action, and desire. Our sin nature is a terminal illness that we are all born with, and without reconciliation to God we are left in a dire condition that leads not only to a physical death, but an eternal physical and spiritual death.

Therefore, what is the smallest possible sin a person could commit, and does it really matter to God? To understand this, it might be useful to first consider the vilest sins a person could commit. Take a moment to think of such possible sins. If you need some help, I encourage you to look up the stories behind the infamous serial killers Ed Gein or Jeffrey Dahmer. These men did horrific things to people to include the rape, murder, cannibalism, forming of trophies from their victim's body parts, as well as making suits from their skin.

What if it was one of your family members who were the subjects of these atrocities? Even thinking about it probably makes you angry that someone could engage in such grotesque brutalities, am I right? It incites an emotion in you that makes you want to rage against the injustice of their crimes, because it completely revolts against everything you know to be good and right. This type of sin incites a wrath in you that is motivated by righteous desire. You know their actions are evil, and it makes you mad. This is the wrath of God towards *all* sin. God's righteous wrath is the starting point of understanding how he is so good.

Scripture describes God's wrath as a consuming fire that annihilates evil in his presence, not because of choice, but because God's holiness demands it (Exodus 33:12–18; Leviticus 10:1–2; Psalm 68:2; 97:2–3; Isaiah 33:14; Hebrews 12:29). God's holiness is like the sun. The sun is raw, unchecked energy of epic proportions. It exists 92.96 million miles away from us and yet still heats the entire earth providing the perfect amount of energy we need to survive. Multiple sources seem to indicate that if the earth was to move less than 1 percent of its distance closer to the sun, it would be completely devoid of life from the consuming heat. If the earth were as close to the sun as the moon is to the earth (238,855 miles) it would be completely vaporized! God's relationship with sin is like the sun's energy to physical matter around it—it does not discriminate with its all-consuming energy—it just consumes.

Sinners cannot be around God's pure, unchecked holiness, like the earth cannot come close to the sun without being destroyed (1 Timothy 6:16). The sun would not choose to destroy the earth, rather it is the nature of raw energy to do so—and so it is with God and sin. Our only heat shield from God is righteousness, and in our sin, we are not righteous. This may be why the spiritual world is now separate from the physical world, and the clouds of heaven will one day open and unite the two at the end of time (Daniel 7:13; Matthew 26:64). There is no God-to-sinner distance like the earth-to-sun distance that could put unreconciled sinners far enough away from the destructive power of God's infinitely holy presence.

Many people assume that God's wrath stems from an authoritarian nature, which places a negative connotation on it. This is a misguided assumption. God is wrathful because he is pure, unadulterated righteousness. To a being who is this holy, the smallest white lie incites the same righteous anger that those things we view as truly evil incite in us. As mentioned above, apart from God, evil is a relative thing to humans. God has a righteous standard, and that standard is the highest of standards. God's pure hatred for all evil leaves him with the *necessity* to unleash his wrath on all those who would sin against him. We can understand this as a good thing if a righteous wrath were unleashed on people like Ed Gein or Jeffrey Dahmer, but it is rather difficult to accept ourselves as the subjects of such wrath.

In our heart of hearts, do we really think we are underserving of God's wrath? Are the small white lies that we commit daily actually over that line for God? As previously mentioned, the problem is that as humans with a prideful sin nature, we measure goodness by using ourselves as the standard of goodness, rather than using God as the standard. We believe someone to be good if they are equal to or "better" than ourselves and we believe them to be bad if they engage in activities we would view as deplorable. However, from God's perspective we are all bad people in our sin. The ugly truth is that because of our sin we have a lot more in common with Ed Gein, Jeffrey Dahmer, and even men such as Joseph Stalin than we do with God.

Humanity is therefore left in a predicament with a wrathful God. Through our choices, we have placed an infinite gulf between ourselves and God. His wrath and hatred of evil must be satisfied before a human being can enter his presence and live. How then is humanity able to know that God is good if our evil nature has placed us so far from him that like Moses (Exodus 33:18–20), we cannot even see him lest we die? The answer is the second component to God's goodness—justice. God's justice allows humanity to know that he is good. If God chose to arbitrarily pardon sin and give mercy to sinners, then there would be a contradiction in his character. He would not truly be a good God if he condoned any degree of evil by allowing sinners to walk free.

This is the heart of misunderstanding for people who ask the common question, "How can a good God allow so much evil and suffering in the world?" It is an understandable question to ask, but the issue lies in that the question assumes that God condones evil. He most certainly does not condone evil. As discussed above, he cannot even be around it! The question that should be asked is, "*Why is there evil in the world if God does not condone it?*" As we have already discussed, every human has sinned and is worthy of eternal separation from God for our sins. This is known as hell. The gospel is the answer that satisfies the above question that all of us so deeply desire. The answer as to why evil is "allowed" to exist for a time is because of Jesus. Christ is God's perfect justice. Remember from the previous chapter, Jesus has an eternal role to play as both Savior and Judge.

> God presented Christ as a sacrifice of atonement, through the shedding of his blood—to be received by faith. *He did this to demonstrate his righteousness,* because *in his forbearance* he had left the sins committed beforehand unpunished—*he did it to demonstrate his righteousness* at the present time, so as *to be just* and the one who justifies *those who have faith in Jesus.*
>
> *Romans 3:25–26, emphasis added*

God's "forbearance" is just a fancy word for his patience. When the Scripture uses the word "forbearance" it is not indicating that God is patient in the way we understand patience. We understand patience with regard to the capacity to endure suffering in the context of the short amount of time that is our life. Remember, God is eternal. God's forbearance is all-inclusive of time. He tolerates evil for the totality of time prior to the final judgement, not to prolong our suffering or to allow evil to abound, but to give everyone a fair chance to accept his salvation offered in Christ. God is good, *all* the time—literally all of it.

However, there will be a point that God determines time to end and it will be at that point that his patience will have run its course.

At that point there will be no more pain or suffering or death (Revelation 21:4–8)—only God's perfect justice. Justice will be served in two ways: we will either stand before God in our sin and try to provide our own justification for them, or we will rely on the shed blood of Christ to wash our sins away so that we may stand blameless before God. We experience God's patience now because it is our opportunity to acquire faith in Jesus and be washed clean by his blood (Isaiah 1:18) before the coming judgement. If we believe in Christ, we will never feel the sobering reality of God's perfect justice at the end of time. If we do not believe in him, it will be too late to acquire such faith—at that moment judgement will be inescapable.

While Jesus is God's perfect justice, he is also how we can understand the third component of God's goodness—mercy. Romans 6:23 claims, "For the wages of sin is death, but the gift of God is eternal life in Christ Jesus." Christ is the perfect balance of the four components of God's goodness discussed in this section. God hates sin and must enact justice, but through the gift of his Son we are also able to find mercy as a substitute. This mercy miraculously coincides with justice. Apart from Christ, justice will be served. In Christ, mercy is given.

We have become slaves (Romans 6:15–23) and prisoners of hell if we are not justified to God. However, there is an individual debt that God requires each of us to pay so that we may have life. Paradoxically, we cannot pay this debt to save our self, because the required payment for our salvation is our very life (Psalm 49:7–9). We cannot give up that which we are trying to gain in this exchange. The exchange must be life for life. God does not want us to try and make this payment on our own, however, because it is not possible to do so. God wants all people to be saved, and the only way is through his Son (1 Timothy 2:4). If there were another way, God surely would not have allowed his beloved Son to be crushed by the hands of his own creation. Jesus, being the only human that was not guilty before

God, ransomed himself for us so that God may extend mercy to us in our helplessness (Matthew 10:28).

Jesus, fully human as we are and fully God as we are not, has the unique ability to endure the wrath of God for every single person ever created (or will be) without being destroyed. Remember, God's omnipotence cannot overpower his own omnipotence. The wrath of God cannot overpower God's ability to endure that same wrath. A human on their own could never accomplish this. Even if a human lived a perfect life and chose to ransom it for another, they would only possess the worth of one human life and therefore could only save one human. Jesus' life was worth enough to save every human who has ever existed, because it is through him that the life of every human came (John 1:3; Colossians 1:16). The wrath and justice that God demands for injustice and evil are perfectly satisfied in the death of his Son, ultimately offering mercy for *anyone* who accepts it. Jesus can and will carry the sins of anyone who will simply give them to him to carry—he can handle it.

This leads us to the final, and most overwhelming, component of the goodness of God—grace. Grace is everything that follows being shown mercy. God did not need to send his Son to die for us so that we might be reconciled to him. After all, we are the ones who committed offenses against him. God did not need to send his Son because he needs us in any way, either. God is complete and content with himself. So why did he do it? God did it because he is gracious in his very being. He delights in showing favor to those who call on his name, and he delights in displaying his glory to all creation through such grace.

It is interesting that I sit here and write about the grace of God, as today is Father's Day. I am incredibly grateful for my earthly father because in many ways he has demonstrated God's grace through his provision for his family over the years. My father did not need me in any way to thrive or survive. I, on the other hand, did need my father. Everything I had as a child was because it was first given to me from the abundance of my father's house. Whether I was throwing a temper tantrum or helping him to push the lawnmower, my father always delighted in showing favor to me simply because I am his son, and he loves me. In the same way earthly parents go beyond the simple provision for the basic needs of their children, our heavenly Father seeks to show gracious favor on his children beyond their basic need of reconciliation to him because he *loves* them (Psalm 103:13).

> In him we have redemption through his blood, the forgiveness of sins, *in accordance with the riches of God's grace.*
>
> *Ephesians 1:7, emphasis added*

Through the saving grace of Jesus, a Christian can draw near to God in spirit and truth. God intends to invade every area of a believer's life when they accept his Son and mold them into the image of Christ's goodness. I am convinced there is no better picture of grace than to be given a relationship and likeness to Jesus Christ through God's image. From this flows the fruit of God's grace in the spirit such as love, joy, peace, forbearance, kindness, *goodness*, faithfulness, gentleness, and self-control (Galatians 5:22, emphasis added).

God Overflows with Generosity, and So Should We

In the *Havdalah* service of the Jewish faith, many families and communities celebrate the end of the Sabbath by prayerfully asking God to increase both their offspring and wealth. The word "Havdalah" itself means "separation" and it points to the time that separates the day of rest (the Sabbath) from the upcoming work week. In the service, there are a few different rituals and prayers that are conducted, one of which is a beautiful example of God's attribute of generosity. This service is significant as it relates to how this attribute is best expressed in humanity. Among other things, a cup of wine and a saucer are two of the necessary instruments used in this service.

During the ritual, wine is poured into the cup in excess to the point that it overflows and fills the saucer below.[13] As the wine is poured, the officiant of the service recites the prayer, "Blessed are you, Lord, our God, sovereign of the universe, who creates the fruit of the vine, Amen."[14] The wine symbolizes the blessings that God has poured out of himself and into the lives of those in celebration of these blessings. The cup, which catches the wine, is symbolic of the lives of those who celebrate the blessings that God pours out. Finally, the saucer which catches the excess wine, symbolizes those in proximity to the Jewish people—those not directly celebrating, but who are peripherally blessed because of the overflowing prosperity, generosity, and abundance of the family that celebrates. This simple service is ultimately conducted as a gentle reminder of a few spiritual truths. First and foremost, the fruit of one's labor *is not* because of human effort but is the result of God's radical blessing. Secondly, this allows the Jewish people to adopt a mindset that everything in their possession was first generously given out of the abundance of God's house and is intended to be used in a similar fashion. This demonstration of generosity is meant to be an outward expression of genuine inner faith.

For us to accurately understand how we are to be generous as God is generous and why we are to be so, I feel it is important to first point out an error in popular understanding of biblical generosity. I would even go so far as to say that this misapprehension is a toxic theology that confuses our understanding of God's heart and causes us to miss out on a great deal of spiritual maturing in likeness to God. The teaching that I am referring to that I have seen many Christians fall prey to is that of "giving out of your need," and the Jewish *Havdalah* service, which is an accurate illustration of God's generosity, plainly contradicts it.

Often, I find myself conversing with believers and unbelievers alike who have heard and believe the message that it is important to give, no matter your *financial instability*. My question is: does generosity have anything to do with finance aside from finance oftentimes being the medium through which a person is generous? How we have missed the mark on generosity if we think that it is about money! There is a famous story in the Bible that is incorrectly cited when trying to justify this concept—the story of the widow's mite (Mark 12:41–44; Luke 21:1–4). In this story, the wealthy Jews are seen ostentatiously giving large sums of money in the temple courts to gain the praise of the bystanders, one of whom happened to be Jesus. While they gave their large sums of money, a widow came up and gave two mites (the smallest of the roman coins). According to the Gospel accounts, these coins were all that this woman had to live on and Jesus commended her actions when he proclaimed that she had given more than any other person, including those who gave such large sums of money.

The widow obviously did not give "more" than the wealthy, but Jesus doesn't lie. So, what did he mean—that she gave "more" *because* she gave something when she had barely anything to give? Was the lesson that Jesus intended meant to be that it is not the amount that matters to God, but that we are to obey God's command to give despite utter deprivation? "Because the widow gave when she had not, we should give when we have not. Giving should hurt, or it is not really giving like God wants you to give." This is a twisted truth—the point of Jesus' teaching was completely missed if this is what we have learned about giving!

If one reads the verses in Mark or Luke through a soda straw with no context, then the moral of the story seems clear: give out of your need, trusting that God will continue to provide after you have given everything away. However, what does the ancient *Havdalah* service detail to us?

In the *Havdalah* service, the cup is filled first. Through our work, God blesses a family with his provision. The amount of wine that God pours out will vary from family to family and so will the size of the cup according to their needs. However, the whole point of the service is that there is never a deficit in the amount of wine that is poured into the cup—for it to overflow it must always be filled to the brim. The *needs* (not wants—and we must be careful in this distinction to evaluate our true needs) of each family are provided for and enough remains for the blessing of others through generosity (Psalm 34:10; Matthew 6:8; Luke 12:31; Philippians 4:19). Then and only then can excess wine fall into the saucer below.

Now, obviously life is not always a pretty picture such as this. People have hard times and get laid off from their jobs. People are victims of other people's sin which could preclude the means to "overflow." People may also not be able to work or materially provide for themselves due to poor health. However, is God calling these people to give what they do not have or to give to the point that they cannot even put food on their own table? Is that really what a loving God would ask of his children—to starve themselves in the name of generosity? Is this the heart of the matter that Christ was teaching about generosity? If this were the message, then the *Havdalah* service should really be that the wine is poured first into the saucer, and then into the cup with the hope that there is still enough wine left over to provide for the family's needs.

Back when the books of the Bible were originally written there were no verses or chapters—only long manuscripts. It was not until AD 1551 that the Bible was broken up into the format that we are familiar with today.[15] This is important to understand because it causes us to place unintended breaks in our reading of stories such as the story of the widow's mite, which often confuses their meanings. In the last verse of the preceding chapter in both Gospel accounts where this story is held, Jesus preached on how the religious officials of that day "devoured the houses of widows." This preaching occurred possibly seconds prior to Jesus looking up and witnessing the widow give all that she had.[16] Is this coincidental? The reality was that widows were preyed on in that day. In a culture where wealth was transferred by inheritance through sons, becoming a widow was a sentence to extreme poverty. Despite this widow's incredibly difficult circumstances, the joy that flowed from her heart in worship to God prevailed, and because of this, God was more pleased with her offering than he was with any other great sum offered that day. Jesus' teaching was not a proclamation that she gave more because she sacrificed all that she had left, but that she gave more because the *attitude of her heart* was the only attitude that demonstrated genuine worship to God.

The lesson that should be gleaned from these Scriptures is not that we should give all that we have even if the power company is about to shut off our lights, but rather that our generosity should have zero ties to our convenience or earthly security. The call of generosity is neither recklessness nor prudence, but rather it is to mirror the heart of God in all our dealings with the things in which God has blessed us. Our generosity should be tied to our love of Christ and our deep faith in the God who became poor so that we might become rich (2 Corinthians 8:9). Our generosity should flow from devoted worship and imitation of God's character *despite* our circumstances—for richer or poorer. Sacrificial giving is admirable, and Jesus commended the widow for this even though some might consider it foolish to handle finances in such a way. Similarly, the apostle Paul commends the Macedonian churches for their extreme gifts despite their poverty (2 Corinthians 8:1–13). However, these commendations were given because the acts of generosity demonstrated extreme satisfaction in the Lord rather than in their worldly comforts. We must be careful not to make poverty or wealth virtuous in our demonstration of generosity—God couldn't care less about a person's means because that is not what generosity is about. Poverty and wealth are both *amoral* positions. Generosity is about the attitude of our hearts.

The interesting thing about generosity when it comes to the giving of finances, however, is that it is not about the money. Oftentimes when we give our money, we think that the amount we give is what is going to make the difference in God's kingdom. God does not need a person's money to advance his kingdom—period. In a psalm of Asaph, one of David's chief musicians, we see this:

I bring no charges against you concerning your sacrifices or concerning your burnt offerings, which are ever before me. *I have no need* of a bull from your stall or of goats from your pens, *for every animal of the forest is mine, and the cattle on a thousand hills.* I know every bird in the mountains, and the insects in the fields are mine. If I were hungry I would not tell you, *for the world is mine, and all that is in it.* Do I eat the flesh of bulls or drink the blood of goats? "Sacrifice thank offerings to God, fulfill your vows to the Most High, and call on me in the day of trouble; I will deliver you, and you will honor me."

Psalm 50:8–15, emphasis added

God already owns every dollar in our bank accounts whether we act in accordance with that truth or not. Money is a medium that humans created to add a universally accepted value to a person's time, talent, and treasure. As demonstrated in the Scripture above, God owns the world and everything in it, including your time, talents, and treasures. So why would he need our money? The answer is that he doesn't. If we can add no value to God's net worth, then there must be an important reason that God calls us to generosity. Being generous goes much deeper than the call to drop a couple of the smaller denominations in your billfold into the offering basket as it comes across your lap so that the church can keep its doors open. Yes, churches use money that is given to them by believers to operate, but can God not provide for his bride, the church, if it is his will to do so? God will not be limited by our limited faith in him!

The reason generosity is our call as God's image bearers is because God is generous in his very being, and in us giving of ourselves we are acting out and growing in a likeness of that attribute. Many of us have read the words of Jesus in the book of Acts, "It is more blessed to give than to receive" (Acts 20:35). Generosity is about much more than our money; it is about the entirety of how we live our lives. Are we living with open hands, or with white knuckles from our tight grip on what is not ours in the first place? The story of the widow's mite was not a story that teaches us we should give out of our need to be blessed by God, to pay our "dues" to church, or to give God's kingdom something that it desperately needs. The story is meant to teach us that living a generous life is the natural response to the one who gave all of himself to us with open and nail-pierced hands.

> "For God so loved the world that he *gave* his one and
> only Son, that whoever believes in him shall not per-
> ish but have eternal life."
>
> *John 3:16, emphasis added*

Giving sacrificially is not giving out of need, but rather it is sacrificing out of the abundance of what you have already been given for the sake of others (2 Corinthians 8:12–15). It is sacrificing some of the comforts of your life above your needs and overflowing that abundance of blessings into the lives of others. This means giving of yourself in every area in which there are blessings to overflow—including your time, talents, and treasures. Understanding the generosity of God is extremely difficult if the only way we understand it is that giving of ourselves should be a burden. Therefore, the apostle Paul wrote in 2 Corinthians:

Remember this: Whoever sows sparingly will also reap sparingly, and whoever sows generously will also reap generously. Each of you should give what you have decided in your heart to give, *not reluctantly or out of compulsion, for God loves a cheerful giver.*

9:6–8, emphasis added

Most of us know the feeling of giving a loved one a gift on Christmas. When you give it to them, you long to see the look of satisfaction and joy on their face. It truly is better to give than to receive. Giving resonates with who we are as human beings. Likewise, in almost every one of God's actions in the Bible from creating humanity and a beautiful world for them to live to giving us eternal life through his Son, Jesus, he does so cheerfully out of the kindness of his heart.

In its essence, to have the image of God means that we function best when we are focused outwardly on the needs of others as God is focused on the needs of others. Jesus taught a parable in Luke 12 about a rich man who was not so focused on the needs of others. This man had an abundant harvest and decided that he would store up the surplus grain into bigger and bigger storehouses, thinking it would provide him security for years to come. His inward focus made him rich, but not rich towards God. Seeing this, God said to the man, "You fool! This very night your life will be demanded from you. Then who will get what you have prepared for yourself?" (Luke 12:16–21). God gave this man much to overflow with generosity, and yet the rich fool thought only of himself. His greed blinded him so far to the point that he had gained the entire world in perceived security, and yet forfeited his soul (Mathew 16:26). Humans were not meant to build kingdoms for themselves (Psalm 119:36). This is not to say that financial prudence is not a good thing. Godly wisdom indicates that one should demonstrate fiscal responsibility, as the Scriptures are steeped with teachings on finance: "The wise store up choice food and olive oil, but fools gulp theirs down" (Proverbs 21:20).

However, the overarching reality is that generosity is a law of the universe in which God created, and we should not try to be the exception to it. God gave humanity his image of generosity so that we may freely give of ourselves to others so that all of creation may thrive as God does within himself. God delights in this. This law of generosity states that a person should not be a dam with their floodgates closed; rather, they should be a lake with a flowing river which generously provides to those downstream (Psalm 36:8). Generosity is the action that allows the world to interact in the same way that God interacts with the world—he gives of himself to glorify himself in the provision of others. In turn, when we give to others, we give glory to God by mirroring this image.

> A generous person will prosper; whoever refreshes others will be refreshed.
>
> *Proverbs 11:25*

The final attribute of God's image in humanity that we will discuss is that of order, or peace.

Prince of Peace

> For to us a child is born, to us a son is given, and the government will be on his shoulders. And he will be called Wonderful Counselor, Mighty God, Everlasting Father, Prince of Peace. Of the greatness of his government and peace there will be no end. He will reign on David's throne and over his kingdom, establishing and upholding it with justice and righteousness from that time on and forever. The zeal of the Lord Almighty will accomplish this.
>
> *Isaiah 9:6–7*

The human heart desires peace above all else—a peace that we were born to experience but have never known. Humanity's best attempt at attaining peace in the fallen world has been through the establishment of government. We live in a world that is ruled by governments and the leaders of them, all in the name of peace. In fact, government as an instrument of peace is a concept that was created by God when he made humanity to eternally live under the perfect governmental rule of Christ (Genesis 9:5–6; Romans 13:1–2). The above prophecy of Isaiah beautifully links the attribute of God's peace to the perfect governing of Christ, which is how the peace of God will most accurately be expressed throughout everlasting life.

To a degree, even in the fallen world we can experience this order and peace while living under our own governments. From this faint understanding we can joyfully anticipate a future world that knows nothing but the order provided by the perfectly just and righteous ruler, Jesus Christ. Our current government offers some protection from those who wish to do us harm or rob us of our life and liberty. Social programs exist to lend a helping hand to the marginalized or offer oppressed peoples a better chance at making a life for themselves. Government provides many things to its citizens that they would not be able to do for themselves if they were to live apart from governmental rule—highways, irrigation, education, and basic mail services to name a few.

The collective innovation and order brought about by a people working together for a common good has produced incredible advancements in technology. In the last century alone the U.S. government has produced innovations such as GPS, the internet (including Google itself), smartphone technologies, Magnetic Resonance Imaging (MRI), the Human Genome Project, civil aviation, and even lactose-free milk.[17] Can you imagine what we as perfected human beings will be capable of accomplishing together under the rule of Jesus Christ?

When you stop and think about it, regardless of your political views or the perceived inefficiencies of our imperfect government, in America we are provided an incredible amount of peace and order in our everyday lives. Most of us do not lie awake at night in fear for the safety of our families as do many unfortunate souls in other nations. When is the last time you have driven through an intersection worried that another citizen will blatantly ignore a stop light and crash into you? Do you ever doubt whether food or medicines with FDA approved labels are fit for human consumption? This is not the case in many places where there is no rule of law, and the lives of those living in those places are characterized by disorder and anguish apart from the peace of Christ.

It is innate in the image of the God of peace that we so desire order and peace in our own lives. We see in the prophecy of Isaiah that Jesus is called the "Prince of Peace" *because* the government will be on his shoulders. In heaven there will be one government for all of God's people and Jesus will be King. There will be no need for social programs that help the marginalized or oppressed because there will be no marginalized or oppressed people. There will be no need for a military because the God of angel armies (Matthew 26:53) will have already defeated his enemies for good. There will simply be a governance of a people who are without sin, living in harmony for the mutual benefit of growing and expanding the kingdom of God forever. Isaiah also declares in prophecy:

> But he was pierced for our transgressions, he was crushed for our iniquities; the punishment that brought us *peace* was on him, and by his wounds we are healed.
>
> *Isaiah 53:5*

"Though the mountains be shaken and the hills be removed, yet my unfailing love for you will not be shaken nor my *covenant of peace* be removed," says the Lord, who has compassion on you. *"Afflicted city, lashed by storms and not comforted, I will rebuild you* with stones of turquoise, your foundations with lapis lazuli. I will make your battlements of rubies, your gates of sparkling jewels, and all your walls of precious stones. All your children will be taught by the Lord, and *great will be their peace."*

54:10–13, emphasis added

Peace is the condition that comes from being given freedom from the oppressive nature, disorder, shame, and guilt that sin brings to all of us. Jesus, the one who frees us from our sin, says to his followers, "Peace I leave with you. *My peace* I give you. I do not give as the world gives. Do not let your hearts be troubled and do not be afraid" (John 14:27). The desire for peace and order within his creation is inherent to God's being—he is peace personified! The rule of law we currently live under is the requirement for people who are enslaved by sin—the law exposes our inability to live holy lives devoted to God (Psalm 81:12; Romans 1:24, 1 John 3:4). There will be no need for such laws in a world filled with people who operate freely according to the peace conferred on their souls through Christ; that is, no laws except one—the law of love.

> God's law of love is the outward flow of his personhood in the constant dispersion of himself to create, uphold and sustain the universe. This giving, outward-moving, other-centered love is the design on which all creation was constructed to operate. The law of love is the principle of selfless giving, which is the foundation upon which all life is built to function. Simply put, the law of love is the law of life! Harmony with this principle

brings life, health, and happiness. Disharmony naturally results in pain, suffering, and death. "We know that we have passed from death to life, because we love each other. Anyone who does not love remains in death" [1 John 3:14]. [18]

God established government and gives government the power to take life in order to punish evil and to establish order in a fallen world. Those in the police and military professions should see themselves in that God ordained role. Also, we must remember that for a time the governments of this world are under the authority of Satan. In Luke 4:5–7 Satan claims to have the authority to give the kingdoms of the earth to anyone he chooses. Jesus does not refute this claim. So, while we are to work for peace, we must also remember that until Christ returns there will always be war. This war is the topic of discussion in the next chapter.

QUESTIONS FOR REFLECTION AND DISCUSSION

What are some of the marks of divinity—the incommunicable attributes of God? Do you believe that God actually has these attributes? If so, what does it mean for all of creation that such a God exists? What does it mean for you that such a God exists? How does this affect your life?

What does it mean to have an eternal perspective? What is time, and how does time fit into eternity? What are the differences between the way that God interacts with time and the way that we interact with it? How does an eternal perspective on time bring clarity to the biblical narrative and the problem of evil?

How do the following communicable attributes of God's image manifest themselves in your life—spirituality, knowledge, wisdom, truthfulness, goodness, love, holiness, peace, righteousness, generosity, jealousy, will, freedom, sovereignty, power, perfection, blessedness, beauty, and glory? In having these attributes, what can we learn about Jesus? What does Jesus, the perfect image of these attributes, teach us about ourselves in that they will be made perfect within us in heaven?

5

What About Satan?

*"The thief comes only to steal and kill and destroy; I have
come that they may have life, and have it to the full."*

John 10:10

In the opening scenes of the popular 1999 film *The Matrix*, the pro-
tagonist, Thomas Anderson (Keanu Reeves), is "living" his normal
life like everybody else around him. By day, Thomas works a mun-
dane job from his cubicle in corporate America, and by night he es-
capes the bland reality of his existence as a hacker operating under
the alias "Neo." On one particular evening, Neo is contacted by a
woman named Trinity (Carrie-Anne Moss) who seeks to broker a
meeting with an elusive figure named Morpheus (Laurence Fish-
burne) who can give Neo answers to his seemingly insignificant life.
Through an interesting turn of events, Neo meets Morpheus and is
ultimately presented with a choice between two pills—the red pill
or the blue pill. Neo is promised by Morpheus that if he takes the
blue pill, he will go on to live his normal life, wake up in his bed,

and continue to believe whatever he desires. If he takes the red pill, however, he will be enlightened to the truth of his existence—never to return. The stakes for Neo have never been higher, and the audience, along with Neo, is asked to consider the question, "Is there more to life than this?"

Without hesitation, due to the overwhelming dissatisfaction with his life and the simplicity of the binary decision to change, Neo takes the red pill. He is freed from the virtual prison called "the Matrix" that enslaves the minds of the entire human race. Neo now realizes that what he thought to be real-life was a façade that enables "the machines" to farm human beings as biochemical energy slaves. The reality is that the vast majority of the human race is not truly alive—they are essentially nothing more than cattle that are used to feed the unseen rulers of the earth. Unfortunately, almost all of humanity is ignorant of the existence of these machines and the power that they have over them. The story that follows Neo's freedom details the war between the humans who have broken free from the Matrix and the machines that seek nothing but their destruction.

Neo's freedom from this false reality came at a price. Living outside the Matrix is a harder life than the blissful ignorance of his past, but he is now *truly free* and able to work for the freedom of others. Our freedom in Christ is similar. In Christ, our spiritual eyes are opened to the reality and truth of authentic life. As it was for Neo's freedom, freedom in Christ is often tougher than continuing to yield to the worldliness around us, but the life that accompanies such freedom is far worth the cost. As we live in this world and go about our everyday lives, there is a ruler who wages an unseen war against us and he seeks nothing else but the utter destruction and continued slavery for our souls (John 14:30). He aims to consume every good thing in our lives so that we may never know the satisfying taste of true freedom (1 Peter 5:8). The ruler I am referring to is Satan.

While inside the Matrix, the image that Neo had for himself was fake—a projection of his mind that was based on a lie sold to him by the machines that he did not know existed. Similarly, Satan attempts to sell each of us a toxic lie while remaining unseen. His lie is that authentic life is found when we humans seek our own way, building an image rooted in the temporal experiences and beliefs of the world rather than living with the conviction of our true identity as image bearers of God. The self-image that we build for ourselves apart from Christ is our own little "Matrix." This is not who we truly are and those living apart from Christ are under Satan's deception. Like Neo was before he met Morpheus, we are incapable of knowing the truth unless someone intervenes—we need someone to break us free from our bondage to sin and open our spiritual eyes to real life. To accomplish this, God has intervened in a special way through his revealed Word and ultimately in the person of Jesus Christ.

Like the offer that Morpheus makes to Neo, Jesus offers each one of us a choice. We can continue to live in the blissful ignorance of the devil's lie and falsely believe that we are living free, or we can follow Christ and allow him to lead us in the truth to actual freedom—both now and for eternity. In learning this truth, we will be free to express the original purpose of our souls—to bring glory to God and find life in his name.

However, what is freedom and why should we so deeply desire it? True freedom is not the ability to do whatever we want in our own little "Matrix" while here on earth. True freedom is Christ. When we know Christ, his Holy Spirit changes our hearts entirely so that we no longer desire the cheap thrills of this world, which are fleeting counterfeits of heavenly pleasures. Rather, freedom in Christ makes us want nothing but the true things of heaven no matter the cost or hardship that comes with them *despite* having to continue to live in this world for a time. We experience such freedom when a person's eyes are opened to heaven through the knowledge of Christ. In knowing Christ, every gift, talent, and calling that we possess is no longer spent on the empty promises of sin, but instead on exploring the limitless glories of God's kingdom, which are better by far (Philippians 1:21–23).

Until a person believes and accepts the "red pill" (the blood of Christ poured out for them on the cross), they will never understand the depths of their bondage to sin and therefore never know the satiating taste of true freedom from it. Their sin will continue to blind them to the truth of the spiritual war that rages around them. Until God's enemies are defeated for good, Satan will work tirelessly to deceive many into taking the "blue pill" so they will continue to be slaves to their sin. Satan, who wants all of us to misunderstand true freedom, works hard to distract us with the alluring things of this life as we pursue meaning and purpose from our limited perspective rather than the eternal meaning and purposes that God has already planned for us.

If we have taken the "red pill" and are in Christ, then we must know that this does not make us immune from Satan's schemes. Much like the machines continued to wage war against Neo following his freedom from the Matrix, Satan's goal is to neuter those who have freedom in Christ through deception and temptation so they cannot triumphantly fight against him and seek the freedom of others.

Satan's greatest crime is that he sought to define the image of God for himself, and he desires for humanity to do the same—to be our own gods. Before we begin our discussion of Satan's impact on God's image, it is essential to understand something about Satan—he has a deep and personal hatred for you. He is obsessed with the desire to see _____ [insert your name here] suffer. Satan seeks to steal your soul, to kill your soul, and to destroy your soul because that is what his pride has done to him. In his all-consuming hatred for God, he naturally hates those made in God's image. Jesus on the other hand wants nothing more than to give you his wonderful life through his image. He came so that your soul may have life to the absolute fullest (John 10:10)!

One of C. S. Lewis' most interesting works of literature is *The Screwtape Letters*, which is a series of satirical letters written from the perspective of an experienced demon named Screwtape to his nephew Wormwood, an amateur demon in training. The work aims to present to the reader insight into the crafty ways in which Satan and his employ of demons try to keep believers in Christ from accomplishing the will of God in our lives. In Letter 8, Screwtape makes obvious the vastly opposing intentions that both God and Satan have for our souls.

> But the obedience which the Enemy demands of men is quite a different thing. One must face the fact that all the talk about [his] love for men, and [his] service being perfect freedom, is not (as one would gladly believe) mere propaganda, but an appalling truth. He really does want to fill the universe with a lot of loathsome little replicas of [himself]—creatures, whose life, on its miniature scale, will be qualitatively like [his] own, not because [he] has absorbed them, but because their wills freely conform to [his]. We want cattle who can finally become food; [he] wants servants who can finally become sons. We want to suck in, [he] wants to give out. We are empty and would be filled; [he] is full and flows over. Our war aim is a world in which Our Father Below has drawn all other beings into himself: The Enemy wants a world full of beings united to [him] but still distinct.[1]

Satan wants to consume and take life from God and humanity. God wants to overflow and give *his life* to humanity. Giving life is a natural thing for God to do because God is *pure life*; he is the one being that requires nothing to live and is the sustainer of all life. God gave life to Satan and Satan squandered it. God gave life and the status as image bearers to humanity and humanity squandered it. Then God gave his own life to redeem his image bearers, and even then, some still choose to squander it by rejecting it—they take the figurative blue pill. Our enemy is working feverishly to keep us from knowing who we are in Christ and living fully for the glory of God. We must resist this enemy and Scripture tells us that when we do, Satan will flee (James 4:7). The unseen war that is waged against our souls is the battle to keep as many lives as possible from reaching God's kingdom through freedom in Christ. Because of the Great Commission (Matthew 28:16–20), a Christian is a threat to the enemy's objective; therefore, spiritual warfare is waged fiercely against us.

I am convinced that most of the church is truly unprepared to fight this war. I would argue that there are millions of churchgoers that do not even know that a war for their very lives is being waged against them. Many even acknowledge spiritual warfare but do not think or act as if they are actively involved in it. If not us, the followers of Christ, then who do we think are going to pick up their spiritual swords and fight this battle? Whether we like it or not, war is upon us. Many Christians, including myself at times, are more convinced of the reality of human wars than they are of the reality of spiritual warfare. The truth is that the wars of humanity are merely shadows of the great spiritual war of unimaginable magnitude and eternal consequence for those involved, which is all of us.

As a Marine Corps attack helicopter pilot, I spend a great deal of time "war-gaming" when I plan for a mission. War-gaming is the process of putting yourself in the shoes of your adversary to accurately predict how they will employ their forces against you. From this, the tactics developed for a mission are produced to make the fight as unfair as possible by avoiding the enemy's strengths and attacking their vulnerabilities. Unlike fighting for sport, there is no such thing as a fair fight in a war—fair fights cost lives and risk mission failure. While the Bible says little about the nature of Satan and his demons, because that is not the intended focus, I think a great deal can be understood by examining the tactics that we do find in Scripture and placing ourselves in their shoes. In fact, "war-gaming" spiritual warfare is an essential skill for any Christian to master so that we are not continually outflanked and outgunned by our spiritual enemies. You can be sure that Satan has had millennia to figure out how to exploit your vulnerabilities and avoid your strengths. He is exceptionally good at it and will not fight fairly against you. Therefore, we must understand who he is, what he wants, and how he will try to get it, so that as a church we may rise and join with Christ to crush him! In fighting such battles, each day we will take on a greater likeness to God as we mature in his image.

* * *

Satan Is Not the Opposite of God

The opposite of a teacher is a student. The opposite of inhaling is to exhale. The opposite of young is old. The opposite of good is ... evil? I would argue that the correct word to finish that sentence is "nothing." There is no opposite to goodness. However, how many of us have it ingrained into our minds that the answer to that statement is "evil"? True opposites are members of a pair that share in the same nature but are antithetical to the other. Surely, good and evil are opposing forces to each other, but do they share the *same nature* to be classified as equal opposition? I believe it is important to mention this distinction, because if we fail to understand the power of evil within the created order relative to the power of goodness, we may subconsciously allow evil to have far too great of an influence in our lives. It may be of use to examine the relationship of another pair of words that have a similar relationship to good and evil—light and darkness.

> In the beginning was the Word, and the Word was with God, and the Word was God. He was with God in the beginning. Through him all things were made; without him nothing was made that has been made. In him was life, and *that life was the light* of all mankind. *The light shines in the darkness, and the darkness has not overcome it.*
>
> *John 1:1–5, emphasis added*

The opening to the Gospel of John uses the metaphor of light and darkness because it is a familiar concept to our experience. We know that wherever light is present, darkness ceases to exist. Darkness on the other hand describes a void—an absence of light. Darkness is not the opposite of light; it is the state in which no light is present. Defining light and darkness as opposites of each other would be like defining a student as the absence of a teacher—this makes no sense. There is no such thing as a teacher if there are no students to teach—education is the defining commonality that makes them true opposites. On the contrary, light and darkness have nothing in common. They cannot coexist in the same place. While they are not opposites, good and evil are often expressed as light and darkness because they share the same relationship.

If we understand how good and evil function together like light and darkness, we can understand how God and Satan function together. Jesus is the quintessence of goodness and is therefore considered "light" while "Satan" is the perfect embodiment of evil; therefore, his works are referred to as "darkness"—the absence of light, or goodness. In the same way that darkness cannot overcome light, because it is the absence of light, Satan cannot overcome God because he is the absence of God.

Satan is entirely evil—he is barren of any goodness. However, his evil nature is not quantifiable as light is quantifiable. His nature is simply darkness. Think of it this way—when someone is going to bed at night, they do not turn on the darkness to go to sleep, they turn off the light. On the other hand, God's goodness is both observable and quantifiable, similar to how light is an energy that can be measured and seen by the human eye. It flows out from him and is experienced by all his creation. For evil to be the opposite of good, it must be a force that possesses equal and opposite power to goodness, yet this cannot be. God and his goodness were all that existed before creation, and so it naturally follows that goodness is the higher, stronger, and eternal state of the created order. Evil is therefore a *temporary state* of darkness that God has allowed *for an ultimate purpose*—so it is with Satan, the archetype of evil. He is a vapor in God's ultimate plan for the world, and his days will vanish like smoke.

Although evil cannot overcome goodness, I want to be careful not to understate the power of evil. The spiritual forces of evil are powerful, and we should be extremely cautious of them as beings who live in a fallen world with a nature that is prone to them. Evil has the power to destroy our lives if we allow it, but the point is that it holds no power over goodness. Rather, Scripture calls us to overcome evil with goodness (Romans 12:21).

While we are currently subject to evil, the fall of Satan described in Isaiah details the power of evil in the grand scheme of God's providence:

How you have fallen from heaven, morning star, son of the dawn! You have been cast down to the earth, you who once laid low the nations! You said in your heart, "I will ascend to the heavens; I will raise my throne above the stars of God; I will sit enthroned on the mount of assembly, on the utmost heights of Mount Zaphon. I will ascend above the tops of the clouds; I will make myself like the Most High." But you are brought down to the realm of the dead, to the depths of the pit.[2]

Isaiah 14:12–15

Satan is God's greatest and most powerful creation. He was the "morning star" (translation of "Lucifer") and "son of the dawn."[3] This is a fitting title for Satan. The "morning star" is traditionally the name that is used for the planet Venus, which shines brightest in the last moments before dawn, the darkest part of the night. However, despite the morning star shining brightest in the darkness, it quickly fades in its beauty and refulgence as it is overcome by the light of the rising sun—what reigns in the darkness cannot overcome the light (John 1:5). Satan possesses more power than any other created being, but the truth is that he is just that—a created being. He is not God's equal opposite. Satan tried to make himself like the Most High, and what happened to him? He was cast out of heaven by God into the realm of the dead and the depths of the pit. In the same way that Venus fades with the *rising sun*, Satan too fades with the *risen Son*—the true light of the world. Considering eternity, the evil plans of Satan cannot hinder the good and sovereign plans of God.

Isaiah continues:

This is the plan determined for the whole world; this is the hand stretched out over all the nations. For the Lord Almighty has purposed, and who can thwart

him? His hand is stretched out, and who can turn it
back?

Isaiah 14:26–27

This is a rhetorical question, and the answer is obvious—no one
can thwart the mighty hand of God. God has no equal. God has no
opposite. In fact, evil is not even truly in opposition to God, because evil is only that which is allowed by God to occur in the first
place. In the book of Job, we are given a glimpse into a conversation that took place in the heavenly realms between God and Satan.
Job is praised by God for his faithfulness, but Satan claims that Job
is only faithful because God has so radically blessed him. Satan believed that if God's blessings were to be taken from Job, he would
no longer be faithful to God. What does God do in response to this?
He *allows* Satan to wreak havoc on the life of Job, taking everything,
including his family from him. Satan is allowed by God to kill everyone in Job's family, destroy all his wealth, and even afflict Job with
sores across his entire body. God's only condition was that the life of
Job is spared (Job 1–2).

If permitted, Satan would take his evil to endless lengths. Fortunately, it can only go as far as God allows it to go and not an
inch further. Satan is under the complete control and authority of
God. God permits him to be the prince of this world for a time
and this is only to accomplish God's ultimate purpose—to bring
glory to himself through the redemption bought by his Son (John
14:30–31). While Satan seeks to oppose God, he is not a worthy op-
ponent to God—no one is! God is always in full control of his creation which includes absolute sovereignty. By understanding Satan's
lack of power compared to God, we can see evil and human suffering correctly through a lens of faith as we live out our God-given
purpose in this life despite living among such evil (Romans 8:28).

* * *

A Note on Human Suffering

God is sovereign and suffering that results from evil exists in the world. In his sovereignty, it is therefore permissible to say that *God allows evil to occur.* Let the significance of that truth sink in for a moment. *God is not the cause of evil* and suffering, but *he allows it.* How can this be? I can think of one reason: for God to allow evil in the world and not create a contradiction of his inherent goodness, the cumulative evil since the fall of humanity through the end of time must be less significant than the good that will come from it. If there is no *greater good* that the sum of all evil and suffering will bring to God's ultimate plan, then God would have never allowed Satan to first sin. However, this is not what happened. Satan and humanity did sin, and suffering abounds because of it. Because suffering and evil exist in this world and God is also good, we must accept that despite the seemingly overwhelming amount of suffering, there will be an infinitely greater good that results from it.

We learn this truth from Job's story. Job was not present when the dialogue between God and Satan took place, and yet he suffered immensely because of Satan's evil acts. His suffering was so overwhelming that Job even cursed the day that he was born (Job 3:1). It must have felt seemingly nonsensical as he lost every important thing in his life despite his righteousness. This probably felt much like the suffering that many of us experience all too often in our lives. Job's story teaches us that not only does a greater good come from our suffering, but there is a purpose behind it even though the reasons for it may not always be perfectly clear to us.

Job was intentionally attacked by Satan in tangible ways, but this was all because God had a plan for his life. Job was very much in the dark as to why he was suffering, but through it he came to know God in a way that he might otherwise never have known and God even restored to him twice what Job lost. God planned to reveal his glory to Job and to the countless people who have learned about God's sovereignty through Job's testimony. Therefore, the message of Scripture is clear: remain faithful regardless of the circumstances and trust God for the results even when we cannot see the whole picture, which is likely all the time.

> For our light and momentary troubles are achieving
> for us an eternal glory that far outweighs them all.
>
> *2 Corinthians 4:17*

God allows Satan to reign over this world for a time, and we must experience the ravaging effects of Satan's oppressive lordship on the present earth. While this seems unfair now, we must see this from God's perspective if we are to have any chance of understanding. The image of God is a process of refinement through the trials of suffering, which create in us a spiritual maturity, and even Satan has a role to play in it. Like a surgery that yields a restored and stronger body through a painful procedure, God in his sovereignty humbly uses our choices, whether good or evil, to restore our humanity and conform us into stronger and more godlike beings in the image of his Son. Of course, as Christians we are always encouraged to choose the former and demonstrate goodness in our lives. Once we understand this, we can see suffering as the process of becoming more Christlike rather than seeing it as nonsensical or undeserved (1 John 3:2).

* * *

Humanity's True Enemy

God is sovereign over all, and he humbly allows his creatures to make real and consequential choices to do both good and evil. Both are true in Scripture, and the effects of each of them are widespread. Yet, God will use each of them for his glory. If evil is something that God allows to occur, then this begs the question, "Who is the spiritual battle of good and evil really against—God and Satan, man and their fellow man, or man and Satan?" It is imperative for us to answer this question correctly. Without defining our true enemy, we will be forever subject to deception and misdirection by the enemy.

The divine discourse in the book of Job shows us that God's sovereignty precludes the spiritual battle from being a war that is waged against him. Satan had only the power to do what God permitted him to do and nothing more. Satan cannot wage much of a war against God when he is subject to God's staying hand. The spiritual battle must therefore be either between humanity and themselves or humanity and the spiritual forces of evil, which is personified by Satan.

In our day-to-day interactions, we often tend to believe that the spiritual battle is against our fellow human beings. The trouble is that we have an exceedingly difficult time seeing beyond the reality of this physical existence of ours. Like the story of Job, behind the scenes of the physical world, God sometimes gives an audience to Satan and to the accusations that he makes against God and humanity. God allows Satan to act against human beings and inflict suffering similar to the way that God allows us to act on the evil desires of our own hearts and inflict suffering on others. Is there a distinction between a human being and the evil that they commit? Do their actions define their humanity, or do they point to something entirely different—humanity's true enemy?

I can remember a time when I was considering which helicopter that I wanted to fly for the Marine Corps. There were three options: the first option was the CH-53E Super Stallion, which transports and supports the Marines on the ground in combat as well as taking on a logistical or humanitarian role; the second option was the

AH-1Z Viper, which is solely designed to kill people; and the third option was the UH-1Y Venom, which is a mix of the two. My gun-loving, American-made childhood desires wanted very much to pilot the second option. What cooler job could a Marine have than to pilot an AH-1Z gunship that is unrivaled on the battlefield?

However, when it came down to the months in which I had to choose, I suddenly realized in my heart that I had never considered the real possibility of taking another person's life. I had a moment of conflict because I was at a decision point in my career which had significant spiritual implications. What was the Lord really calling me to do? Could I stomach working day in and day out to become an expert at killing God's image bearers? Ultimately, as you have probably noticed by this point in this book, I was chosen to fly the aircraft that is solely designed for the purpose of killing people—the AH-1Z Viper attack helicopter. As I matured in my faith, I came to understand that Jesus' teaching on murder provides clarity as to whom the spiritual battle is actually to be waged against.

> "You have heard that it was said to the people long ago, 'You shall not murder, and anyone who murders will be subject to judgment.' But I tell you that anyone who is angry with a brother or sister will be subject to judgment."
>
> *Matthew 5:21–22*

Jesus' teaching reveals humanity's true enemy. Surprisingly, Jesus points out that taking a life is not what makes murder a sin. He taught that the evil attitude of the heart in an angry person is the same evil desire that motivates a person to commit murder—that is the sin. Flying attack helicopters became much more palatable for me because of this teaching. The difference between killing and murder is the motivation of the heart, not the actual taking of life. Murder is when a person succumbs to evil desire and takes the life of an image bearer of God. So long as this distinction is made in the heart, taking life in the profession of arms is waging war against evil for the protection of others. So long as my heart remains pure and my finger is on the trigger, I can stomach the requirements of my profession—fighting against evil, not humanity. While accountability remains with the one who commits evil, it is *evil* that is humanity's true enemy.

Satan is a murderer at heart (John 8:44). When we hate others, we become murderers at heart as well. However, this is not our humanity—it is our evil nature that has robbed us of our humanity. And if evil is our true enemy, then by extension, Satan—the personification of evil—is our enemy. A Christian response to sin is to hate the sin, not the sinner. Paul says in his letter to the church at Ephesus:

> For *our struggle is not against the flesh and blood*, but against the rulers, against the authorities, *against the powers of this dark world and against the spiritual forces of evil* in the heavenly realms.
>
> *Ephesians 6:12, emphasis added*

Our struggle is against the spiritual forces of evil, not each other. The real struggle is not against our fellow image bearers although it is true that we will often find ourselves opposing evil that is working through other human beings (Psalm 109:2–5). Contrary to popular belief, the battle between good and evil is not solely a battle between angelic and demonic creatures in the spiritual realm. That is part of it, but it is also a battle fought here on earth in the hearts of human beings. Because darkness cannot overcome light, the battle must occur through a medium that has the capacity to do both good and evil—human beings. We are both evil in our sin and righteous in Christ, possessing the capacity for both. Because Satan cannot oppose God, he will attack that which God loves—human beings. The battlefield for Satan must occur in the hearts of each of us, as he relies on our weakness to wage his war against God.

Like Job, we are subject to pain and suffering inflicted by Satan, and the way in which we respond to it is critical. Our daily responses to both the devil's attacks and the evil desires within our hearts are the battles won and lost in the spiritual war for our souls. We may not always have a full understanding as to why we are being attacked, but the one thing that we can be sure of is that we *will be* attacked. Our faith in God and the power that he gives us through the abiding presence of his Spirit empower our choices to be of serious consequence in this war (Acts 3:12; 2 Corinthians 4:6–7; 12:9; Ephesians 3:20).

There is beauty in the struggle of good and evil that we face in life. In our current state, we are weak in mind, body, and spirit. Our weakness makes it easier for Satan to win some of the battles, but through this same weakness, Christ's power and victory are made perfect (2 Corinthians 12:9). We can do nothing good apart from Christ, but through him we have the resurrection power that gives us the ability to resist the devil and know that he will flee in the presence of Christ's goodness (James 4:7). Our reactions to the day-to-day attacks of Satan and his demons could be like Job's, praising God despite our suffering and thereby walking in a manner worthy of the gospel (Colossians 1:9–14). The other option is to allow ourselves to continue to be shackled by our sin and the lies of Satan even though we have the power to overcome.

As God's image bearers we have the desire to demonstrate love as God demonstrates love and Christ gives us the freedom from sin to do that. The sin that another person commits is not what defines that person, God's image is where their identity is found. Therefore, we are not to hate each other, but instead we are to hate the sin and the one who first tempted us to sin—Satan. While it is not the focus of the greatest commandment of loving God with all that we are, it is consistent with the nature of God to hate that which is evil, and for that reason it is not sinful to hate the paragon of evil, Satan

(Psalm 97:10; 139:21). John Piper takes this a step further, stating that hating Satan is actually a necessity for those who love God: "Not to hate an impenitent fountain of evil is not to love the good."[4]

Jesus was not fooled by Satan's misdirection of him being the true enemy, and we must not be either. When Jesus told his disciples that he must die so that he can be raised to life and accomplish his mission, Peter pulled him aside to give Jesus some words of wisdom on what the Son of God ought to do for God's kingdom:

> Peter took him aside and began to rebuke him. "Never, Lord!" he said. "This shall never happen to you!" Jesus turned and said to Peter, "*Get behind me, Satan!* You are a stumbling block to me; you do not have in mind the concerns of God, but merely human concerns."
>
> *Matthew 16:23, emphasis added*

Ouch! What a name to be called by the Son of God! However, was Jesus really calling Peter "Satan"? It was not Peter who was trying to thwart the plans of God, but Satan himself. While Satan did not force Peter's hand, he used Peter's weakness to attempt to thwart God's plan for the salvation of all humanity. Jesus saw right through Peter to his true enemy and he called Satan out for it. We therefore must learn to see past the shortcomings of our fellow image bearers, deal with them in love, and oppose our true enemy—evil.

Satan has had thousands of years perfecting his craft of fooling humanity to oppose the will of God in thought, action, and deed. He is so good at it that most of the time we do not even realize we are buying into the lies the devil is selling to us. If a person knew they were being duped, they would not act on such deception. No one is convinced of a blatantly obvious lie, but a truth that is slightly twisted, one might be tempted to believe.

* * *

Did God Really Say?

Have you ever heard a piece of advice and acted on it as if it were true, only to find out later that it was a myth? Some examples of this might include: "shaving for the first time makes your hair grow back thicker," or, "eating food you dropped on the ground is safe so long as you pick it up within five seconds," or "turkey makes you tired," or "urine heals a jellyfish sting." These are all silly examples that most of us have heard at some point, but they illustrate a profound truth. As human beings who are always maturing, we act on what we believe to be true, regardless of whether or not it is the truth.

As it turns out, when you shave hair for the first time, you simply create blunt tips on the hair follicles, which gives them the appearance of being thicker after they grow back. Additionally, the food you dropped was dirty the instant it hit the ground; cheddar cheese has more tryptophan than turkey, so it was probably the overeating at Thanksgiving dinner that made you so tired;[5] it would have been better to leave the jellyfish sting alone because urine causes a jellyfish's nematocysts to inject more venom at the sting site. We are so easily fooled by bad advice! Why on earth do we believe it?

The deception that goes unnoticed is how Satan operates as well. He knows that humanity is gullible, and he never intends his deceit to be obvious to us. His lies seem appealing to us because they typically offer a bit of truth to them. Satan takes the truth and twists it ever so slightly so that we believe him when he tempts us with seemingly appealing things. However, the nature of truth is that even the slightest twist in it precludes it from being truth altogether. The great lie of the Thanksgiving turkey is not the deception I am referring to—that is just a silly misunderstanding. The lies I am referring to are those that Satan tricks the members of the church into believing, and they typically have consequences in how we approach our faith in God. Most of them sound like they are scripturally based, and they seem harmless, but they produce the exact results that Satan desires. Our belief in them can cause a person to miss out on the great life that God has for them.

"God won't give you more than you can handle," is a twisted truth pulled from 1 Corinthians that is thrown around quite often in our culture. It sounds so optimistic towards God, but is it true? Would God *really* never give you any circumstance that you cannot rise above on your own volition and strength? It sounds like that theology does not leave much room for God to work a miracle in a person's life because they will never have to rely on the strength of God to handle anything. This pulls the Christian's focus away from their faith in God to overcome adversity and towards reliance on self—what Satan desires of them. Relying on oneself is a one-way ticket to hell for the unbeliever, so why should the believer in Christ follow such advice? Our own salvation is proof that there are things that we cannot handle by ourselves! This is what the Scripture actually says:

> No *temptation* has overtaken you except what is common to mankind. And God is faithful; he will not *let you be tempted* beyond what you can bear. But when you are tempted, *he will also provide* a way out *so that you can endure it.*
>
> 1 Corinthians 10:13, emphasis added

The Scripture says that you will not be tempted with evil past what you can bear. It says nothing about every difficult circumstance in life. The truth is that God does his greatest work when a person is burdened beyond what they can bear, excluding temptation, because it leads a person to a place of total dependence and surrender to God's sovereignty in their life.

"Money is the root of all evil," is another common lie inserted into 1 Timothy 6:10. While it is often misquoted, Timothy emphasizes the *love* of money as a root of all kinds of evil, rather than the money itself. Timothy infers that money can create a condition of the heart in which humanity elevates money above God in importance. The natural conclusion that we draw from excluding the teaching about the condition of the heart in our beliefs towards money is that God hates money; therefore, anyone who tries to follow God must live in poverty and also hate money rather than use it according to the purposes made clear by Scripture. It makes people feel bad about having money or wanting money because the message they constantly hear is, "money is evil." The reality is that money has incredible power to do a lot of good in God's kingdom, and it is a blessing from God that we are to use for his glory and our enjoyment. God only asks that he is above everything in our hearts and that we make him the center of our worship, not money. *After that*, there is nothing wrong with having or even wanting more money.

"You need to be married to be happy," and "Marriage is the ultimate goal of living a fulfilled life" are crippling lies that are permeating the church which effectively destroy the noble position of single people. If you are young and single, you know exactly what I am talking about. Even if this is never overtly stated, many of us feel the reality of this message, and it greatly impacts our focus in our life. If both Jesus and Paul were single, then where are we getting this theology from if not Satan himself? Paul conceded that being married was perfectly acceptable, should a person choose to marry, but he did not say that it was the preferred state of living—he actually said the opposite (1 Corinthians 7:7).

Paul boasted that singleness is the best way for anyone to live, and we base most of our understanding of the faith in his teachings. Yet, for some reason we have left this teaching out in the way many churches approach singleness. They often place Christian marriage on a pedestal above singleness. This is similar to how singleness was viewed as a curse before Paul taught the church of Corinth that it allows a person to focus more on Christ and his priorities. In fact, this book is a great example of how singleness has been a blessing to me. If I had not been a single man as I wrote this book, it would probably not exist. I wrote the first draft before I met my now wife, Holly, and by the grace of God I wrote the second draft while deployed overseas—in my final moments as a single man. This book is a product of the freedom that singleness has given me to spread the message of Christ's salvation, and Paul encourages all single people to courageously use their gift of singleness for God's glory.

Other cultural lies that Satan has inserted into our understanding of God that are hard for us to accept include: "You are saved as soon as you believe in Jesus," when James 2:17 says intellectual assent is not saving faith, but rather demon faith.[6] "Good people go to heaven," when the truth is that *forgiven* people go to heaven, and those we believe to be "good people" go to hell because in God's eyes there are no good people (Psalm 14:3; 53:3; Romans 3:10). "Church is not necessary to be a Christian," when the one person who did not have to go to church, Jesus, made it a point to attend church every week (Luke 4:16). "God hates sex," when he is the one who created sex and desires for it to be richly enjoyed as it was originally intended, within the marriage covenant, rather than see his image bearers create a cheap imitation of God's ultimate wedding gift (Proverbs 5:18–19; Song of Songs 7:6–12; Hebrews 13:4).

> "He was a murderer from the beginning, not holding to the truth, for there is no truth in him. When he lies, he speaks his native language, for he is a liar and the father of lies."

John 8:44

Jesus said it best when he called Satan by his true title, the father of lies. Satan is a liar. He has no power over God, and so his only effective strategy is to slander God's name and to accuse God before us through lies and deception. In our pain Satan tells us that God is not good, and in our pleasure, he tells us that God cannot satisfy us above what he can offer (Matthew 4:8). He is a master manipulator that confuses humanity by finding creative ways of asking the original question that he asked Adam and Eve in the garden of Eden: "Did God really say...?"

The goal of Satan in the great unseen war for our souls is to distort our view of God by twisting the truth of God's Word. In distorting our understanding of God, Satan distorts our understanding of ourselves in the image of God. If we do not properly understand the image of God then we cannot understand ourselves and therefore cannot understand Christ, who is the perfect image of God. How easy would it be to understand Jesus Christ if we did not allow ourselves to be constantly misinformed with such bad advice?

> The god of this age has blinded the minds of unbelievers, so that they cannot see the light of the gospel that displays the glory of Christ, who is the image of God.
>
> *2 Corinthians 4:4*

* * *

Satan Was Made Good

Why is it necessary to spend an entire chapter discussing Satan if this book is about the image of God? What does Satan have to do with God's image? While Satan possesses far more power and other traits that human beings do not have, he possesses a surprising number of traits that we do have in God's image such as reason, a responsibility to God, and function as detailed in chapter 2. Satan also has many similar limitations to us. He does not possess any of the incommunicable attributes that are unique to God. For example, Satan cannot be in more than one place at one time and he cannot know your thoughts (Isaiah 46:9–10; Mark 13:32). However, he does have an incredible number of demons in his employ to carry out his will and he knows how to tempt us into wrong thinking.

Due to the unanimous testimony of the Scriptures and our current experience of the fallen world as proof, we know that Satan has no good in him (John 8:44). However, he was once a member of the heavenly host of angels that were created *good* (1 Timothy 4:4). If Satan was part of this original good creation, then how did he get to the desolate position he is in today? Where did his evil originate if he was the very first being of all creation to commit an evil act, and what is to be learned from him falling so far from God?

It is exceedingly difficult to find the answers to such questions because the Bible does not go into explicit detail on the matter. The answers may be too far from our ability to comprehend on this side of heaven. No one tempted Satan to sin in the way Satan tempted Adam and Eve in the garden, and yet he still sinned. While the garden was paradise for Adam and Eve, the adversary, Satan, was already fallen and present when humanity was created (Job 38:4–7). One thing is certain: his evil did not come from God—that is completely contrary to God's character, and Scripture is extraordinarily clear about that (1 Chronicles 16:34; Mark 10:18; James 1:17). It is only logical that such evil came from deep within him—that it is a *necessary possibility* that exists within a being that possesses free will and is not God.

As mentioned in chapter 3, beings that possess a high enough consciousness to partake in the same kind of relationship that God has within himself as a Trinity, must possess free will. While part of that freedom includes the choice to love and obey God, by necessity there must also be the possibility to do the opposite. If free will does not allow for the possibility to not love and not obey, then it is not truly *free*. One could never understand or give sincere love to God because all of creation would be an elaborate puppet show for God, with every being obeying God's every command.

God already had profound joy within himself, so he desired to freely share it with his creation and for them to reciprocate it. While it is difficult to definitively say that angels and demons possess the *imago Dei*, they do possess free will. We know this because humanity's rebellion was the result of free will and this came only after Satan first rebelled—indicating that he has free will as well. This, however, still fails to answer the question of the source of Satan's evil in a world where it did not previously exist.

To understand why Satan is evil, let's review why God is good. God is good for the simple reason that he is God—he is the standard of goodness. His created beings, both angels and humanity, were created good because they were created by a good God and, in the case of humanity, in the image of him. However, an important distinction to note is that the goodness of the creation is not qualitatively the same as the goodness of God—it is merely an expression of God's goodness. God's goodness springs from the infinite attributes that make him God: beauty, omniscience, omnipotence, eternity, spirituality, righteousness, omnipresence, love, peace, joy, order, immutability, wisdom, generosity, faithfulness, etc. Because of these attributes, God is who he is as a "good" God (Exodus 3:14). The merit of goodness is solely based on God's attributes, and unless a created being possesses the fullness of them, they do not possess the same goodness of God. No one is good but God alone (Mark 10:18).

Because God is good, he cannot commit evil. It is not that God could not commit an evil act due to lack of ability, but that it is outside the *realm of possibility*, because that would require God to change his *immutably good nature*. However, God is so complete in his wisdom, understanding, love, joy, and peace, that every other possible course of action besides his goodness is already known by him to produce less than the amazingly good life that he already has.

It is therefore understandable that even if God could choose to do evil, he would not do so.

Created beings do not have this perspective. God's beings were created innocent and without an evil nature, but with inexperience comes naivety. Satan was naïve to think that God's way of life was not the best way for him to live. In fact, he was naïve in that he failed to recognize that it was the only way for him to live—that is, the only way that does not produce death (Romans 6:23). It was inevitable that Satan would make the free choice to define life for himself, which in the end led to his spiritual death. How was it inevitable one might ask? It is easy to sit in a broken world and wonder how he could be so foolish, but when there was nothing but good in the world, how could he have known that his choice to rebel against God wouldn't work? Why does a parent tell their child not to touch a hot stove? They do it to protect the child from the inevitable result of getting burned, but until a child experiences the pain of a burn, they will never appreciate the loving wisdom of their parents.

Likewise, we as human beings who live in the aftermath of our own rebellion to God realize only now that we should have listened to God from the start—so it is for Satan except for the fact that Scripture claims he is unrepentant to the very end (Revelation 20:10). The inevitable necessity of choosing to not obey God has occurred and continues to occur daily, as evil from deep within us wages war with our longing to have life with God. Fortunately, our assured faith in Christ is working to remove this inevitable necessity from our very nature—never to occur again when we are in heaven.

While Satan wrongly tempted humanity in the garden and humanity wrongly tried to become their own gods when they ate the fruit, Christ is bringing Satan's words to bear against him in making us like God, knowing both good and evil, but being unable to commit evil: "For God knows that when you eat from it your eyes will be opened, and you will be like God, knowing good and evil" (Genesis 3:5). In his free choice to disobey God, Satan tempted humanity who took the bait, leaving none of humanity in good standing with God. Through this original sin, we have all fallen short of the glory of God's image, attempting to define our own image. By defining God's image for ourselves we are willfully believing just another piece of Satan's bad advice.

QUESTIONS FOR REFLECTION AND DISCUSSION

In the most existential sense, what does it mean to be truly free? What does it mean to be a slave to your sin? How is the work of Christ inextricably tied to true freedom? Do you consider yourself to be involved in spiritual warfare on a daily basis? If so, how do you prepare for battle?

How would you define the relationship between good and evil? Biblically speaking, what limits of power does evil have over the life of a Christian? Why does God allow evil to exist in the world? To what end?

Why is Satan, the personification of evil, humanity's true enemy? What does the spiritual battlefield between good and evil look like? As it relates to humanity's involvement in the spiritual war, what role have we to play?

What methods does Satan use to deceive people? Why does Satan want to deceive people? What are some examples of the lies that Satan tries to sell us? What must we believe to be true about God before we can believe these lies? What are the consequences of believing these lies? How does one's relationship with God suffer?

Is Satan made in God's image? As the first being to ever sin in a world without temptation, where did Satan's evil originate? What was lacking in Satan's soul that allowed him to sin in the first place? What do we lack in our souls that allows us to continue to sin?

6

⚜

Falling Short of Our God-Given Image

For all have sinned and fall short of the glory of God.

Romans 3:23

Why do children ask the notorious question on car rides, "Are we there yet?" If they had arrived, wouldn't they know it? Yet, regardless of their parent's response, the question is asked repeatedly. Unlike an adult, a child has an undeveloped concept of time. They struggle to see beyond the present moment to the outcome of their journey. Perhaps this is because of their overall limited life experience. To a child, five minutes may as well be five hours or vice versa depending on the situation. The restless anticipation of the pleasures to come in reaching their destination causes them to unceasingly probe their parents for a more satisfying response. However, as much as a child desires the journey to meet its end, they are ultimately just along for the ride—they have no consequential choice to alter their course or speed it up. They are fully surrendered to their parent's sovereignty, whose hands are literally and metaphorically on the steering wheel of their life.

Unlike a small child, we as morally responsible individuals are not so limited in our ability to alter our own courses in life as we navigate our faith and seek our ultimate destination, which is heaven. While little children ask their parents, "Are we there yet," do we not also ask our heavenly Father this same question in our inward groanings and selfish desires of the flesh? In the deepest reaches of our souls, we long for heaven. We long for the peace and security that it provides in Christ, but in our flesh, we often try to attain heaven on our own terms, even knowing this is an impossibility. The difference between ourselves and little children in a car is that we actually have a consequential choice to veer off the path that God has set for our lives to reach our final destination—we can choose to take the painful backroads of a worldly life. In our sin we would take matters into our own hands and try to navigate life without a map, rather than trust the directions that are provided in God's Word. In this way, time and again we fall short of God's glory that he intends to reveal in us (Romans 3:23).

The roadmap for our lives is clearly laid out to us in the Bible, and it depicts every way that leads to the fullest possible life for those who bear God's image. Yet, we constantly push back and defy the commands and wishes of our heavenly Father under the same pretense that we have figured out a better way to navigate this life from our own limited experience. In reality, our understanding of life is no more complete than a child's understanding of time.

In our independence from God, we can often satisfy our immediate desires as we attempt to speed up the journey or alter course to reach our destination, but it is usually to our detriment. Approaching our faith with such confidence in our own experience and wisdom is an incorrect attitude of our hearts towards God. A person who is truly wise will understand that the dependence they once placed on their earthly parents to direct their course in life should only serve to increase their level of dependence on God for direction now. Jesus points this out in the book of Mark:

> But when Jesus saw this, he was indignant and told them, "Let the little children come to me, and do not hinder them! For the kingdom of God belongs to such as these. Truly I tell you, anyone who does not receive the kingdom of God like a little child will never enter it." And he took the children in his arms, placed his hands on them, and blessed them.
>
> *10:14–16*

Jesus taught us that the correct way to approach our faith in God is like a little child—with complete dependence (1 Thessalonians 2:7, 11–12). We are to come to our heavenly father with total dependence and trust if we desire to honor him and grow in likeness to him most fully. Unfortunately, we are often unsatisfied with the responses that God gives us to our inward groanings of, "Are we there yet?" And so we take matters into our own hands, ultimately falling short of the glory of God that could be revealed through us. Does God put these seemingly unsatisfying answers in place because he is trying to prolong our painful anticipation of arriving to our destination? By no means! They are in place because God loves his children, he wants the best for us, and he knows the most direct path to get there. The most direct path for us is to know God and experience life by abiding in him and we can do this best when we become more like him by following his perfect will.

In this chapter, we will unpack some of ways in which we fall short of the glory of God's image when we stray from his will. As stated in previous chapters of this book, the image of God has infinite implications in our lives, and it would be impossible to go through each specific way in which we fall short. Therefore, this

chapter will discuss only a few areas that my experience has led me
to believe are the most overarching shortcomings in our present culture. In this way I hope this offers relevant perspective for you to
investigate your own life and examine how you may better follow
God's calling for yourself.

> "For my thoughts are not your thoughts, neither
> are your ways my ways," declares the Lord. "As the
> heavens are higher than the earth, so are my ways
> higher than your ways and my thoughts than your
> thoughts."
>
> *Isaiah 55:8–9*

* * *

Idols

In Exodus chapter 20, God provides the infant nation of Israel with
the Ten Commandments. The first four of them point to humanity's relationship with God and the latter six point to humanity's
relationship with their fellow humans. In the first and second commandments, God states that we are to have no other gods before
him, and that we are not to make any images (idols) to be worshiped, including even images of heavenly things (Exodus 20). God
forbids this because when we create an object of worship, we are
in effect reducing our worship to the material world—to something
that falls far short of the intended design for our worship. The intent behind our worship is much grander than this. From God's perspective, worshiping an idol is like picking up a single grain of sand
at the beach and expecting to find the fullness of your beachgoing
experience in that single grain of sand. Surely much of the experi-

ence would be missed if we were to depend on a grain of sand to satisfy us. Likewise, God in his infinite glory cannot be reduced to something that is only a tiny part of his creation. We will surely miss out on the fullness of him!

It makes sense that God would command humans to make no images of him, because that is something that he has already done in creating humanity—we are the living, breathing images (idols) of God. It is our role to conduct worship of God, not to make additional images to worship (Romans 12:1). An inanimate object can neither conduct worship of God, nor represent him in the same way a human being can do as his image bearer; therefore, God detests such things (Psalm 135:15–18). However unfortunate, we are all guilty of idol worship. We fall short of the glory of God's image by forgetting our role as God's image bearers when we idolize the things that we create—material things or even other human beings.

Allowing idols to take hold of our hearts removes God from a position of sovereignty in our lives and instead replaces him with created objects that could never satisfy the human soul. Idolatry is a deceptive trap for a Christian because it is rooted in a desire to fulfill the natural inclinations of the heart. We want to worship. We were made to worship. God created humans as images of himself to worship him alone for his glory and our enjoyment, and so it is only natural for us to desire to worship something, even if this worship is misplaced with idols. Whether we believe it or not, every human soul will worship something. We have a common desire for something far beyond ourselves or what we currently have in this world. God has intentionally given us, as image bearers, a divinely implanted awareness of eternity, and therefore we each long for something that is much more permanent than anything this world could provide.

He has made everything beautiful in its time. *He has also set eternity in the human heart*; yet no one can fathom what God has done from beginning to end. I know that there is nothing better for people than to be happy and to do good while they live. That each of them may eat and drink, and find satisfaction in all their toil —this is the gift of God.

Ecclesiastes 3:11–13, emphasis added

King Solomon, the author of Ecclesiastes, understood that we would never be able to fully understand the complexity of God's eternal plan for the world, but that we as humans have a deep desire built into the fabric of our souls to know and to please our Creator while living on this earth. Even though we often attempt to fill this God-sized hole in our hearts with something less than God, part of each of us knows that we will still have the irritating feeling of homesickness in the pursuit of such things. Every feeling of loneliness, worthlessness, depression, anxiety, and fear that we have ever experienced is proof of this. In our hearts we often think that we desire anything but God, but the truth is that the only real desire we have ever had is God—everything else will simply leave us feeling incredibly homesick and unsatisfied.

> *If I find in myself a desire which no experience in this world can satisfy, the most probable explanation is that I was made for another world.*[1]
>
> **C. S. Lewis**

The desolate state of the human soul can be satisfied only by God, because the home that he designed us to live in, heaven, is not the broken and corrupt home in which we currently reside. If humanity could find complete satisfaction in this broken world, what need have they for God? Of course, contemporary Christians are not making golden calves to worship in the twenty-first century, but there are still many idols that have become "gods" in our lives. Our golden calves in this age are phones, cars, clothes, alcohol, *College GameDay*, the house on the lake, a spouse, sex, another degree, the perfect job, or even success itself. What does worship of these idols look like in practice? Let's take a moment to investigate the idol of success to see how dangerous idols can be when they become the center of our worship.

As a warrior in the United States Marine Corps, I get to work with some of the best individuals that our nation has to offer. Part of the ethos of being a Marine is the pride we have in being the best of the best. Our organization does more with less, fights and wins our nation's toughest battles, and has a long history to prove it. To acquire such a reputation, we must constantly strive for excellence in all that we do. However, as a Marine Corps officer and a follower of Christ, I cannot help but see my profession through a lens of faith. I have noticed that there are many in this organization that worship their career, and there was a time when I was one of these individuals. For those who worship the Marine Corps, I have noticed that being the best is sometimes the motivation for everything in a Marine's life. This was certainly true for me before God became the center of my worship, and it cost me much to worship my career.

Although I have spent my entire adult life in the military, I imagine idolizing professional success is not unique to my community, but a commonality across our success-driven culture. Is there anything wrong with achieving greatness in our work? Absolutely not. As followers of Christ we are called to work as if our employer was God himself, and as such we should give God the absolute best of our efforts (Colossians 3:13–24). The distinction I intend to make is that for some, a career has become their highest calling. The career itself has become the *end-all* of all their toils. They do not recognize it to be what they do, but rather who they are. For many, to lose their career would be to lose their identity. Some are even willing to go so far as to make sacrifices on the altar of their career, the false god of success. The sacrifices I am referring to are often relationships with family, friends, and co-workers.

Success is a very deceptive idol. As Solomon said in the Scripture above, satisfaction in our toil is a gift from God. This Scripture goes on to say that we have these satisfactions in life so that we are in awe of the greatness of God. This is not because the satisfaction of work or the glory that we receive from it is the ultimate good, but that our work is meant to arouse an outcry of praise to the one who has given us such a great gift. However, what does it look like when success becomes an idol? King Solomon is the perfect example in the Bible, but to illustrate this point in a way that we can comprehend in the twenty-first century, I will use a more contemporary name that epitomizes success by American standards—Tom Brady. This man has it all, from the world's standards: money, fame, success, athleticism, and a picture-perfect family. Maybe football is not your niche, but imagine if you had Tom Brady's level of success in whatever area of life you are most passionate about. Would you feel accomplished? Would you feel completely satisfied in your success?

In 2005 Tom Brady was the subject of an interview by CBS 60-minutes. His response to a simple question absolutely amazed me, because it pointed to an even grander reality of the current world that we live in. Without even knowing it, Brady repeated the truth of Solomon's observations on the eternal state of the human heart:

> **KROFT:** This whole experience—this whole upward trajectory—what have you learned about yourself? What kind of an effect does it have on you?

> **BRADY:** Well, I put incredible amounts of pressure on me. When you feel like you're ultimately responsible for everyone and everything, even though you have no control over it, and you still blame yourself

if things don't go right—I mean, there's a lot of pressure. A lot of times I think I get very frustrated and introverted, and there's times where I'm not the person that I want to be. Why do I have three Super Bowl rings, and still think there's something greater out there for me? I mean, maybe a lot of people would say, "Hey man, this is what is." I reached my goal, my dream, my life. Me, I think: God, it's gotta be more than this. I mean this can't be what it's all cracked up to be. I mean I've done it. I'm 27. And what else is there for me?

KROFT: What's the answer?

BRADY: I wish I knew. I wish I knew. I mean I think that's part of me trying to go out and experience other things. I love playing football, and I love being a quarterback for this team, but, at the same time, I think there's a lot of other parts about me that I'm trying to find. I know what ultimately makes me happy are family and friends, and positive relationships with great people. I think I get more out of that than anything. [2]

If Tom Brady made it to such a high level of success in life and concluded that there must be more to life than success itself, then we are all in for a life of disappointment if success is our highest calling. If we are made in the image of a God whose very life is defined by loving relationships that are meant to glorify himself, then it is not possible for anything to fulfill the human soul apart from him. We can ignore this truth and pursue meaningless idols for the rest of our days, but like Tom Brady, we will always wonder if there is more out there for us—and there is, but not in this world. As we appraise our lives, what images have we made and worshiped to satisfy our homesickness for heaven?

* * *

Vices

While an idol is an external thing that we tend to elevate above God in worship, a vice is the behavior that results from idol worship. A vice is a disease that incubates in the heart and festers because of sin. This behavior taints the very soul which was designed to worship God in complete purity. Like our discussion in chapter 5, vices and virtues share a similar nature to good and evil. In the same way that evil is the absence of good, a vice is the behavior resultant from the absence of virtue.

The discussion of vice and virtue is as old as time. If you have ever taken a class on philosophy, you are probably familiar with the names of many ancient Greek thinkers—Aristotle being the most prominent of them. Aristotle understood virtue to sit in the middle of two vices on opposing ends of a particular sphere of action. He called these vices of excess and vices of deficiency. Too much or too little of any specific behavior results in a vice, but when opposite vices are balanced, you are left with virtue. To Aristotle, a person could be a coward, or they could be rash, but if cowardice and rashness are balanced, one is left with the virtue of courage.

From a Christian standpoint I tend to disagree. Virtue does lie in the middle of two extremes of excess or deficiency of a particular vice, but Aristotle seemed to think that virtue is a delicate balance that can swing either way if too much or too little of a behavior is displayed. If a person has too much courage, they would be rash, and if they have too little, they would be a coward. Christian virtue demonstrates goodness and therefore cannot be taken too far. A person cannot be "too virtuous" or "too good" to the point that they would be demonstrating a vice. While Aristotle would see virtue to lie in the center of a horizontal line, I believe that it is found at the top of a bell curve that has no limit to its height.

Take someone's physical well-being for example. A person can make their health the most important thing in life, eventually breeding a mentality that leads to the vice of body worship. Conversely, they could completely neglect their health and suffer the unfortunate medical consequences. It is when a healthy diet and exercise regimen are balanced with work, spiritual discipline, and relationships that the virtue of health is found. In doing this they not only reap the benefits of physical health, but they may also have healthy relationships, a healthy spiritual walk, and a healthy work life—all things that would not be possible if a person erred too far on the sides of body worship or neglect. Of course, this example is not perfect. There are plenty of people who suffer from poor health despite making virtuous, God-honoring decisions regarding their lifestyle. This is part of living in a fallen world.

As discussed above with idols, it may be of use to pick a specific example in this section for each of us to examine our life to become more virtuous. Charity is a virtue that is lost for much of our nation. As a twenty-six-year-old who has experienced three major financial crises in my formative years (Dotcom Bubble of 1999–2000, Housing Market Crash of 2008–2009, and the current 2020 crisis of COVID-19), I have noticed a unique role that debt plays in a person's life as it relates to their faith walk. Currently in America there is $10.3 trillion owed on mortgages, $1.56 trillion owed on student loans, $1.14 trillion owed on automobiles, $1.02 trillion owed on credit cards, and $130.3 billion owed in personal loans.[3] These numbers are quite difficult to comprehend because of the sheer size of them, but I think it is safe to say that Americans are addicted to debt. What do the national debt levels have to do with masking God's image in us through vices?

When debt is used inappropriately, it becomes the opposite of the virtue of charity and generosity. It is the indulgence in oneself when it goes beyond its use as described in the Bible (Leviticus 25; Deuteronomy 15:1). Many people in our nation would not even dare to categorize the excessive utilization of debt as a vice, because they believe it to be a necessity of fiscal responsibility. From a young age, most Americans are taught that the credit score is necessary to live your best life. The reality is that it has only either ravaged the lives of those who are ignorant to the dangers of hyper-consumerism or perpetuated a mediocre financial life for those who idolize the FICO score through revolving offerings of interest to the bank in pursuit of a better score.

There are two primary motivations for unbiblical uses of debt, and both are vices. The vice of excess that debt causes is greed. Greed is the selfish desire of wanting more than a person can afford on the income that God has given them. Conversely, the deficient vice caused by debt is stinginess. When a person is strapped with debt, they are unable to live a life centered around the virtue of charity—a God-centered perspective on material resources.

Gaining freedom from the burden of debt has allowed me to make some observations on what it is that debt truly does to a person's life. If you think of your income as a pie chart, you will have several categories of expenses, savings, and giving that would make up the whole circle. In a healthy financial life, a person or family balances the necessities of life, saving for the inevitable rainy day, and charity into their income pie. When they desire something that is larger than their monthly income pie, they typically have two choices apart from using debt—to save up for it or to purchase something that is more within their means. If neither of these options seem acceptable, many of us succumb to greedy desire and decide to leverage the item with debt to make it "fit" into our pie as a small sliver of a monthly payment. This might be justifiable in the case of a home, but this ultimately becomes greed when a person fails to see large-ticket items for their true cost and instead views them as small slivers in their income pie.

This cycle of breaking down large-ticket items into small payments becomes a lifestyle for many. By doing this, one is effectively making the decision to maximize their lifestyle within their income until their pie is completely consumed by monthly payments. This insidious pattern ultimately renders them a slave to the banks that hold their notes and steals any margin they could have had to be charitable (Proverbs 17:18; 22:7). The natural reaction of a person who has no margin in their financial life due to overwhelming debt is to swing in the complete opposite direction from greed to stinginess.

Debt often breeds a mentality of "maximizing my life" rather than living a life that is centered around maximizing the lives of others. As mentioned in chapter 4, a person cannot be generous when their cup is not overflowing. When a person is strapped with debt, they cannot effectively mirror the generosity of God. This may be why only 3 to 5 percent of Americans in the church tithe regularly, and the average giving in American churches is only 2 percent of their gross income. In fact, the Health Research Funding organization's statistics on American tithing states, "People who tithe regularly typically have less debt than other demographics—eight out of ten have zero credit card debt and 29 percent of them are completely debt-free, including not having a mortgage."[4] Debt has become a vice in our culture that has precluded charity. I wish this were only my biased opinion, but the numbers speak for themselves.

I understand that some Christians may object on the basis that life has dealt them a difficult hand in terms of their income and they are left with no choice but to borrow money to cover the bills. I am in no way intending to shame the marginalized in the church by posing such strong opinions on borrowed money. My point is that our lives need to be put into proper perspective. Those who are below the poverty level in America, for the most part, are still in the top 1 percent of the world in terms of wealth. There are 736 million people worldwide who make less than $1.90 a day, and each of these people bear the same image of God as us Americans—that is less than $700 a year in annual income. In stark contrast, it is widely accepted that a conservative daily take of a panhandler in the U.S. is about $30—that is a $10,950 of tax-free money annually. It is our perception of scarcity that is skewed. Compared to the rest of the world, we are all rich. Therefore, the real issue at hand is, "What are we to do with the margin in our lives?" Rather than use debt to force an increasingly excessive lifestyle into the margins, we should decrease our lifestyles and increase our charity as God would have us do.

Here is a litmus test for each of us on greed and stinginess: Would you rather give $10,000 of your time or $10,000 of your money? If you are like me, your first inclination would be to give your time. Many of us would consider ourselves as generous people using the scapegoat of "giving our time" so that we can justify not giving what we really value—our money. Giving our time is undoubtedly important, but the question is intended to prove that it is not about the money, it is the attitude of our hearts towards charity. The Bible says that where your treasure is, so will your heart be (Matthew 6:21). If we have a tight grip on our money, our hearts are not and cannot be generous. God knows this; otherwise, why would he be so adamant that we give our money? Why is it so hard for a rich man to enter the kingdom of heaven (Matthew 19:24)? It is because money can take a powerful hold over the heart of *anyone*. It can be an idol, and our interaction with it could produce a vice.

Life is hard, and money is a way in which we perceive it to be made easier or add significance and value to our lives. However, many people spend their entire lives chasing material wealth, only to lose it all when they die anyways (Psalm 49). The second and third order effects of operating on the world's financial advice will rob us of the life we desire. The above numbers of debt in America are proof of this. Debt causes people to become wage slaves, suffer from depression and hopelessness, and live vain lives from excessive consumption. In John 16:33 Jesus says to his followers, "In this world you will have trouble." Praise be to God that he did not stop there. In the same verse, he goes on to say, "But take heart! For I have overcome the world."

Instead of running to the bank every time life gets hard, we should put our trust in Jesus Christ to deliver us from such hardship. If your money stresses you out, that should be proof enough that it has not and will not give you the peace you so desire. The lie of debt cannot put anyone in a position to overcome such hardship, so why bother with it? Our souls, as made in the image of God were made to function best when they operate according to the constructs of the Creator's character, which includes a heart for charity (2 Corinthians 9:7). Overcoming greed and stinginess is found in the exercise of the muscle of generosity, because it will transform us more into the image of God.

In general, vices are the result of listening to the world's advice on how to take corrective action to the spiritual dissatisfaction in our hearts. Because we were not meant to live in this broken state, there is an irritating itch of insignificance in each of us. This truth can be universally applied in examining the motivations for any vice. People gossip about others to elevate the perception of themselves by comparison, yet gossip only serves to destroy trust and relationships (Ephesians 4:29; James 1:26; 3:9; 4:11). Substance abuse, such as excessive alcohol consumption, only serves to numb the inner pain of life. If a person cannot enjoy their life without first lowering their inhibitions and dulling their senses, then they cannot deny they have some real inner pain they must deal with (Proverbs 23:33; 1 Corinthians 6:10; Ephesians 5:18). No matter the vice a person struggles with, take heart that we have it in us to live a life of virtue because a virtuous life was the original design for our souls and there was one who came and showed us the way to do so—Jesus Christ.

* * *

Image of Self

> But the Lord said to Samuel, "Do not consider his appearance or his height, for I have rejected him. The Lord does not look at the things people look at. People look at the outward appearance, but the Lord looks at the heart."
>
> *1 Samuel 16:7*

In my college days, I was a member of the varsity men's gymnastics team at the Naval Academy, which is one of the few remaining colleges with NCAA Division I Gymnastics. The team practiced each afternoon from the end of classes until the evening meal for the Brigade of midshipmen. The gym was on the top floor of the main sports complex at the Naval Academy, between a weightlifting gym, a volleyball court, and boxing gym. Having spent a substantial portion of my time in college training at the gym, I was able to see how often people frequented the adjacent facilities. At a military school, fitness is a way of life for many. However, each year there was a period that could be predicted with incredible precision for the weight and cardio gyms to be completely packed—the thirty days that preceded spring break.

The stampede of midshipmen that flocked to the gyms following afternoon classes during this time of year was truly a sight to behold. Why did it happen every single year without fail? In the military, we take pride in our appearance. The Naval Academy expected each midshipman to be in pristine physical condition. The two large mirrors in each of our rooms reinforced this fact. One of these mirrors was placed on the back of the door to the only exit of the room, which subtly reminded us that the image we present to the world is incredibly important.

The period from January to March that leads up to spring break is referred to as "The Dark Ages" at the Naval Academy. It gets its name because midshipmen are typically in class from sunup to sundown due to the shorter days in the winter months and their rigorous academic course loads. Inclement weather and heavier winter uniforms could lead one to be less concerned about physical fitness because it is easily hidden under the cover of cloth and darkness. However, with warmer weather and spring break on the horizon, many midshipmen seemed to simultaneously come to the realization that the weight gained over the winter would soon be exposed for all to see. Hundreds of them went into "panic mode" as their mirrors pointed out the inadequacies of their physical condition.

When it comes to our physical appearance, however, it is not only Naval Academy midshipmen that go into "panic mode" when a mirror is placed in front of them after a long winter of gaining weight. Society at large is overly concerned with the image that we portray to everyone else around us. We are obsessed with creating a perception of perfection to the world. If you do not believe me, log onto your Facebook or Instagram and start scrolling. These mirrors, whether literal or figurative, are a tool that we use to examine ourselves and locate the deficiencies that the world deems unattractive.

Mirrors breed a lifestyle of obsession over our physical image and many will stop at nothing to change them.

Epsom salts, saunas, Whole30® diets, cleanses, yoga, massage therapy, workout programs, and the like are the things we do when we look in the mirror and seek to improve our image to impress others. We also buy things, go on vacations, and hang around certain people to improve our image. In truth, none of these things are necessarily bad. A good diet and proper exercise have proven physical, emotional, and spiritual benefits. However, like the thirty-day mission to the gym at the Naval Academy to lose a few pounds, as God's people we often miss the mark when we seek to build up an outward image of ourselves to the world, rather than focus on building the inward image of our souls in likeness to God (1 Timothy 4:8).

God's Word is the mirror to our soul—it is the mirror that shows us our real motives and our everlasting image (Hebrews 4:12). This image is not one that can be easily posted on social media or seen by others, and so it often gets neglected. It is, however, the image that we will wear for eternity in heaven. Now, in contrast, let us compare the differences in the outward and inward images. Which is better—to have six-pack abs for a coming vacation, or to be free from a decade of pornography addiction? Is it better to fit into that wedding dress that is one size smaller than your natural weight, or to be free of the anxiety about your impending marriage relationship? Is it better to drive the fancy car and go out to fancy dinners so that the Joneses are impressed, or to have financial peace and a generous heart? Imagine the feeling of freedom we could have in our lives if we decided to focus our efforts on losing the extra "weight" from our spiritual lives. The image that we portray to God is the one that truly matters!

God does not care for the vain portrayals that we try to make of our life to the world. God cares about the character that we are developing in our hearts and his image in us. In the Bible, there is a principle called the Law of the Harvest. The basic concept is that there are three rules that apply to sowing crops in a field: you reap what you sow, you reap it later than you sow it, and you reap much more than you sow. If we sow nothing but selfishness and vain conceit in our pursuit of a good self-image, then what would the Law of Harvest say is the likely outcome?

* * *

Private, Blind, and Demon Faith

> *"There are three things you don't talk about in public: money, politics, and religion."*

Satan

Obviously, this is not an actual quote, but most of us have heard these words spoken in some capacity. Money, politics, and religion are topics of conversation in which people hold polarizing beliefs. Some people often find themselves in serious contention when discussing these topics due to the strong emotions that surround them, and this has caused them to become social taboos for our society altogether. On a large-scale, society in twenty-first-century America believes a person's faith to be a private matter both socially and individually despite our Pledge of Allegiance claiming that we are, "One nation, under God." We may have been "under God" as a nation at one point, but I have witnessed the utter elimination of God's influence over both public and private institutions in my short life. The simple proof of this is the unease that many of us feel in expressing our faith in certain public spheres. Societal norms have burdened the church with paralysis in bringing the gospel to places that are in desperate need of it because of extreme hostility towards God. However, are we really called to restrain the spread of the gospel because of social taboos or are we commanded to spread the message of salvation despite them?

What would the world be like if Jesus did not openly discuss his faith because of an aversion to conflict? The world would surely be doomed because no one would have heard his good news of salvation! Fortunately, Jesus was incredibly open about his faith, and although there was conflict, he shared it with great love. Likewise, for us today, spreading the gospel to those who do not believe is the heart of the Christian faith, and Jesus is the perfect model for it. As God's image bearers, we are Christ's ambassadors to all people who do not know him (Matthew 28:16–20). Our God-given appointment is to proclaim the good news of salvation to the ends of the earth, but the sad reality is that many of us will fail to share the gospel with a single person over our lifetimes.

Before Jesus ascended to heaven, he did not leave them with a final teaching, but a command for his followers to tell people the good news of his salvation and a promise of his abiding presence. Telling people about the Savior of their soul is the most important thing a follower of Jesus can do. If we do not do this, can we really say that we are following him? As Christians in America, we often focus our efforts on every other aspect of the Christian life except the simple task of sharing the gospel. How unloving is it for us to have eternal salvation and not to share this knowledge with someone who will experience eternity in the agonizing despair and suffering of hell without Jesus Christ? It is a tragedy that we fail to share Christ with our fellow image bearers because of our aversion to conflict stemming from societal norms.

I cannot count the amount of opportunities that I have missed in this area of obedience. I grew up under the same societal pressures that faith is one of the "big three" you should not talk about. In my own prayer, I must constantly be reminded that my life and the mission that God has given me is not about me, but about *him*. Therefore, my faith should be anything but private for the sake of those who do not yet know Jesus.

What are some of the reasons that people do not share the gospel? From what I can tell, there are a few reasons. Some may be afraid that they will not have all the answers. I understand this sentiment because I felt this way for a very long time in my early days of walking with the Lord. So imagine for a moment that you are telling someone about the goodness of God, and they interject with, "Oh yeah, well, how come my younger sister died in a car accident last fall? How can God be good when bad things happen to good people like her?" How would you respond? Many of us do not have a defense readily available for why bad things happen to good people, especially in the face of real suffering in someone's life. That is okay. You are not going to "ruin God" for them—that is something only they can do in their own heart. God can handle their criticism. Our job as Christians is to walk in obedience with what we do know about God and to share *our personal* testimony with others (Revelation 12:11). Failing to share the gospel for the reason of not knowing all the answers is to assume that a person's salvation is dependent on you and not on Jesus Christ.

Another reason that people might not share their faith with others is because they struggle deeply with ongoing sin in their life. That is okay too. If every person who wanted to tell someone about Jesus did not do so because of sin, then no one would ever hear about Jesus! We all struggle with sin and are all sinners. It is true that unrepentant sin is a legitimate hindrance to both our faith walks and witnesses, a fact that needs to be addressed, but this should not preclude us from proclaiming the name of Christ to others. People identify with imperfect people because we are all imperfect. The message of salvation is much more believable when we are telling Christ's story from our personal life experience. After all, if we were perfect, we would not have a story of Christ's work in our life to tell because there would be no redemption and sanctification.

Think about how hard it was for Christ to share his own gospel. Christ was the only perfect person to ever walk the earth and he had to spend three years of hard work to get twelve of his best friends to believe in him. On the contrary, Peter, the one who denied the Son of God three times, convinced three thousand people with one unimpressive speech in which he insults his audience's faith by telling them that Jesus is their long-awaited Messiah (Acts 2:41). This story in Acts proves Jesus' claim that we will do greater works than him after he departs (John 14:12).

Still others might not share their faith because they simply do not know how to share it. When I was a brand-new Christian, one of my best friends who walked alongside me and discipled me told me that his mother used to say to him, "If every Christian just lived according to what they say they believed, then no one would ever have to tell anyone about Jesus." What is the point of this statement? It is that we must live a life that begs the question of who Jesus Christ is. We must be so different and obedient to God in every area of our lives that when someone sees the way we react to bad news, or how quick we are to forgive, or what comes out of our mouths when we stub our toe, they see the image of God in us and ask why we are the way we are. They will see something different in us and ask why we do not conform to the pattern of this world (Romans 12:2). We can respond with a simple answer that Jesus has changed our life, or we can give them our entire testimony. The more the image of God is displayed in us, the more the world will see Christ. Private faith will naturally become public faith without you ever having to feel like you are cramming your faith down someone else's throat.

Private faith is dangerous because we are failing others in our most basic job as Christians, but *blind faith* is dangerous because we are failing ourselves. One of the biggest hindrances to possessing true, saving faith is when people fail to understand why they believe what they believe. I was the perfect example of this. Because of my lack of knowledge on my surface level beliefs growing up, I walked away from God because I did not understand God in the context of my own religion. I was a member of the Catholic Church and went to Catholic schools growing up, yet I did not understand a single thing about the faith—there was no depth to my beliefs. I knew what I was told to believe but had no reasons as to why I believed them nor conviction that I truly believed them at all. When life started to happen, I found myself standing on a foundation of shifting sand and my faith crumbled under the immense weight of my burdens. Likewise, I think many people who sit in churches week after week are in similar situations. I cannot speak for other denominations of the Christian faith, but I know for a fact that there are thousands, if not millions of Catholics in this nation who are like the old me and have no clue why they believe what they believe if they believe it at all. Can you genuinely believe in something you do not understand?

Personally, walking away from the Catholic Church was exactly what I needed to reconcile this issue. Now, if you are Catholic, I am not advocating for you to do the same. My intention is not to place any blame on the Catholic Church, as I know many incredible and godly Catholics, including members of my immediate family and the Catholic schools I attended in my youth. The Catholic faith was not the issue when I was younger, but rather my rebellious heart. My only hope is to challenge you to be able to give a defense for your faith (1 Peter 3:15). Instead of doubting your faith or walking away as I did when it does not make any sense, lean in and ask the questions. Trust me, God can handle them. Seek and you will find (Matthew 7:7). There is nothing his Holy Spirit will not make clear to you if you earnestly seek him (Jeremiah 29:13). In doing so, clarity on who you are as God's creation and who Jesus is as his perfect image will begin to come into focus.

I can remember being taught in religion class about the holy sacraments of the Catholic Church. My classmates and I received the sacrament of the Eucharist (celebratory ritual commemorating the Last Supper) when we were seven years old, and the sacrament of Reconciliation (confession) when we were nine years old. We were taught that to receive the Eucharist at church, you must first confess any "mortal" sins lest you commit another "mortal" sin by partaking in communion prior to absolution.[5] The Eucharist was supposedly enough to absolve a person from any "venial" sins they have committed.[6] I am in no way claiming to have a perfect understanding of Catholic doctrine. My point is, this is what I was taught, and I did not question it. Truthfully, I have not gone back to figure out if I was schooled correctly. The Bible is God's inspired Word, and by God's grace he gave me the ability to understand it for myself. I hold fast to the notion that each person should look at the Scriptures themselves to test the accuracy of what they have been taught. If it cannot be found in the Word, it should not hold any weight in the practice of our faith. Believe it or not, believing the correct things about God has eternal implications for a person. If it did not, then any world religion would be equally valid to enter heaven because many of them make claims about God.

Instead of reading religion textbooks, literature such as this book, or seeking another person's opinions, we as individuals need to find out what God himself says about these subjects. If someone were to tell me today that I need to confess my sins to a human—a mediator between God and myself other than Christ—in order to be forgiven, I would tell that person with gentleness and respect that they have missed the message of the gospel of Christ (1 Timothy 2:5).

Paul says this regarding forgiveness:

Bear with each other and forgive one another if any
of you has a grievance against someone. *Forgive as the
Lord forgave you.*

Colossians 3:13, emphasis added

We forgive each other because we *are already* forgiven. Forgiveness is something that has already happened when we chose to believe in Christ, and that forgiveness was perpetuated from our first
breath to our last (Acts 10:43). Choosing to believe in Christ must
be accompanied by humbling oneself and confessing sin to the only
mediator who can truly be your advocate to God the Father—Jesus
Christ. Without confession to fellow believers, there is no spiritual
maturing or sanctification for the believer; however, absolution is
not something that comes from confession to an earthly mediator
such as a Catholic priest or a Christian brother or sister. It is unbiblical to say that a person must be absolved for "mortal" sins by the
religious ritual of confession when Christ already washed away every
sin with his blood. Because we are stuck in time, we often think that
sins we have not yet committed will not be forgiven until we take
some sort of action to ritually purify ourselves. However, the simple truth of the gospel is that Jesus was the final sacrifice who perpetuated forgiveness throughout eternity for all those who believe
in him. That includes every past sin, every current sin, and any sins
that you will commit from this moment until your death.

Therefore confess your sins to each other and pray
for each other so that you may be healed. The prayer
of a righteous person is powerful and effective.

James 5:16

Notice that James, the brother of Jesus, does not say we are to
confess to be forgiven. He says we confess so that we may be healed.
A believer in Christ is already completely forgiven, but they still
may be harboring up a mountain of shame and guilt from their actions. While they are forgiven, Jesus wants us to also find freedom

in our hearts from such guilt. He does this through other members of the church, who are his hands and feet (1 Corinthians 12:7). Paul admonished believers to bring every sin into the light because of the shame that results from keeping sin a secret (Ephesians 5:11–14). Forgiveness was accomplished on the cross, but freedom and healing from the effects of sin are accomplished through honest confession to each other so that we can share the weight of each other's burdens! Confessing sin in a sound-proof Catholic confessional to a total stranger who has taken a vow of confidentiality does not seem consistent with the teaching of the Bible. Here is the funny thing about confession anyway:

> If we confess our sins, he is faithful and just and will forgive us our sins and purify us from all unrighteousness.
>
> *1 John 1:9*

Not only do we sometimes believe the wrong things about our faith, such as confession, because we have not examined the Scriptures for ourselves, but sometimes we also fail to believe what the Bible says regarding these beliefs even when we have read the Scriptures. Many of us do not take God at his Word when he says that he will purify us if we confess our sins (James 1:6–8). How many of us fail to confess our narcissism, our pride, our alcohol problem, our porn addiction, our anger, or the like because we are not truly convinced that we can be free from them? "I'll never be free of this," is a lie that Satan rejoices in you believing. It is true that freedom does not happen overnight for most issues.

For me, I was freed from an eight-year nicotine addiction overnight. I tried quitting for years, but the moment I tried after I started to follow God, the burden of dependence was lifted from me, and I have never gone back. With lust and pornography, this was not so. I have been scratching and clawing to remain pure since the day I first confessed my sin, and I still fight the daily battle for my soul. However, because I wrestle with God daily, I am in a much better place now than I was then and am confident God will see me through to the end in purity (Romans 7).

As a church, we must understand the correct things about God if we are going to live well as Christians. It seems that many people place more trust in their denominational beliefs and church traditions than in what the Bible teaches. These beliefs are supposed to be derived from the Bible, so why not fact-check it for ourselves and make sure we believe the right stuff? Incorrect teaching and examples have devastating effects on a person's faith walk and lead to nothing but meaningless ritual, which places us far from the heart of God. God does not care for our meaningless rituals (Isaiah 1:11–17). He wants us—our hearts, our souls, our lives. He wants the image of himself in you.

Here is a hard to accept truth: A person with *blind faith* is in grave danger of having *demon faith*. What is faith, and how are we to be sure that we truly have it so that we may inherit eternal life? Charles Spurgeon believed there are three components to faith: knowledge, belief, and trust. For someone to place faith in something, they must first hear what there is to believe. After one hears the information, they must then make mental assent to the truth of it and believe it with all their soul. While Spurgeon did not stop here for the recipe of faith, I would argue that this is where many churchgoers stop with their "faith." We believe that Jesus is the Son of God. We believe he died and rose again on the third day. We believe he will come back for his church. But what about trust? Do we believe it enough to trust it? And does trusting it have implications for how we are to live? For Spurgeon, there is no saving faith without completely leaning on and trusting in Christ. This trust means that our entire beings are to be wholly devoted to Christ.[7]

Trust is an action. I believe in gravity; therefore, I do not jump off buildings because I trust in the certainty of -9.8 m/s^2 (the force of gravity) and the fact that asphalt will not give way to me when I hit it. When it comes to our faith, many Christians say that they have faith in Jesus; however, nothing in their life would indicate they trust him in the way they trust in gravity—it does not seem to affect their lives. In the Upper Room Discourse Jesus says: "If you love me, keep my commands" (John 14:15).

Loving Christ means that we are to obey his words, not merely make intellectual assent to their truth. It is not enough to believe in who Jesus is! According to James, even the demons believe these things—and shudder (James 2:19). Does that mean that any "Christian" that does not earnestly strive to obey the Lord's commands has demon faith? Scripture seems to indicate that it does. If both humans and demons believe that Jesus is the Son of God, then why do we think demons will go to hell at the end of time and we will go to heaven? Where is the distinction? Both demons and humans believe the same things, but it is trust and obedience to Jesus Christ that differentiates the two. Faith, without deeds, is dead (James 2:26). While it was the work of Christ that truly saves a person, *true faith* is indicated by surrendering to Christ and sharing in his sufferings.

Making a verbal claim to your faith with no accompanied action is kind of like joining a gym, but never going to work out. Great! You joined the gym, and now have the same option that everyone else has—the ability to go to the gym and get in shape. However, what good is a membership if you never go? You will never get in shape. Likewise, what good is it to say you believe in Jesus if you never act on that belief? Everyone has the same access to Jesus like everyone has access to a gym, but if they never go to him for guidance, correction, confession, and forgiveness, and do what he says then what good is their faith? You will have a head knowledge that there is a God that loves you and wants the best for you, but you will still be out of spiritual shape, precluding yourself from eternal life. Salvation is not the result of good works, but good works will be present if there is truly salvation (Ephesians 2:8–10). You cannot have one without the other.

If we take an honest look at our churches and see the amount of people who claim to be Christians, how many are actually living out their faith? Why does Jesus teach, "Wide is the path that leads to destruction and narrow is the path that leads to life" (Matthew 17:13–14)? Jesus knew there would be other world religions that would miss the mark. He knew there would be plenty of atheists who would hate him and would not believe. However, I do not think he was talking to them in this Scripture because it immediately precedes Jesus defining "false disciples," or people who think they are following him but really are not. Jesus was talking to the "cultural Christians" of the day who would claim to believe in him, only to later perish for having stopped inches short of trusting and saving faith.

> "Not everyone who says to me, 'Lord, Lord,' will enter the kingdom of heaven, but *only the one who does the will of my Father* who is in heaven. Many will say to me on that day, 'Lord, Lord, did we not prophesy in your name and in your name drive out demons and in your name perform many miracles?' Then I will tell them plainly, 'I never knew you. Away from me, you evildoers!'"
>
> *Matthew 17:21–23, emphasis added*

The people who said this are those same people who sit in church week after week, thinking their belief apart from obedience to God's will is good enough to get them into heaven. Will they be surprised on that day when Jesus turns them away? Absolutely! How could anyone give a defense for themselves to the God of the universe who sacrificed his own Son to get them back? We have all sinned and fallen short of the glory of God's image, for we were designed for lives of committed faith, not religious veneer.

In *Crazy Love: Overwhelmed by a Relentless God*, Francis Chan wrote, "Our greatest fear in life should not be fear of failure, but of succeeding at things in life that don't really matter."[8] Keeping one foot in the world waters-down a person's faith until it looks like "cultural Christianity," but this type of Christianity already has a name—unbelief. This is not about being a "good Christian" who lives out their faith or a "bad Christian" who does not. The person that does not live out their faith is simply not a Christian. We are not afforded the opportunity to pick and choose what living a Christian life means and then call ourselves "Christians." The title we give ourselves is not the ticket into heaven; our relationship with Christ is, and that relationship is defined in the Bible.

The Bible outlines very carefully what the Christian life is and what it is not. Salvation comes through grace alone, not works, but our works are the proof that we have true and genuine faith. Let's be honest. As hard as we try, our works still are not that good. Fortunately, the performance of Christ on the cross was good enough. Believing in Christ means trusting him enough to do what he says. The image of God does not call for lukewarm Christianity or a half-hearted commitment to Christ. The image of God looks like the commitment that Jesus had to his Father, which was his very life. We are not expected to be perfect, and when we have seasons of disobedience, that does not mean we are no longer Christians. However, you know deep down if you love the Lord with all your heart, mind, *nephesh* (soul), and strength because of the indwelling Holy Spirit and the conviction that comes from knowingly living in disobedience.

Now, I want to take a second to pose a question to you, but before I do, I want to warn you: if you are not prepared to give your entire life to Christ, put down this book and read no further. Otherwise, this question may ruin your life as you know it. If you have already given your life to Christ, then this is not directed towards you. Here goes:

If you have not been all in, are you now willing to step out in obedience and trust Jesus Christ for your salvation (in other words, are you willing to make changes in your heart knowing that your life will now be marked by a self-sacrificial love for others as Christ's life is marked by self-sacrificial love for you)?

My prayer is that you will not remain one of the many who will say, "Lord, Lord" when you have your divine appointment with the Almighty. I pray that no one reading these words will be turned away because they never truly knew Jesus. This is the most important question that any of us will ever answer for ourselves. I should insert an apology at this point because if you are still reading, I just ruined your life as you know it if you are on the fence with God. As of this day, ignorance is no longer bliss. You will no longer be able to say, "Lord, Lord, did I not ... [insert lukewarm Christianity here]," because God will reply to you and say, "What about on [insert to-day's date] when you read about true faith in my Son, and you didn't accept him as Lord?" My friends, we all have been presented with a choice.

Now, how will you respond?

QUESTIONS FOR REFLECTION AND DISCUSSION

What is idolatry? Why are human beings predisposed to idolatry? What is the deepest desire of the human soul—the great void of every human heart that is always searching for answers? What are the idols of our day? What are the promises that these idols make to satisfy the great void? How short do they fall from doing so? Why do they fall short?

What is the difference between an idol and a vice? What are some common vices and virtues? How do vices affect our walk with God? How does a virtuous life display God's image?

What mirrors, whether literal or figurative, exist in your life? How have mirrors shaped your self-image and identity? In your life, how has God's Word been used as the mirror to your soul? When you look into this mirror, do you see God's image?

Is sharing the Gospel a priority in your life? If so, do you experience any difficulty in sharing it with others? What specific challenges make it difficult for you? How can these challenges be resolved?

What are the core beliefs of your Christian denomination? Are they your beliefs? Why do you believe them? What is the biblical proof of these beliefs? Have you investigated the counterarguments to them? Is there biblical evidence to the contrary? If so, how have you reconciled your beliefs as the correct beliefs? When it comes to your faith in Jesus, do you believe in him enough to entrust him with your entire life? What is the proof of this?

7

⦿⦿⦿

The Image of God Manifested: Jesus the Christ

The Son is the radiance of God's glory and the exact representation of his being, sustaining all things by his powerful word. After he had provided purification for sins, he sat down at the right hand of the Majesty of heaven. So he became as much superior to the angels as the name he has inherited is superior to theirs.

Hebrews 1:3–4

A long time ago, a man was born who was so influential that we continue to acknowledge his existence and influence by the very year on our calendars some 2,020 years later. This man's birth literally split the reference system of time. His name is the standard to which every event of human history is either referenced as pre-

204 - J. W. SAUERS, JR.

ceding or occurring thereafter using BC (before Christ) and AD (anno Domini, or "in the year of the Lord"). Even those who seek to remove the mention of his influence in human history by changing the calendar reference to "before the common era" (BCE) and "common era" (CE) still acknowledge that moment in history when everything changed. To some, his name is a swear word and to others his name is "Savior." Millennia after he walked the earth, businesses continue to close as secular and religious peoples alike celebrate his birth, death, and resurrection whether they believe in the work he completed or not. His fingerprints are on the very fabric of every society on earth, touching everything from family life, to government, to education, to business, to science, to healthcare, and the arts. Despite this, there has never been, nor will there ever be a person as polarizing as the one whose name is Jesus Christ. The entire biblical story of the fallen world, and its redemption, is focused on God's revelation of himself as manifested through the person of Christ.

Before the incarnation of Christ, the nation of Israel viewed God as a power that could never be understood or communed with, but only worshiped out of reverence for his power. Through Christ, that same God literally put on the fragility of humanity, coming in the form of a humble servant so that humanity could come into true communion with the God of the universe. It is almost inconceivable that God would leave his heavenly throne of endless glory knowing that he would be rejected by his own creation.

Humanity had significant messianic expectations for their God, and Christ fit none of them. So how is the corrupted human race expected to respond? Christ had a mission to accomplish on earth, which included rejection by people who despised him, but from that was born a body of believers that has persisted and flourished through the ages, despite aggressive persecution. Through Jesus Christ, the world has been given the answer to our fallen condition.

We can now understand who we are, who we come from, and what our ultimate purpose is in this temporal life on earth. Jesus Christ, being the perfect image of God, has bridged the eternal gap between humanity and God. His perfect and miraculous existence as the God-man enables us to understand what it means to be human and bear the identifying divine mark of God on our souls. This chapter will explore four words that qualify Christ as the perfect image of God and will detail why each is significant for us. The words are *image*, *man*, *God*, and *God-man*.

* * *

Image

When we think of an image, most of us think of a picture—a visual representation of the external form of something. We live in an age that is inundated with images due to the rise of social media and the ubiquity of mobile devices with built-in cameras. Whenever we go anywhere worth going or do anything unique, the experience is often meticulously documented with images because we find value in what they represent. What better way to describe the incredible mountainside vista that you experienced on a backpacking trip than to show a friend or family member a picture of it? Surely the image is not the same as standing in the place itself, but to someone who has not been there, it is the closest that they can come to understanding the beauty of it. Likewise, we as human beings are ourselves images, however imperfect and inexact. We are not God like a picture of a mountain is not the mountain, but we possess in ourselves a representation of God that looks very much like him. The primary distinction is that the image of God that we possess is infinitely more dynamic than the mountainside vista because the former is the image of the living and infinite God.

Jesus Christ, as mentioned in the introduction to the book of Hebrews, is the exact image of God. He possesses a perfect likeness to God, because he is both the perfect God and the perfect human. Christ in his perfect, sinless humanity brings into focus what it means to be made in the image of God. If the image of God was a Polaroid picture, Jesus is the perfectly exposed and developed Polaroid and we are a Polaroid that is still in the development process. However, unlike an actual image, the entirety of this book is devoted to a concept that surrounds the representation of the form of something that cannot be seen in a picture, but actually *in* the person of Jesus Christ.

Rather than pixels or colored ink, God uses *words* as the medium to describe what makes humanity "like" God by having his *image*. My words are only an attempt to describe the application of the image of God as I understand it, but God's words in the Bible are in themselves the image. They are the story of God working in and through his creation; they record and preserve his mighty deeds in order that humanity might come to know him perfectly. The opening sentences of the book of Hebrews are noticeably clear and offer us a summary of the entirety of God's character and glory as revealed throughout Scripture in the image of one person—Jesus Christ. In reading the Word of God, we are given a clear picture of God through the one who is himself the Word of God (John 1:1). Christ is the fullest revelation of God to humanity. He is the exact representation of God's Word because he himself is God. More than that, he is also a human who possesses a likeness to God in his own image. In Christ, humanity is given the clearest picture of Genesis 1:26–27, where God first made humanity in his own image.

It is interesting that the Bible says that Christ is the perfect image of God but gives us almost no depictions of Jesus' physical appearance. To me, this indicates that the image of God is not focused on what can be seen on the outside, but rather what is on the inside. This makes sense because two members of the Godhead are spirit and do not take physical form (John 4:24). Even when describing Jesus, who does possess physical form, we are not given a description of his appearance, but rather a word picture of *who* he is and *what* his character is like, which is far more important.

It is important to make the distinction that the physical appearance of Christ is unimportant because we live in the physical world and we deeply desire to know what Jesus' physical image looks like. However, if you consider yourself a follower of Jesus Christ, it is because you place your trust in who Jesus is as the Son of God and that his promises are true even though you cannot see him (Hebrews 11:1). God's perfect image of the Son as revealed through his Word becomes the ultimate source of attraction for anyone who knows Christ. He is indescribably beautiful, yet we do not know what he looks like. I find it fascinating that the Savior of my soul, being Jesus Christ, is in my opinion the most attractive human to ever walk the earth, and I have no clue what he looks like. Even in reading the Gospel accounts I cannot help but project my Americanized view of Christ on the stories as they play through my head when I read them.

Christ was probably far from the 5'9" white male with long brown hair that I have seen depicted in so many artist renditions or movies. He could be a 5'4" balding Middle Eastern Jew who looked like anyone else from that era and area of the world, which is more reasonably the case. Isaiah 53:2 gives us the only glimpse in the Bible of what he looked like, and it says that he was physically unattractive to the point where no one would desire him! The images that we portray of Christ are clearly not of much importance, because Christ's inner beauty is what has attracted more people and followers as his bride than anyone else to ever walk the earth. Rather, the character and actions of Christ in the Gospel accounts are what best portray the image of God and display Christ's ultimate beauty.

> But the Lord said to Samuel, "Do not consider his appearance or his height, for I have rejected him. The Lord does not look at the things people look at. People look at the outward appearance, but the Lord looks at the heart."
>
> *1 Samuel 16:7*

As God's image bearers, we must be mindful of this so that we always remember to seek after the heart of Christ in all that we say and do.

* * *

Man

> Jesus left there and went to his hometown, accompanied by his disciples. When the Sabbath came, he began to teach in the synagogue, and many who heard him were amazed. "Where did this man get these things?" they asked. "What's this wisdom that has been given him? What are these remarkable miracles he is performing? *Isn't this the carpenter? Isn't this Mary's son and the brother of James, Joseph, Judas and Simon? Aren't his sisters here with us?*" And they took offense at him.
>
> *Mark 6:1–3, emphasis added*

Which is harder to believe: that Jesus is fully man or fully God? I would argue that for most of us living in the twenty-first century, that it is the former, rather than the latter. The high impact works of Christ detailed in the Gospel accounts such as quieting a storm with the sound of his voice or walking out of his own grave are obvious proof that he is more than a man. Is he *only* more than a man as the divine Son of God? Or is he also in the *fullest sense* a normal human being? I use the word "normal" not because there is anything normal about the perfection of Jesus' humanity, but to allude to the fact that Jesus is as normal of a human being as any one of us apart from our sin nature. That's right. Jesus is no less human than you and me. In fact, I would argue that Jesus is more human than us. Think about that for a minute. What does it mean to be human in the first place?

As a human being, the life of Christ was remarkably similar to our lives. Jesus was born of a human mother. He was once a child who needed to be reared. He had a physical human body that grew, thirsted, hungered, tired, and died. He had a human mind that learned, reasoned, felt every possible emotion, and required sleep. In his human spiritual life, Jesus prayed, experienced spiritual hills and valleys, fasted, and was tempted to sin. He experienced those exact intense desires to seek his own will that we all feel, except that he always chose to follow the will of his Father. I find this to be the most amazing part of the humanity of Christ.

> For I have come down from heaven not to do *my will*
> but to do the will of him who sent me.
>
> *John 6:38, emphasis added*

Jesus Christ, as a human being, had his own unique human will that was separate from the will of God the Father. The will of Jesus, that he claims he has not come to accomplish, cannot also be the will of God because his statement would then become contradictory. The will of Jesus, if it must be aligned to his Father's, cannot also be God's will. Jesus has his own personal human will and, in his humanity, he had to choose to align it to that of God the Father. Aligning the human will to God's will is the essence of the Christian walk (1 John 2:6) and makes us fully human as Christ was fully human. This has been the defining principle for humanity since the garden of Eden.

In the garden, the expectation of humanity was that they would stay within God's will for their lives. It was an amazingly simple concept to understand for Adam and Eve: *Do not eat from the Tree of Knowledge of Good and Evil.* When presented with a choice as they were tempted by the serpent, Adam and Eve failed to be fully human. They became something less than fully human when their wills were not aligned with God's. What exactly did Satan do to them? He presented them with a choice, challenging the notion that God's will was the best thing for their human life. Satan never called humanity to follow him as God; he called them to follow themselves—to do their own will. Satan does not need followers. He knows God's way is the only way that leads to life, and anything outside of the will of God brings forth pain, suffering, destruction, and death (Genesis 3:6). Man following his own will is exactly the aim of Satan—it is a *mirror image* of what Satan himself did when he fell from heaven (Isaiah 14:13–14; 2 Thessalonians 2:3–4).

Every person who follows Christ is following the perfect example of what it looks like to surrender your own personal will to that of God. While we are the old Adam, Christ is the new Adam. He is humanity as originally intended. The difference between our humanity and Jesus' humanity is that Jesus never sinned. To sin is to oppose the will of God in thought, word, or deed. As the Creator of humanity, God designed us to live inside his will and remain unstained by the ugliness of sin. Because Jesus is fully human, it is not surprising that those described in the passage from Mark 6:1–3 (quoted at the beginning of this section) were so astonished by Christ. To them, Christ was as human as they come! The people who knew Jesus the best had a much more difficult time understanding that he was God, rather than a normal human being who was the son of Mary. How could he also be God if he was just like the rest of them?

> Therefore, just as sin entered the world through one man, and death through sin, and in this way death came to all people, because all sinned. ... For if, by the trespass of the one man, death reigned through that one man, how much more will those who receive God's abundant provision of grace and of the gift of righteousness reign in life through the one man, Jesus Christ!
>
> *Romans 5:12, 17*

As a human, Christ bears the image of God, and that image is evident to us in his humanity as he perfectly submits his will to the will of the Father. This is how the author of Hebrews can make the claim that Jesus is the exact representation of God as a human being. God created us to also be the exact image of God, and Jesus is the only human that has perfectly presented that image to the world. Therefore, as a human who is holy and righteous, we can understand God the Father as we gaze upon the Son (John 14:9).

* * *

God

> For in Christ all the fullness of the Deity lives in bodily form.
>
> *Colossians 2:9*

In chapter 4, we discussed the attributes of God's image in terms of those he does and does not communicate through humanity. Those attributes that are said to be "incommunicable" are specifically withheld from humanity because they are what differentiates the divine from creation itself. The church has spent a great deal of time through the ages proving the deity of Jesus Christ through the evidence provided by the Scriptures. What better way to understand Jesus as fully God than to understand him as perfectly possessing all the incommunicable attributes of God as revealed through God's Word?

While the fullness of Jesus' humanity is necessary for Christ to be an acceptable sacrifice to God in place of humanity and for us to understand ourselves as made in God's likeness, it is equally important for us to understand the fullness of Christ's deity. It will be difficult for anyone to come to faith in God and have assurance of their salvation if they do not fully understand Jesus as God. The wages for our own personal sin are death (Romans 6:23). We cannot make the physical and spiritual payment for our own sin and then walk out of the grave and into eternal life with God. Eternal life is only possible for us if someone else covers the debt that we owe. Unfortunately, every other human that has ever walked the earth except for Christ has their own debt to pay and is therefore incapable of covering someone else's debt.

Who can possibly make this payment except for a perfect human? We have proven Christ is the perfect human. That may be understandable, but a perfect human is only enough to stand in the place of one human. Therefore, the deity of Christ is essential for us to understand. If humanity is to be saved through Christ, then he must possess the infinite worth of God in order to pay for the sins of everyone who believes in him. He must possess the infinite ability to endure and satisfy the full, unchecked wrath of the infinitely powerful God to cover the sins of all humanity through his death and still pull off Easter! If Christ is not divine (fully God), then we who believe in him are not saved. Throughout his life, however, Jesus proved that he was the Son of God and the perfect image of the Father.

What are the marks of Jesus' divinity?

The most obvious of his divine attributes is *omnipotence*. The Gospel accounts record the many miracles Jesus performed from turning water to wine, walking on water, healing the sick, casting out demons, feeding the masses, calming storms with the sound of his voice, and raising the dead. The closing to the Gospel of John indicates that there is not enough space in the world to contain all the books that could be written of everything that Jesus did. Jesus was also omniscient. He knew people's thoughts as well as events that would come to pass with incredible precision (Matthew 12:25; 26:34; John 2:19–22).

Jesus is also *immortal* and makes the claim that he will not only complete the seemingly impossible by rising from the dead, but he would do it by his own trinitarian power (John 10:18; 1 Timothy 6:16). In Jesus making these bold claims, he also makes the claim that he is sovereign over all creation. It is fitting that Christ claims this authority before he acts, completes the work he predicted, and then reminds his disciples of his authority in the Great Commission after he has proven to be true to his word in every way.

This gives the reader of the Bible confidence that Christ can be trusted to possess the other attributes that are unable to be recorded in the Bible but are still mentioned in the Great Commission (Matthew 28:18–20). These attributes are Christ's *omnipresence* and *eternal nature*. In the last verse of the Great Commission, Jesus makes the claim that he is both: "... and teaching them to obey everything I have commanded you. And surely *I am with you always, to the very end of the age*" (Matthew 28:20, emphasis added).

* * *

God-Man

As I mentioned in the Preface of this book, the only credentials I hold to write this book is the wondrous and miraculous work God has done in my own life. I chose to write this book solely because of the great work that God has accomplished in my life through the saving power of Jesus Christ and the redemption provided through the Holy Spirit. I have no platform that would qualify me or give me credibility to reach the masses with this book, and so quite honestly, I wrote it for the benefit of my family and friends. My hope in the writing of this book was to simplify concepts surrounding our understanding of God, which in turn affect the way we live our lives. Unfortunately, this section on Christ as the God-man is not one I can simplify. This section could in theory be simplified, but I am not willing to explain Jesus' dual nature (both human and divine) in simpler terms out of fear of making a grave theological error. Therefore, I will attempt to systematically describe Christ's dual nature as the God-man as I understand it.

The doctrine of the hypostatic union of Christ is quite possibly the most wondrous truth about the Lord Jesus. Quite frankly, I must admit that I do not understand it perfectly and am unable to unwrap it fully for the reader in this book—many books could be written on this piece of doctrine alone. However, I believe in the truth of it and because I believe that it helps us to bridge the gap between our understanding of the image of God with respect to Jesus Christ, I will cover it.

Put simply, the hypostatic union of Christ is the union of the human nature and the divine nature of Christ into one being. At first glance, this doctrine seems like something that most Christians have claimed to believe their entire lives, but when you start to peel back the onion on this definition, you realize there are significant implications contained within it. Consider these two Scriptures. The first was said to Jesus by his disciples, and the second was said by Jesus himself:

> "Now we can see that *you know all things* and that you
> do not even need to have anyone ask you questions.
> This makes us believe that you came from God."
>
> *John 16:30, emphasis added*

> "But that day or hour no one knows, not even the
> angels in heaven, *nor the Son*, but only the Father."
>
> *Mark 13:32, emphasis added*

It seems paradoxical that Christ could be both omniscient as God and yet not know things as a man while existing as one person. While it is an entirely different discussion, God's Word is inerrant and consequently both verses must be true. How can the human mind fully rationalize a being that possesses both a fully human and a fully divine mind? How can the fundamental limitations of human nature coexist with the limitless nature of God within one being?

Theologians wrestled with this concept for the first four centuries of the church, debating and rejecting heretical understandings of the incarnation of Jesus Christ, until AD 451 when the Chalcedonian definition of the hypostatic union of Christ was produced. It has largely been accepted as the standard definition by most church organizations including the Catholic, Protestant, and Orthodox branches of Christianity since that time. It may be of use to review the key takeaways of the council regarding the essence of Christ's existence that apply to the image of God:

1. Christ is both *truly God* and *truly man*, possessing a soul and body.
2. Christ is *consubstantial* (of the same nature/substance) with the *Father*, and *consubstantial* with *humanity*.

3. Christ is to be acknowledged in *two inconfusedly, unchangeably, indivisibly, and inseparable natures.*

4. The distinction between these natures is *not diluted* by the union of the two, but rather each nature is perfectly preserved and occurs in the *one person* of Christ.[1]

These statements of truth concerning the nature of Christ might bridge the gap in understanding seemingly paradoxical portions of Scripture. However, if you are like me, you would want to know how this is possible. I believe that the reason divinity and humanity can have communion with each other within the one person of Christ is because both Christ's humanity and divinity can be fully displayed without the nature of the other being forfeited. I understand this to be possible because of the *eternal nature* of Christ as the God-man. For Christ to be eternal, he must exist completely outside of time. This is not to say that he cannot enter time, but that he must encompass the totality of existence outside of time. To be outside of time means that the progression of time is an irrelevant concept to him. His eternal nature was not "paused" while he came to earth. He did not "miss" thirty-three years of eternity while he was on earth. His existence is simply ever-present. When it comes to time, Christ is before it, over it, around it, and after it. He is both *immanent* (operating within time) and *transcendent* (operating outside the material universe). The Alpha and the Omega, if you will.

"I am the Alpha and the Omega, the First and the Last, the Beginning and the End."

Revelation 22:13

Because of this, Christ, as the God-man, must be immutable. Change is a function of time, and a being who is ever-present cannot change. From my understanding, Jesus eternally exists as the hypostatically united God-man. Our limited experience and capability as human beings allows us to understand Jesus inside of time. We see that his hypostatic nature includes his existence in time for us to experience him, and yet he has also always existed outside of time. It is his nature as God to do so. As mentioned in chapter 4, God's eternal nature experiences all of time as the present moment. Even while Jesus was dying on the cross as a human in time, his divine nature was "at the same time" also present outside of time as well. This means that Jesus is (present tense) the same Jesus before the creation of the world, when he came into the world, and is (present tense) in his resurrected form as we *will* (future tense) experience in heaven. There is no beginning or end to Christ as the God-man—he is eternal, without beginning or end. We as humans are everlasting meaning our souls have a beginning, but no end.

As God, Christ must be forever outside of time or he would cease to possess an eternal nature, but Christ is not *only* God as we sometimes incorrectly understand God. As a human he can be inside of time as well, experiencing the limitations of humanity. Christ's humanity can be weak inside time, and yet he can still be the sovereign God of the universe who is outside of time. The two natures of Christ are not and cannot be mutually exclusive, because Christ is, always has been, and always will be the God-man. Christ's nature is like a Venn diagram with the left circle being eternity and the right circle being time. His existence, as made possible by the incarnation, is within the overlap of the two circles. We as humans are located only in the far side of the right circle and see Christ as God and man from inside time, but Christ also exists in eternity as both God and man in the far-left circle. This will be our experience of Christ when we enter eternity in heaven.

> The Son is the image of the invisible God, the firstborn over all creation. For in him all things were created: things in heaven and on earth, visible and invisible, whether thrones or powers or rulers or authorities; all things have been created through him

and for him. He is before all things, and in him all things hold together. And he is the head of the body, the church; he is the beginning and the firstborn from among the dead, so that in everything he might have the supremacy. For God was pleased to have all his fullness dwell in him, and through him to reconcile to himself all things, whether things on earth or things in heaven, by making peace through his blood, shed on the cross. Once you were alienated from God and were enemies in your minds because of your evil behavior. But now he has reconciled you by Christ's physical body through death to present you holy in his sight, without blemish and free from accusation.

Colossians 1:15–22

This eternal existence of Christ as the God-man has implications for us, both now as we are in time and for when we leave time as perfected beings in Christ. In time, his perfect humanity and perfect deity bring into perfect focus the image of God. We were made in the likeness of the God who himself possesses our same humanity in Christ. Christ is the image of the invisible God existing as a human being and thereby gives humanity an example to emulate in our lives for moral purity (1 Peter 2:21). We can confidently follow his words and actions because he is God himself and he lived a full life as a human being, experiencing trial and temptation beyond anything that we will experience (Hebrews 4:15; 5:8). All things, including humanity, were created through the same God that walked the earth and shared in our struggles. He is not a far-off distant God who arbitrarily demands that we act in a certain way to have the best life. He lived it and knows what the best life is!

As fully God possessing all the attributes of God and fully human possessing all the attributes of humanity, Christ is the example of what it means to be an image bearer. The pattern of the creation of humanity came from the humanity of Christ (Genesis 3:8; Hebrews 1:10–12). Our humanity as originally created, mirrored the preexisting nature of the humanity of Christ. He did not become human when he came to earth; he already was human through eternity past. We were created in his image, not the other way around.

And just as we have borne the image of the earthly
man, so shall we bear the image of the heavenly man.

1 Corinthians 15:49

As human beings created by and through Christ, we inseparably possess the image of God and the humanity of Christ. Through our own selfish will, as naïve children, we have all gone astray defining good and evil for ourselves. As indicated by 1 Corinthians 15:49, the story is not over yet. In fact, it is just beginning. As created beings, it is impossible for us to share in eternity past because we are not God. We must therefore have a starting point for our journey as everlasting beings created to enter eternity. Our starting point is this broken world—broken due to our sin—and redeemed in Christ as part of God's greater plan for preparing us for eternity. Not only that, but as we shall see next, the fall of humanity was *necessary* to accomplish God's will for us.

QUESTIONS FOR REFLECTION AND DISCUSSION

Why do we place so much value on physical depictions of Christ? Is the physical appearance of Jesus unimportant as it relates to God's image? Why? How is the image of God perfectly represented through Jesus Christ in the Bible?

What does it mean to be human? How is Jesus fully human? While Jesus *is* the image of God, in his humanity, does he also *have* the image of God?

What does it mean to be fully God? How is Jesus fully God? What are the marks of Jesus' divinity?

How is Jesus both fully human and fully God? Given the fundamental limitations of humanity and lack thereof in God, how can both natures coexist within the person of Christ?

In what ways does the perfect image of God, Jesus Christ, give us examples on how to live a morally pure human life? How does Jesus' humanity help us to understand what humanity will look like in heaven?

8

A Reason for the Fall of Humanity

*And we know that in all things God works for the good
of those who love him, who have been called according to
his purpose. For those God foreknew he also predestined
to be conformed to the image of his Son, that he might be
the firstborn among many brothers and sisters. And
those he predestined, he also called; those he called, he
also justified; those he justified, he also glorified.*

Romans 8:28–30

One of the most difficult questions for us to answer—"What is the meaning of life?"—is a question we often avoid altogether, because it seems impossible for anyone to answer with certainty. Limitless possibilities give way to doubt that we can ever truly know the answer before we die. Even from a Christian worldview, the understanding of life's meaning raises many additional questions that need to be resolved for us to be fully convinced of the truth of it:

- Who am I?
- Why are we here?
- Why would God create a person if he knew that in the end, they would spend eternity in hell? Wouldn't it be better for that person to have never been born?
- If the garden of Eden were truly paradise, then why would God place a tree in it that gave humanity the possibility to sin in the first place?
- Why would God create Satan knowing that he would rebel and cause immense pain and hardship for the rest of creation?
- What end is God pursuing for this world?

These are the questions that I wrestled with for some time, and the answers that I found led to the genesis of this book.

Even before I could rationalize these topics of theology, I believed in the truth of the gospel. I believed that Jesus Christ is the Son of God who left his heavenly throne to rescue humanity. The unfathomable change in my own life after I met Christ was explicit proof of this belief. Yet, the more I pondered the problem of evil, the more difficult it became for me to reconcile Christ's identity with the fact that God allows the *overwhelming majority* of people who have ever lived to face eternal separation from him in hell (Matthew 7:13). Is there really a greater good if such an inconceivable number of people are going to eternally perish? Many of those who will perish are just blindly searching for meaning in life, and eternal damnation, torment, and misery seem like too harsh of a punishment for most of humanity given their fundamental limitations and inexperience.

However unlikely it would be, maybe if you or I were in the

garden of Eden we would have made a different choice than Adam and Eve. Maybe our choices would have spared humanity from this state of worldly decay that we are in today. Would our descendants have made the same choice? Or is the choice to reject God an inevitable decision of spiritually immature beings? Yet, regardless of the choices we may or may not have made, we all suffer from the fall of humanity. In Christ, we are provided with God's solution to buy back what was lost in humanity from the fall. However, there are so many legitimate questions that we desire answers to before we can fully reconcile this plan for salvation in our minds so that we may fully believe it. Infant mortality, unreached peoples, people of different faith backgrounds that grew up under different religious influences, and modern science are a few areas in which many people struggle when attempting to understand divine punishment and the purposes of the Christian God. From what I can tell, the answer to all of them, including the meaning of life, are found in understanding the image of God.

* * *

Tree of Life versus Tree of Knowledge

In the garden of Eden, man and woman were in paradise. Or were they? In the Genesis account we are given a beautiful depiction of a sinless world in which humans were operating within the constructs of their design by the Almighty Creator. There was beauty, peace, work, love, and genuine relationship. God gave humanity free reign to do whatever they pleased. They were to enjoy creation and rule over it. However, there was one rule:

And the Lord God commanded the man, "You are free to eat from any tree in the garden; but you must not eat from the Tree of Knowledge of Good and Evil, for when you eat from it you will certainly die."

Genesis 2:16–17

The garden of Eden was likely vast in beauty and magnificence, but even amid the splendor of God's creation, the spotlight in the Genesis account is placed on only two trees—the Tree of Life and the Tree of Knowledge of Good and Evil. In their sinless condition, humanity could eat of every tree except one—the Tree of Knowledge of Good and Evil. A few questions immediately arise. God's creation was good, but was it good for Adam and Eve? Why would God place the Tree of Knowledge of Good and Evil in the garden in the first place? The tree symbolized the detrimental effects of disobedience to God, but it offered something to humanity as well—the knowledge of good and evil. To have this knowledge was to be "like" God in that respect (Genesis 3:22). The tree was the constant reminder that humanity must choose to obey God and deny their desire to live life on their own terms whenever they walked by it. This choice had both life and death consequences.

Did Adam and Eve even know what "death" meant when God told them that death would be the result of their disobedience? There had never been a death before, both physically and spiritually. Death was about as foreign a concept to the first humans as belly buttons. What could the promise of death have meant to them? It is hard to imagine them feeling the need to avoid that tree at all costs when the totality of their experience had been loving communion with God and abundant life. What wrath had they to fear? God had no reason to unleash his wrath on creation up to this point. Prior to their disobedience and taking the knowledge that was not theirs to take, they walked around naked like children without shame. Only when they fell from God's grace through their sin did they first experience the reality of their disobedience. This disobedience moved them to cover themselves with fig leaves and hide from God in their shame. Because of their sin, they were permanently banished from the garden of Eden.

At first, their exile from the garden may have seemed like punishment for their sin, but it was intended for their own good. We often forget that God is a loving Father when we read the Scriptures. The truth is that he loves his children, and good parents discipline their children in such a way that will benefit them over the long haul (Proverbs13:24; Hebrews 12:11). While Adam and Eve freely chose to disobey, the consequences of their rebellion served to protect them. Along with their sin came a corrupted nature. They could not be allowed to continue to eat the fruit of the Tree of Life, lest they live with this corrupted nature forever (Genesis 3:22). God in his grace shielded humanity from this unfortunate fate by placing them outside of the garden and guarding the entrance with cherubim until humanity could be brought back into right standing with God through Christ Jesus.

Some theologians have suggested that humanity could have attained the knowledge of good and evil if they had only obeyed God and not taken such wisdom for themselves through the fruit of the tree. Obedience to God was the requirement for humanity to continue to live in harmony with God, but I do not believe that obedience would have allowed us to understand the knowledge of good and evil—a requirement of a spiritually mature being as God desires us to be. The argument that God would have given humans the knowledge of good and evil in his own good time suggests that humanity's actions can thwart God's sovereign will. This is not possible. It is true that *God is fully able* to give humanity this wisdom (1 Kings 3:9). However, because he did not provide it to them in the garden, it is reasonable to assume this was not God's will for humanity.

To say that humanity could have acquired such a knowledge to be "like" God through obedience is to say that they forced God's hand to execute a backup plan when they ate of the tree. God does not have backup plans, however, because there is no being whose actions could get in the way of his primary plan. Everything that has come from the fall of humanity has been according to the will of God since before the foundation of the world, as indicated by Romans 8:28–30 in the beginning of this chapter. The fall of humanity was never God's "Plan B" for humanity; it was always "Plan A."

There are naturally some immediate concerns that arise from this way of thinking. If the fall of humanity was always part of God's plan, did God cause it? The answer to this is an unequivocal no. The fall of humanity could not have been caused by God, because God has no evil way in him to tempt or commit sinful acts. The fact that the fall occurred only indicates that God, in his sovereignty and omniscience, created a world in which this order of events could and would take place. The ability to choose to love God must be accompanied by the ability to choose not to love him as discussed in chapter 5. This order of creation was intended so that God may glorify himself through it, which is always the root of God's purposes.

The culpability for the fall remains solely with humanity, as it rightfully should. Even if something is part of God's will, that does not mean that immoral behavior is ever condoned. Nowhere in the Bible is sin excused by God, but there is justification for the evil that exists in the world. God works through evil to bring about his glory (Genesis 11:4; Isaiah 10:5–7; 37:36–37; 48:9–11). If God's greatest glory and good can be achieved through evil, then there is no contradiction within his character. If the greatest good is the end result, then God remains true to his name.

We must therefore accept that humanity was always going to eat of the tree, not because they were forced to by God, but because God predestined it to be so through the way he made the world and those in it. By doing this, God may subsequently call his people back to him through the eternally preordained role of his Son as the Savior of the world.

As mentioned in chapter 5, Satan was the first to sin against God. The Bible does not give us a timeline as to when or where this first rebellion occurred, but we do know from the Genesis account that Satan was present in the garden of Eden in his fallen state. If the fall of humanity was not God's Plan A for humanity, then what purpose could it have served to allow Satan in the garden among such naïve human beings who know nothing but trusting love? It sounds like nothing short of a disaster waiting to happen.

While we are currently living in the middle of the biblical story, it might help to look to the end of the story to see the answer to these difficult questions. In the book of Revelation, there is also a mention of trees as there is in Eden, but of only one type—the Tree of Life. John gives us a beautiful prophecy regarding the paradise that God always intended for his creation, and he uses similar language to that of the Genesis account. However, the Tree of Knowledge of Good and Evil is not mentioned. Obviously, humanity will have already acquired such knowledge by the time we have arrived in heaven! Additionally, Satan will not be present to tempt a once again sinless human being into taking for themselves what God has decreed as his alone.

> Then the angel showed me the river of the water of life, as clear as crystal, flowing from the throne of God and of the Lamb down the middle of the great street of the city. On each side of the river stood the tree of life, bearing twelve crops of fruit, yielding its fruit every month. And the leaves of the tree are for the healing of the nations. No longer will there be any curse. The throne of God and of the Lamb will be in the city, and his servants will serve him. They

will see his face, and his name will be on their fore-
heads. There will be no more night. They will not
need the light of a lamp or the light of the sun, for
the Lord God will give them light. And they will
reign for ever and ever.

Revelation 22:1–5

The Tree of Life that is mentioned in the book of Revelation acts
almost as a hyperlink to the opening of the biblical story. When
I read this description in Revelation, I imagine the same focus on
the Tree of Life as described in Genesis. However, this description
mentions only one tree. By mentioning only one tree, the Scriptures
paint the picture that resembles the beauty of the garden, but with
the possibility of sin removed—something accomplished by Christ
on the cross. In their fully mature state in heaven, humanity will no
longer possess the naïve nature that could fall prey to temptation as
they did in the garden of Eden. Even if there was a possibility to be
the subject of temptation such as in the garden of Eden, humanity
would never again fall into sin. The price that was paid for them to
acquire such a spiritually mature nature with the profound understanding of the knowledge of good and evil was far too great. Satan
will be eternally defeated, and there will be only one tree that will
bear fruit every month that is once again safe for humanity to eat
for life everlasting—the Tree of Life.

* * *

The Progressive Trinity

What exactly happened when Adam and Eve fell into sin and were
cast out of the garden of Eden? Often as Christians we use the

churchy term "sin nature" when describing the sickness that each of us inherited from our parents and can be traced all the way back to the garden. How does this nature relate to the image of God? The simple fact that humanity took on a sin nature way back in the beginning of the biblical story proves that the image of God was not complete in humanity. If humanity possessed a fully mature likeness to God, then they would have understood the moral implications of seeking their own way apart from the Lord; they would have already had the knowledge of good and evil. If humanity possessed a sinless nature, as well as an exact likeness to God in their endowed image, it would have been outside the realm of possibility for humanity to sin like it is for God.

The image of God described in the creation account was not complete in that humanity did not possess the fullness of God's image regarding the Trinity. It is true that to have the image of the Father means to have the image of the Son, which means to have the image of the Holy Spirit. The triune nature of God's image manifested itself in Adam and Eve by making them equal in being and relational capacities. We see this in that humanity was created equally as male and female to have relationship with each other like the relational capacities of the members of the Trinity. However, the part of the Trinity that was lacking in humanity's image was not in their equality in being because each of them possesses exact likeness to the others (John 14:20). Rather, the roles they assume mirror those of the Trinity. The Father is different from the Son and Holy Spirit because he *initiates* salvation for humanity. The Son is different from the Father and Holy Spirit in that he *accomplishes* salvation. The Holy Spirit is different from the Father and Son because he *applies* the salvation of the Son to those who are saved by sanctifying them and growing them in spiritual likeness to God. Now, as it relates to Adam and Eve, how are they to be in likeness to the roles of the Trinity that have not yet been accomplished in them?

God the Father declared it from the beginning that he desires to have many children, with Christ as the firstborn of them all. We know this because God bestowed us with his image so that we too may be called sons and daughters of God through adoption into his family at the completion of his saving, sanctifying, and perfecting work.

> The Son is the image of the invisible God, the firstborn over all creation. For in him all things were created: things in heaven and on earth, visible and invisible, whether thrones or powers or rulers or authorities; all things have been created through him and for him. ... For God was pleased to have all his fullness dwell in him, and through him to reconcile to himself all things, whether things on earth or things in heaven, by making peace through his blood, shed on the cross.
>
> *Colossians 1:15–16;19–20*

The image of God is perfected in humanity by the execution of each individual Trinitarian role. Those roles, while eternally set in place by God, are played out in time. For events to play out in time, they must happen in sequential order as experienced by those of us who live in time. By implication, we cannot understand the completion of these roles as beings who are still in time and in the middle of the process. In our present state, we possess a base likeness to the Trinity. However, when the roles that each member of the Godhead plays are brought to completion at the end of time we will possess the fullest likeness to each of them. Just as our salvation is contingent on Jesus' work on the cross, which happened in time, being conformed into his image occurs over time as well. We must be careful to remember that our current perspective on God's plan is far grander than our individual lives—we are a tiny piece of an infinitely complex narrative.

As stated in Romans 8:29 at the beginning of this chapter, being conformed into the image of the Son is something that occurs in our life here on earth. Adam and Eve were born with the image of God, but their transformation was not complete, and Paul affirmed this in his letter to the Romans when he stated that humanity must be conformed into the image of the Son in order to become the younger brothers and sisters of Christ. Being conformed into the image of Christ is to take on Christ's spiritual DNA, which humanity did not possess in the garden of Eden or even fully today. We are given this DNA by taking on the Trinitarian role of Christ, which is to honor and obey the Father's will—the same role that Christ embodied during his life and death on the cross. We are conformed into sons and daughters in God's image by following this same pattern. Through this beautiful plan, humanity has been given a way to be grafted into the family of God.

Throughout history and even today, some theologians have insisted that Adam and Eve lost part of their likeness to God when they fell into sin in the garden of Eden. I do not think this is a plausible reality. Rather than losing likeness to God in the fall, I believe that it is more plausible that there was something in humanity's image that was lacking that enabled them to sin in the first place. Scripture indicates the opposite of losing likeness to God in Genesis 3:22 when God said, "The man *has now become like one of us*, knowing good and evil." In reality, we became more like God when we fell into sin in that we came to know the difference between good and evil. However, we accomplished this through sinful means, which was why we were alienated from God.

As mentioned in chapter 5, it is outside the realm of possibility for God to commit an evil act—something that is fully within the realm of possibility for humanity. This is evident in the fact that humans continually sin. If humans possessed a full likeness to God, we would not have sinned nor would we continue to do so. We proved exactly how unlike God we are in our rebellion to him! God's eternal plan must therefore be to conform us into beings that are one day incapable of corruption, as God is incapable of corruption through the redemption of the fallen world in Christ. If Adam and Eve really had the full, complete image of the Son, they would have also embodied the perfect obedience of the Son to the Father and resisted temptation in the garden. Sadly, for them, this was not the case.

Therefore, to have a complete image of the Trinity, humanity must gain a sense of spiritual maturity to be like God in all aspects, including the willful obedient nature. However, to have the fully mature image of God, the roles of the Godhead must be brought to completion. The execution of the roles of God, in Christ, is that which bestows humanity with the fully mature image. Without the salvation procured by Christ and the application of it by the Holy Spirit, no one could ever come to be more like God. In fact, without salvation the entire discussion of God's image becomes irrelevant because we would all be eternally separated from him as we endlessly pursue our own image.

In being cast out of the garden, God initiated the first act of salvation for humanity and the possibility for us to be conformed into the image of Christ. To be like the Son, we must possess the sacrificial and obedient mature nature of the Son, but before this can happen the Son must first demonstrate this love to us through his own sacrificial and obedient nature. While humanity may have possessed a likeness to the Son in physical form (Romans 5:14), we did not possess the qualitative nature of the Son in spiritual form. This image of the Son was not attained in the fall, but it was made possible for us to receive it by being in a place that we can be redeemed from the fall.

The eternal role of Savior that God the Father appointed to Christ necessitates that Christ has a people to save. Humanity was created for that purpose—to be not just a people for Christ to save, but an entire race of people in his image. To deny that humanity was created for this purpose, one must first deny that Christ has always been ordained as our Savior. I find it fascinating that the Scripture quoted above from Colossians indicates that because all things that require redemption were created by Christ and for Christ, it is also the work of Christ that will bring humanity to the fullness of God's image that dwells within him! Christ is the reason for our creation, the reason for our rebellion, the reason for our redemption, and the reason for our sanctification. Christ is all and is in all (Colossians 3:10–11)! The incarnation of Jesus Christ and his death and resurrection has given humanity the way to become like God's Son through the work of the Holy Spirit. As we mirror the Son's obedience, we are transformed more and more into his image.

It is beyond comprehension that God would create a being that is capable of sharing in his eternal nature. The basic nature of created beings is that they are not eternal in the first place. The image of God is therefore not a completed mark of "God-likeness" when we were created, but of a naïve child who is capable of corruption. Except for the fact that we are born with a sin nature, Adam and Eve's fall into sin is like the way each one of us loses our innocence through our own sin.

To possess the fully mature image of God and to share in the incorruptible nature of God himself, humanity must go through a process of refinement in the way a sculptor meticulously chips away at a formless block of marble in order to create a masterpiece. The Holy Spirit is the sculptor, we are the formless block of marble, and the fullness of Christ within us is the masterpiece. The current state of the world that has been saved through the work of Christ is the penultimate stage of God's redemptive plan as we wait in joyful hope for the return of our Savior so that this sanctification may be brought to completion. This refinement process was never promised to be easy for us (John 16:33), but we should rejoice that as we share in the sufferings of Christ, we are conformed more and more into his image.

* * *

An Important Point to Consider

How many fathers would give up the life of their son for the sake of their enemies? Was God surprised by human rebellion and therefore *compelled* to sacrifice his Son to redeem them? Could he not just as easily have wiped out the earth, sent Adam and Eve to hell, and still rightfully be praised and worshiped by the legions of angels in heaven? Yet, this is not what he chose to do. Instead, God chose to send his only Son to die in the place of those who hated him. Why? This is so important to understand, because Scripture is clear that everything God does is for his greatest glory which is the only end worthy of God. Consequently, sparing humanity from deserved judgment through the sacrifice of his Son must result in God's greatest glory. If this is true, then what glory did God's deferment of punishment from humanity to his Son accomplish?

As God's image bearers, proper understanding of ourselves as humans is a function of our understanding of God. Because we are made in the image of him, we must first know him to know ourselves. However, there are facets to God's being that we can only know through his interaction with the fallen world. We understand that God is good, but this is only because we understand what is not good in the context of this evil world. Wrath, justice, mercy, and grace are attributes of God's goodness, but these attributes would have never been revealed to us if we did not first fall into sin. Because of the fall of humanity, God has revealed to his creation unique aspects of his character, and from this we can understand ourselves better in his image—an understanding that Adam and Eve could have never gained if they continued to live without sin.

The attributes of goodness that were demonstrated as a result of the fall are perfected in Christ. First, God's *full* cup of wrath was poured out on Christ (Matthew 20:22). While the wrath of God is evident in the biblical narrative and in world events throughout history, we have not seen anything close in magnitude to that which Christ suffered on the cross when God the Father turned his face away. Second, the justice of God was displayed through the sins of the world in that the wages of *all sin* (past, present, and future) were satisfied through the blood of Christ (Romans 6:23). Third, the mercy of God is radically poured out to *those who believe* in the work of Christ (Titus 3:4–7). Mercy is judgment withheld on the guilty. Since Eden, humanity has needed God's mercy and in Christ, God is merciful (Ephesians 2:4–5). Fourth, the grace of God was shown in that while we were *still sinners*, Christ died for us (Romans 5:8).

Because of Christ, we can now understand dimensions of God's goodness that quite possibly would not have been revealed to us had the fall of humanity never occurred. The requirement of God's perfectly just nature is punishment for sin, but God is also perfectly merciful and therefore must provide a way for sin to be forgiven. However, sin cannot be arbitrarily forgiven lest God impugn on his own goodness. Justice must therefore be served on *someone*. When evil is present in the world, God's nature as a good God is seemingly paradoxical. Jesus Christ removes any paradox in God's character by providing both justice and mercy. Without Christ, there could never have been a created order where sin is a possibility because God could not be both just and merciful. Without mercy in Christ, justice must be served on humanity and God then fails to be perfectly merciful—this is an impossibility. Perfect justice and perfect mercy can only exist in God through the perfect mediator, which is

Christ. Contrarily, with Christ the Savior, an unfallen world is an impossibility because he has eternally existed as such. The revelation of these attributes of God was made possible through the sacrifice of Christ and was orchestrated by God the Father to occur in this way since before the foundation of the world. It is the requirement of a wrathful, just, merciful, and gracious God to be what he is in the context of his creation.

It is important to understand that humanity's actions add nothing to God's character. God is who he is. His humble choice to allow his will to be accomplished through a fallen world allows his creation to better understand him. God's will for our lives is for us to be like him. As sentient beings, we cannot strive to become qualitatively like someone who we do not know. Our ability to know and be like God is rooted in our understanding of the person and the work of Christ. As we live out our faith and make God-honoring choices in a fallen world, we share in the goodness of God through Christ's sufferings and form in ourselves a character that will remain with us for eternity (Romans 5:3–5). The spiritual character that we form now while we suffer will go with us to heaven. When every tear is wiped from the faces of humanity and death becomes a distant memory, there will no longer be similar character-forming trials for us to face. In the trials we face, our character and faith are strengthened to be more like God. Therefore, it is imperative that we not discount these sufferings, but instead allow them to be used for God's glory, as Isaiah did when he was cleansed with the burning coal at the start of his prophetic ministry (Isaiah 6:1–8). We should take heart that the God of the universe thinks this painful, but purifying, plan of refinement in a fallen world is important enough for our spiritual maturing that he was willing to pay the *infinite cost* of his Son to buy us the ability to be like him.

> I want to know Christ—yes, to know the power of
> his resurrection and participation in his sufferings,

becoming like him in his death, and so, somehow, attaining to the resurrection from the dead.

Philippians 3:10–11

So, if his greatest glory is the end result of God choosing to sacrifice his Son instead of dealing with our sin in another way, a single question remains: Is God bankrupt from having paid the infinite cost of his Son for our redemption? In sacrificing his Son, God put everything on the line to save humanity. However, it is not possible to define infinite cost for a God of infinite worth. While the cost was everything to God, he lost nothing. On Easter, Jesus defeated death like he was always destined to do. Shortly thereafter, he ascended to heaven to be seated at God's right hand, but now he has a redeemed people to bring back with him.

Because God lost everything through the sacrifice of his Son, but also lost nothing in Christ being raised back to life, gaining back spiritually mature, perfected image bearers served only for God to bring glory to himself (Revelation 5:12). This is an unprecedented and ingenious act of love! While we add nothing to God regarding the perfection and completeness of his being, God created us in his image and placed infinite worth on us. To God, the infinite value of his Son is worth the infinite cost of you and me, and as the recipients of both the life of Christ and our own worth, we should be eternally grateful.

* * *

An Elected People

The doctrine of predestination, also known as election, is very difficult for some to accept. Simply put, predestination is the act of God choosing some humans to be saved and others not to be saved, based on the knowledge of God before creation. This doctrine has been highly debated in the church, because it seemingly contradicts the free will of human beings and the inherent goodness of God. The argument goes, "If God predestines or reprobates someone, then they really have no consequential choice in their life." This is surely not the case, which will be addressed below. As God's image bearers, it is important for us to understand and accept the truth of Romans 8:28–30, the Scripture cited in the opening to this chapter. The fall and redemption of the world was necessary for humanity to one day fully reflect the image of a triune God. Predestination is incredibly important, as it relates to this since it proves that God's eternal plan is not arbitrary, but rather a calculated decision that will manifest the greatest glory for himself as it makes possible our freely given, genuine love for God.

The question that I have pondered in my own maturing is, "If God chooses only some to be saved and inherit eternal life, then wouldn't it be better for those who are not chosen for salvation to have never been born?" It seems extremely unfair for God to determine that many will not be saved, that he knew this fact from before the beginning of time, and that he still chose to create them. However, if God is good, then it must not be wrong for him to create these people. Some argue that the responsibility for personal salvation must therefore lie with human beings. However, humans cannot save themselves. So God creates people predestined for hell, and humans cannot do anything about it. The argument goes around and around in our finite minds. To completely understand how God's sovereignty and human free will work together is beyond human capacity. Once we accept that God's thoughts and ways cannot be fully understood from a human perspective (Isaiah 55:8–9), we can then acknowledge God as the Bible reveals him to us and know that he will keep our paths straight (Proverbs 3:5–6).

No, we declare God's wisdom, a mystery that has
been hidden and that God destined for our glory before time began. None of the rulers of this age understood it, for if they had, they would not have
crucified the Lord of glory.

1 Corinthians 2:7–8

When left to our own understanding, we completely misunderstand God's purposes. We see this in the way the Son of God was
treated in his death. The world was so blind to God's purpose and
plan to redeem humanity that their limited understanding was the
very thing that God used to procure our salvation. Our spiritual
blindness is the very thing that led us to nail Christ to a cross. The
interesting thing about the passage above is that it claims that God's
wisdom is intentionally hidden from the world. Even in the Upper
Room Discourse, Jesus told his disciples that the world would not
accept his Spirit because it neither sees him nor knows him, but that
it would be the Spirit of God that makes known God's wisdom to
those who accept him (John 14).

Only those who have the Spirit of God after they have accepted
Christ's death and resurrection can truly know God's purposes.
Therefore, it makes sense that Paul would say that they would not
have crucified the Lord of glory. The Holy Spirit had not yet been
given to God's people to make known the plan for salvation through
God's Son. This is the key to understanding the doctrine of predestination. We cannot know God, his purposes, and his plans if he does
not first reveal himself to us. Even then, in our sin, we often miscon-
strue the character and purposes of God.

There are many alive today that still do not understand God's
plan for humanity like those in Jesus' time. The irony is that the
people in Jesus' day who were the furthest from understanding God
were the religious elite—the people who were supposedly closest to
God. They did not understand God or his wisdom, because if they

had, as Paul mentions, they would not have killed Jesus Christ who is the exact image of God (Hebrews 1:3). However, since the fall, humanity has been in a hopeless condition because of our sin. Even before we are old enough to understand our hopelessness, we have contracted a terminal disease with hell as our final destination.

However, indulge me in a hypothetical situation for a moment. What if for some reason every person on earth was aware of their sin nature? What if every unbeliever knew that the only way to be freed from their inevitable demise is through a Savior who, by nature, must be a human soul (see chapter 1), must be worthy of atonement (see chapter 4), and who is tempted as we are tempted and yet remains free of sin? If they understood this, then when Jesus came on the scene, they would have recognized his sinlessness, that he is the fulfillment of God's Law, and that he is God incarnate as demonstrated by his teaching and his works—that he is the only one who can provide atonement for humanity. If that were so, imagine how the meeting of the top religious leaders might go: "All right everyone, we have determined that Jesus is the Christ, the Messiah in which we have long awaited to eternally deliver us from our sins. Who wants to be the one to kill him so that the rest of us can be saved? Any takers?" (Crickets)

Fortunately for us, that is not what happened. In our sin, we refuse to see what is right before our eyes, and that is why God's plan worked. That is why God's plan was always going to work. God uses the spiritual blindness of humans and spirit beings (Luke 22:3) to accomplish his sovereign will so that we may receive sight. Because of our sin, Jesus had to go to the cross (Acts 2:23; 4:27)!

Some may say, "Well, it still doesn't seem very fair or just that God would select only a specific group of people to be his elect. What about the rest of us? What about those whom God used in the Passion of Christ such as Judas, Caiaphas, and Pontius Pilate? They were instrumental in God's plan unfolding as it did, so did they have

consequential choice to not be who they were predestined to be?"
My response to these types of questions is that it was not fair for
God to give up his Son to be killed for our willful rebellion, but God
did so not because we deserve it but because his character demands
it. However, just because his Son had to assume the role of Savior
to accomplish this does not take responsibility away from humanity for the conscious choices we make to sin against him—including
those used in the passion of Christ.

It was *willful disobedience* that set humanity apart from God. Predestination does not preclude our free will. Foreknowledge by the
God of the universe who is not bound by time does not change the
fact that it is the inward, willful choice of each human heart to accept or refuse the gift of salvation. Secondly, there is something remarkably interesting about the doctrine of predestination, which
can only truly be appreciated and understood from those who are
on the "predestined" side of it—only those who have gained eternal
life can understand the doctrine. Paul continues this line of reasoning in 1 Corinthians 2:9–10:

> However, as it is written: "What no eye has seen,
> what no ear has heard, and what no human mind has
> conceived" the things God has prepared for those
> who love him—these are the things God has revealed
> to us by his Spirit.

It is God's Spirit who reveals God's identity to us, the knowledge
of our salvation, and the knowledge of our predestination. Only
those who have accepted God can know that they were predestined
in the first place! Personally, never once did I wonder if I was "one
of the elect" as an unbeliever. It is a silly thing for a person to wonder anyway, when all it takes to know for sure is to accept Christ.
So, if you are not sure if it is you and want it to be you, how do
you become sure? The answer is this: Jesus said, "Come to me, *all*
you who are weary and burdened, and I will give you rest" (Matthew

11:28). How is it that God predestines only some, and yet he also says, "come one, come all"? It is because the invitation is for everyone. God in his omniscience knows that not all will accept it; therefore, he can write a statement of fact in the Bible that there would be only a select group who will be saved. That does not mean that God takes pleasure in the knowledge of those who will not accept him. In fact, the prophet Ezekiel specifically deals with God's heart agonizing over the wicked.

> "Say to them, 'As surely as I live, declares the Sovereign Lord, I take no pleasure in the death of the wicked, but rather that they turn from their ways and live. Turn! Turn from your evil ways! Why will you die, people of Israel?'"

Ezekiel 33:11

God is dying (literally) for every person to have eternal life (1 Timothy 2:4; 2 Peter 3:9), but he knows that not everyone will choose to turn from their evil ways and accept his Son (Matthew 25:31–46, John 12:44–50; Hebrews 10:26–29)! Free will reinforces the truth of election rather than precluding it altogether. Therefore, not only are the elect chosen by God for his glory, but those who are reprobated by God will have no one to blame but themselves for their own damnation! These people grieve the heart of God by failing to repent. Even amid their eternal destruction in hell, God's glory will radiate to all creation because of his perfect justice (Isaiah 5:14–17). So, what do you get when there is a God who *longs* for everyone to know him, who *knows* those who will and who will not accept him, and then *inspires* an eternal Word in the form of the Bible that is read by humans of finite understanding who are constrained in time? The answer is the doctrine of election.

If you want to be in the "club" of God's elect, then coming to Christ is all that is required. It is that simple. By accepting Jesus as your Lord, you will be given his saving grace, and the Holy Spirit will come into you and teach you that you are in the "club." It suddenly does not seem so unfair that God would have an elect group of chosen people, because the elect are only actually selected because of God's knowledge of their willful choice to be saved in the first place. Even the Pharisees, who hated God and killed his Son, could have accepted Jesus after his resurrection. If they did, then they too would have been predestined since before the foundation of the world.

There is no one that God would create for the sole purpose of eternal suffering. Each person makes the choice not to accept him, therefore removing all blame from God for a person's failure to accept his gift of life. This includes, as far as we know, Judas, Caiaphas, Hitler, Stalin, Saddam Hussein, Osama Bin Laden, Ed Gein, and any other person who, as it seems, did not choose to receive the free gift of everlasting life in Christ. None of them or what they did is beyond God's saving grace. In fact, Jeffrey Dahmer, the rapist/murderer/cannibal described in chapter 4 was reportedly saved while in prison. If you are one of the elect, you may find yourself standing next to him one day in heaven worshiping the same God of immeasurably calculated love and forgiveness.

* * *

Judgment Day: Every Wish Granted by God

Many people view judgment day to be the final point in time when God, in his wrath, deals out eternal punishment for disobedience on some and rewards for obedience to others based on exceptionally convoluted scales of justice. However, if it is true that anyone can choose to receive God's blessing of salvation, then is it not more likely that judgment day will simply be the day that God gives each of us the desires of our own hearts—to be far from God or close to him? I must be careful to point out that I am in no way attempting to diminish the seriousness of the judgement seat of Christ—that the sins of even the believers could be on display before the resurrected church. I am also not intending to diminish the reward aspect of the judgement seat. Rather, I am speaking in generality about the inward longing of the heart of each human being—a heart that either desires God or wants nothing to do with him. Heaven would be miserable for a person who has hated God for their entire life and continued in their hatred. God is everywhere in heaven! In life, if someone has chosen to reject God's offer to cover their debt of sin because they refuse to believe that they have such a debt, then God will allow them to try to pay it on their own in hell.

Yet, I believe that many people also do not have an accurate understanding of hell. I do not think hell is like the traditional understanding of it, being some kind of semblance to Dante's inferno described in the epic poem *Divine Comedy* where each soul is forever tormented in a manner fitting to their sins committed during life. It does not seem consistent with God's character to thoughtfully create a place of intricate suffering for those whom he created. This is reinforced by the fact that Scripture does not go into any significant detail on it.

Rather, it makes more sense that hell is a chaotic place where God, or any of his good creation is not present—forever. Every gift that is from God, such as love, joy, laughter, compassion, friendship, peace, beauty, and music will be absent in hell—forever. The things that come from rebellion against God, such as fear, shame, anxiety, despair, anger, jealousy, treachery, greed, violence, lust, self-indulgence, and sorrow will be ever-present and inescapable in hell—forever.[1] However, those who go to hell will only be there because they decided in their hearts that they would rather pursue the image Satan wants for them rather than the image that God wants for them. This is the reality of judgment day.

So, to those reading who have ever thought, "Eventually ...," this is written for you.

"I will eventually deal with my sin that separates me from God."

"I will eventually deal with that irritating urge to look into this faith thing a little deeper."

"I will eventually..."

This is what Jesus has to say about judgment day, and it does not have an "eventually" disclaimer in it:

> "Therefore keep watch, because you do not know on what day your Lord will come. But understand this: If the owner of the house had known at what time of night the thief was coming, he would have kept watch and would not have let his house be broken into. So you must also be ready, because *the Son of Man will come at an hour when you do not expect him.*"
>
> *Matthew 24:42–44, emphasis added*

Jesus will return like a thief in the night (1 Thessalonians 5:2; 2 Peter 3:10; Revelation 16:15). There is no place in Scripture that indicates we have time to delay in figuring out our faith. Anytime other than right now is nothing more than a gamble with horrific consequences. I do not think that Jesus will return today or tomorrow, but it is surely possible (2 Peter 3:9). I think that it is more likely that physical death will come for us before Christ. In fact, for the sake of those who do not yet know Christ, I hope that it does.

Like the impending return of Christ, death does not exactly come at a convenient time for anyone. *From humanity's perspective*, it does not consider whether we have had enough time to figure out our salvation—this has been determined by God's wisdom apart from our knowledge (James 4:14). You may not have cancer or another disease in which you can see an expiration date on your earthly life drawing closer which might motivate you to get your spiritual affairs in order. You could be hit by a car on your way to work tomorrow or be the victim of yet another tragic mass shooting. This is not intended to be a scare tactic I am using to get people to come to the faith; this is simply a reality of life. I do not think it is necessary to cite statistics on human mortality, because I am confident that the rate is 100 percent (with the exception of Enoch and Elijah). God has promised forgiveness and an abundant eternal life, but time for procrastination in answering the question of who Christ is was never included in that promise. In fact, Scripture strongly warns against it. The time for that decision is today (2 Corinthians 6:2).

Why do we say, "Eventually ..." when it comes to answering questions of faith anyway? I do not think it stems from disbelief in the truth of the gospel. Rather, I think we fear the implications of the truth of the gospel. If we decide to have the true faith as discussed in chapter 6, that means a major shift in what we value in life. If Jesus really is who he says he is, that means we must make radical changes to our lives. If we are honest with ourselves, that scares us. Many of us are not convinced that this change is in our best interest, because we are holding on to the cheap idea of life that we have built for ourselves here on earth. However, the reality is that true life is only found when we live a life according to the fullness of God's image.

If we are taken by surprise due to our own procrastination, whether by death or the return of Christ, it will be too late for us. On that day "at the name of Jesus every knee should bow, in *heaven* and on *earth* and *under* the earth, and every tongue acknowledge that Jesus Christ is Lord, to the glory of God the Father" (Philippians 2:10–11). On judgment day, every person that has ever existed will be raised and will acknowledge that Jesus is King, and it will not be a matter of free will to accept him. There will be no doubt as to who Jesus is—every tongue will confess it. He will be in his full glory with the full power of God and legions of angels by his side. No one will be able to deny or oppose him, his eternal Word will cut down every evil thing in his path (Revelation 19:15). Do not delay!

While I am not convinced that hell is a thoughtfully designed place of suffering, I am confident that heaven will be designed beyond our wildest dreams. In the Bible, Revelation mentions that the streets of heaven will be paved with gold that is as pure as transparent glass (Revelation 21:21). When I first read this, I did not really understand its significance until I thought about the picture that it portrayed. Gold has existed for millennia as the most precious metal on earth. The amount of gold that exists on earth is far less significant than one would assume. In fact, if all the gold on earth that has been mined up until this point in time were collected, melted down, and formed into a cube, its length, width, and height would be only twenty-one meters. That could easily fit inside a baseball infield. That amount of gold is estimated to be 76 percent of all the gold on the planet.[2]

Imagine if this amount of gold was divided over the earth's population. Each person would receive only a miniscule amount—a small fraction of the gold that makes up a wedding ring. Its rarity makes it so precious. In heaven, this "precious metal" will be so common that it will be used as asphalt to be trampled underfoot. In fact, to contrast a twenty-one-meter cube of gold to the amount of gold needed to pave the streets of heaven, one needs to know the size of the city described in Revelation. The New Jerusalem will be 1,400 miles in length and equal to that in width and *height* (Revelation 21:15–16).

Everything in heaven will be beyond our wildest comprehension. We will possess a likeness to Christ that will absolutely love everything about heaven, and we will wonder why we clung so tightly to the "precious metals" of our earthly life. Considering eternity, earthly precious metals are nothing of significance. Many of us refuse to believe that there is a God out there whose goodness is as scandalous as the God who saves. Yet, if there is a God who is worthy, should we expect anything less from him? So, to answer the question posed at the beginning of this chapter on the meaning of life, I would argue that our purpose in life is to know God and to glorify him by allowing him to conform us into the image of his Son. In doing so, we fulfill God's purpose and our destiny to share in the inheritance of the King of kings.

QUESTIONS FOR REFLECTION AND DISCUSSION

Was it God's plan all along for us to attain the knowledge of good and evil—even before humanity ate from the tree? What did the Tree of Knowledge of Good and Evil represent to Adam and Eve, spiritually immature human beings? What did the tree offer to them? In eating fruit of the tree, did Adam and Eve thwart God's plan for humanity?

How are we made in the image of the Trinity? As humanity currently exists, how are we not in the image of the Trinity? What are the three eternal roles that the members of the Trinity possess? How are those roles executed in time? Why is the execution of those roles necessary for God to complete the image of himself in humanity?

What does the fallen world that is redeemed through Christ demonstrate to us about God's character that would not have otherwise been shown if humanity never sinned? How do the trials we face in a fallen world strengthen our character and likeness to Christ?

What is free will? How do we know that we have it? Does predestination preclude free will or reinforce it? How do we know if we are one of God's elect that is to be conformed into the image of his Son?

As an image bearer of God, what is the meaning of life? In the specific circumstances of your life, what is your purpose—in your family, in your friendships, in your line of work, in your hobbies, and in your personal time?

9

Soul-Sending

Then Jesus came to them and said, "All authority in heaven and on earth has been given to me. Therefore go and make disciples of all nations, baptizing them in the name of the Father and of the Son and of the Holy Spirit, and teaching them to obey everything I have commanded you. And surely I am with you always, to the very end of the age."

Matthew 28:18–20

Imagine the experience of skydiving for the very first time. Whether you are a thrill seeker or not, what would you feel as you take that leap of faith out of a moving aircraft and free-fall to the earth? I am willing to bet that it would be much different than your current state of existence. When you make the jump, your sympathetic nervous system would completely overwhelm your emotional, psychological, and physical state as the flood of epinephrine enters your bloodstream. This is ultimately why people go skydiving—to experience the overwhelming adrenaline rush and heightened acuity of the senses. It makes them feel "alive" in a way that cannot be replicated in normal life.

While skydiving, a person's entire being is experiencing the reality of their life in a few short moments, but this is only because they are so close to the reality of certain death apart from the intervention of a parachute. When it comes to recreational skydiving, we place a great deal of "faith" in the reliability of our parachutes so that we may experience the thrill. However, it all comes down to whether our parachute is packed properly. The key to enjoying skydiving is obvious—don't die. With a properly packed parachute, our faith enables us to find that which we sought in taking the leap—the thrill of skydiving. But if our parachute is packed improperly, we will experience only a brief thrill followed by sheer terror and certain death. In a similar way, the message of the gospel presents us with a choice in life. In what or whom are we placing our faith to both save us from certain death and to supply a thrilling life?

Living by faith in Christ is like making the jump in skydiving with a parachute that is packed by a professional. In doing so, we receive both the thrill of an abundant life and an escape from certain death. Conversely, if we fail to acquire genuine faith in Christ, we are skydiving through life with parachutes that we ourselves have improperly packed. We may be experiencing what we believe to be a thrill for now as we navigate life by indulging ourselves with the world, but there is only one way that this jump will end—a reality that we would rather not have come to fruition.

Christ calls all of humanity to step out in faith and trust him for eternal life instead of trusting our own understanding of what "the good life" looks like. This starts by experiencing the thrill of this life by trusting him right now, and it continues into eternity. Sadly, we are often the skydiver who chooses to hold tightly to our ways and not trust that Christ has our best interest in mind. We believe the popular lie that we must look out for number one, not knowing that in doing so we are choosing to go down the road that leads only to death. God does not want us to pack our own parachutes in this life. The truth of living out God's image in our lives is this—if we are not ready to give up our lives by trusting in Christ, then we are not ready to truly live.

> Then Jesus said to his disciples, "Whoever wants to be my disciple must deny themselves and take up their cross and follow me. For whoever wants to save their life will lose it, but whoever loses their life for me will find it. What good will it be for someone to gain the whole world, yet forfeit their soul? Or what can anyone give in exchange for their soul? For the Son of Man is going to come in his Father's glory with his angels, and then he will reward each person according to what they have done."
>
> *Matthew 16:24–27*

Jesus Christ, being the perfect image of God, was obedient even unto death. His claim, which he backed up through his resurrection, is that he is the way, the truth, and the *life* (John 14:6). As God's image bearers, we will experience the thrill of "the good life" to the degree that our lives approximate the life of Christ. This likeness to Christ even includes the same radical abandonment to the gospel and God's kingdom that Christ demonstrated in his life and death. A follower of Christ would be hard-pressed to argue that Jesus' life was not the fullest life of anyone who has ever lived. Every person, Christian or not, is seeking the best and fullest life for themselves—this is a reality of humanity's self-oriented nature. Are we going to allow the Creator of all life determine what a full life looks like, or are we going to continue to define it for ourselves? If we claim to follow Christ, then we must first admit that the fullest possible life a person can live is a life that looks like Christ's, which oftentimes is vastly different than the one we are currently living. It is radical for Christ to call people to this level of reckless abandonment to him, but the promised reward for doing so is far more radical than what we can hope to gain in our own strength!

Therefore, what would be better: to live an abundant life that closely approximates the life of Christ, or to live a life that approximates the status quo of a temporal, human perspective? Anyone can attempt to keep up with the Joneses, believing that life is found in the comforts of this world. The truth is, they will never have enough in their eyes (Ecclesiastes 5:10–11). Anyone can hit the bars every weekend, believing that life is found in the party. The truth is, they only do so because they are spiritually hungover and depraved and would seek to numb the pain. Anyone can have an average marriage, believing life is found in the security of their spouse. The truth is, they might be married and yet have never felt more alone, as true companionship is found in the abiding presence of God. These things that we place our faith in to provide us with the "thrills of life" will never fully satisfy. Those who seek a full life in this world apart from Christ receive the unfortunate results listed above, but those who place their faith in the Lord will experience the joys and the pleasures of the Lord forever.

> You make known to me the path of life; you will fill
> me with joy in your presence, with eternal pleasures
> at your right hand.
>
> *Psalm 16:11*

In our search for identity and purpose in this life, we as Christians have undeniable proof that we are made in the image of the God of love. Since before creation, God has predestined us to be conformed into the image of his Son so that we may share in his Son's inheritance and life. As sons and daughters, we are to live according to the purposes of our God and Father, which is to help build the ever-expanding, never-relenting kingdom of God. We are blessed to have the opportunity to share in the building of God's kingdom as our souls are sent out into a world that does not yet know the one true God of the universe. This chapter will explore a few of the many ways that we as Christians can best approximate the image of God in our lives as humble servants of Christ Jesus. In learning to trust Jesus with our life, as we would trust a properly packed parachute in skydiving, we will experience the thrill of an abundant life here on earth and throughout eternity.

* * *

Seek First His Kingdom

In American life, most of our days are spent on only a few things: sleeping, eating, working, childcare, household necessities, driving, and leisure activities. In fact, according to the annual Time Use Survey conducted by the Bureau of Labor Statistics, the first five of those activities consume 18.8 hours of our day alone.[1] If we examine our daily lives, it is quite clear that there is not much margin with our time. We are experts at making every minute count by spending our time doing the things that are most important to us. Relationships are a great example of this. Think of the most important relationship in your life in the context of your busy schedule. Maybe it is your spouse, or your child, or a friend. How much time over the course of knowing that individual have you put into deepening your relationship with them? Probably a great deal, and that is why you consider that relationship to hold so much value. The intimacy you share with that individual did not materialize by chance but was the result of concerted effort in coming to know and care for that individual. Consequently, we can only have a limited number of relationships that are as deep as our most intimate relationship, because there is only so much time available to invest in them.

In these hectic lives that we live, how are we to find the time required to develop a relationship with God that is more intimate than our closest earthly relationship? Is an hour a week at church enough? Would it even be possible to have a more intimate relationship with Christ than we have with a spouse or our closest friend if we only spent an hour a week at church deepening that relationship? Based on common experience of our closest human relationships, it would not be possible. From my observations on our culture, our jam-packed schedules seem to be one of the biggest barriers for many of us to attain true intimacy with God. Many people even express desire to have a relationship with him, but the pressures resulting from other obligations often trump developing a deep and abiding relationship with God.

Most American Christians simply settle on being acquainted with God, using him as a spiritual vending machine when it suits them rather than God being their sustaining fountain of life. Is the burden of knowing God this heavy (Matthew 11:30)? Is God asking too much for him to be the center of our entire life when we have so many people to see and so many things to do? Many of us feel that we do not have the time to attend church, let alone the time to read our Bibles every day, to fellowship with other believers, to seek opportunities to serve, to pray, to witness, etc. How are we to attain such intimacy with God? Biblically speaking, attaining intimacy with God should be the easiest thing a person ever does. Let me explain.

As mentioned in chapter 1, the human soul is a person's all-encompassed life, and it was created specifically to commune with God in every possible way. Therefore, in the same way we prioritize spending time with those who are closest to us, we must also prioritize spending time becoming closer to God in the way we were created to do so. The good news is that deepening our relationship with God should not prevent us from meeting other obligations. Knowing God is to commune with him and to worship him through every circumstance of every second of every day. We cannot know who God is and what his will is for our life if we do not know and study his Word. Bible study is a time commitment, but in general, having God's image allows us to focus on our relationship with God twenty-four hours a day, seven days a week, for the rest of our lives. There is no earthly relationship that offers this level of access to intimacy compared to what God individually offers each of us, and yet it is wholly up to us to respond and acknowledge him.

> Therefore, I urge you, brothers and sisters, in view of God's mercy, to offer your bodies as a *living sacrifice*, holy and pleasing to God—this is your true and proper worship. Do not be conformed to this world, but be transformed by the renewing of your mind. Then you will be able to test and approve what is the good, pleasing, and perfect will of God.
>
> *Romans 12:1–2, emphasis added*

Seeking God in our everyday lives allows us to deepen our relationship with him. Communing with God is not only for church on Sundays, nor in our bedtime prayers as our head hits the pillow, but rather in the way we live our entire lives. We should not view our responsibilities that take up the 18.8 hours of our day as tasks to be accomplished for only the purposes of success. Rather, they should be used to pursue the kingdom of God and intimacy with him. In everything we do, we must "seek first his kingdom and his righteousness, and all these things will be given to [us] as well" (Matthew 6:33).

What good is it for a person to gain the whole world, and yet forfeit their soul (Matthew 16:26)? Success is not wrong, but if our success is more important to us than our relationship with God, then we have missed the rudimentary calling of humanity. Whether we consider our day-to-day activities as "just getting by," "normal life," or "success," it makes no difference. All these things we prioritize in our lives are but a vapor—here one moment and gone the next (James 4:14). If we spend our time focusing solely on accomplishment for the sake of accomplishment, then what is the point of our efforts (Ecclesiastes 4:13–16)? Are we any better prepared for eternity in heaven? Are any more people going to be in heaven because of our efforts?

As a church we need to encourage each other to transform our priorities from temporal concerns to eternal concerns that are focused solely on Christ. If it is God's will for us to achieve success in the world because of faithfulness to him, then so be it! The point is, we do not have to rely on our own efforts to achieve success in life. For sure, we should put forth effort in all that we do. At the same time we must place our faith in God, in all circumstances, trusting him to work through them to accomplish his will—whatever it is. Jesus teaches us that if we seek God's kingdom first, all these things that we worry about will be given to us in addition to his kingdom. Does he mean that everything *we are seeking* will be poured out abundantly on us in this life? Certainly not! Some may if they are according to his will, but to Jesus, our earthly lives are incredibly short, and not the end goal for *his kingdom*. Jesus brought glory to God by staying focused on God's priorities (John 17:4); therefore, we should do the same. In doing so, we are better able to glorify God in every circumstance of life.

As followers of Christ, we should let the world worry about security, success, and happiness. A Christian is not to worry at all, because they have a heavenly Father that knows everything we need, and he rejoices in giving it all to us (Matthew 6:32). He made the promise that we will be provided for with security, success, and happiness in heaven. If time were even a quantifiable metric considering our eternal security in Christ, then how small would these temporal struggles seem ten thousand years from now? Or one million years? Besides, there is a good bit of irony in the remedy to the pursuit of worldly security, success, and happiness. The anxiety that comes from the pursuit of such things will end at precisely the point that we stop trying to find them in our own strength. It is when our hearts are content with the security of heaven provided in Christ that we can chill out down here on earth. This allows us to use the day-to-day events in our lives as a means for us to seek first the kingdom of God rather than the kingdom of self!

This was an incredibly difficult lesson for me to learn when I was a new believer. My life seemed so different than what I read about in Scripture regarding what a properly lived faith walk looks like. It was difficult for me to see how every aspect of my day could be centered on my relationship with God. Eventually, I began to see how God's will really started to work through the circumstances in my life when I relied on his strength rather than my own. A good example of this is my work. As an AH-1Z Viper pilot for the U.S. Marine Corps, my career brings me a lot of praise. Whenever I spend time with family or friends, they always ask about the latest stories from flying and for me to recount my experiences in the air. If I am being honest, it is a pretty cool job. Apart from God, this career could be the pinnacle of my working life. There are not many jobs in this nation that are as cool as one that allows me to turn vehicles into crumpled up soda cans in a fiery blaze of American justice. If my ego were left unchecked, it would be very easy for my worldly success to get to my head, and I would begin to think too much of myself regarding my own abilities and strengths. I would begin to think that the success I have been given at this point of my life was from my own doing. The next verse of Romans 12 quoted above says this:

> For by the grace given me I say to every one of
> you: Do not think of yourself more highly than you

> ought, but think of yourself with sober judgment,
> according to the measure of faith God has given you.

Romans 12:3

Thinking too highly of ourselves and our abilities only serves to cap our potential as Christians (1 Corinthians 4:7). God has incredible plans for each of us, but they will only be realized in an attitude of humility. We must humble ourselves like Christ humbled himself before the Father in order to be of any use to God. In humble obedience to the Father, Christ set aside his eternal glory and came to earth to die for us and God raised him from the dead and lifted him up above all things. If we humble ourselves before God, then he will likewise exalt us (1 Peter 5:6) as heirs of the promise and sons of inheritance (Galatians 4:7). With God's help, you can reach heights that you never imagined, but it cannot come from pride in your own abilities—it can only come from the position of laying prostrate before the cross.

What we are doing may not always seem important to God. I could not have ever imagined how an attack pilot could be useful in God's kingdom. But here is the beauty of being made in God's image: I know that whatever I do, God has plans to prosper me (Jeremiah 29:11). While I am serving in this capacity, God is using my career to develop me as a warrior for his kingdom. I could never imagine that the God of the universe has plans to use an attack helicopter pilot, a career that preaches violence and death, to preach his gospel of peace. He has blessed me with an awesome job so that I am able to use my talents to enjoy *and* lead those around me to his Son.

No matter the field of work you are in, God has put you there for the same reason. Who can reach a lost soul in a field of work apart from someone who understands their struggles? A professor at a liberal arts school would probably have a tough time relating to people who fly attack helicopters. Likewise, we Marines who have a stigma for eating crayons for breakfast would probably not be able to speak into the life of a college professor—that is, we are better known for our brawn than our brains. We probably would not have the cognitive abilities or similar experiences that would enable us to relate to them! Nevertheless, both the Christian college professor and Christian attack pilot are called to seek *first* the kingdom of God and proclaim the good news of salvation in the line of work which God has entrusted to them.

* * *

Adore the Trinity

Seeing God as triune is essential to understand our purpose as his image bearers. If we are to live a life that is seeking God's kingdom above all else, then we must be sure to have the proper perspective on who God is and how he operates. We should use our understanding of the Trinity as the lens that brings the beauty and complexity of human interaction into focus. As mentioned in chapter 3, God is three persons of one divine essence. All three are fully God, and yet they function together in subordinate roles within their relationships. Therefore, since humanity possesses a likeness to the Trinity in this respect, our lives should be ordered according to these truths. As it is with the Son and Holy Spirit, God the Father should be the object of all our adoration and motivation in life. Jesus, the standard for properly lived out relationships, made everything in his life about glorifying God the Father. If glorifying the Father was the ultimate motivation of God the Son, it should be ours as well. In this way, we mirror the image of God best.

We must also remember that roles are not to be confused with equality. The current state of the world equates subordinated roles with lesser value. This is contrary to the value system in heaven; the last shall be first, and the first last (Matthew 20:16). All three members of the Godhead share in equality and worth, and yet they are all as different in their roles as the east is from the west. If we desire to bring a little heaven into our lives, we must mirror the Trinity in the way that we value all of our fellow human beings. They are all of equal status as image bearers and yet function differently in the roles they assume. This applies in the workplace, in marriage, in our friendships, and within the body of believers.

Additionally, we must remember that while God is one being, he is three different persons, which necessitates that we relate to him in three different ways. We cannot approach all members of the Trinity in the same way, because each one offers a different dimension to our relationship with God. God the Father sends his love and will, Christ the Son demonstrates and procures the Father's will, and the Holy Spirit applies the work of the Son to creation. Each person of the Trinity deserves equal attention in our adoration of God, and we must be careful to give such adoration.

Practically speaking, how are we to apply this to our spiritual walks? Prayer is the most obvious example. Our prayers should always be addressed to God the Father, because he is the ultimate object of our adoration. It is also the Father's will that each of our prayers must be aligned with for God to answer with a resounding yes. With prayer, Christ the Son intercedes with God on our behalf (John 16:23). He presents our requests before the Father, because he alone is our High Priest—the only person worthy to stand before God blameless and vouch for us. We as sinful beings are not worthy for even our prayers to be in the presence of God without the mediation provided in Christ. The Holy Spirit's role in prayer is to apply the work of the Son by interpreting our prayers to God (Romans 8:26). God's Holy Spirit searches the depths of our hearts and translates the imperfect groanings of our prayers into ones that fully represent our true requests. Have you ever been surprised by the way in which God answers some prayers in life? It is probably because the Holy Spirit corrected and polished your prayers into what you really need, so that God may provide you the perfect answer according to his good and perfect will.

In making the Trinity the source of our adorations, our eyes will be opened to the bigger purposes of God as we see him work in new dimensions that we never imagined possible. In attempting to mirror the roles and relationships within the Trinity, our lives will continue to grow in the image and likeness of God.

* * *

Remain in Community

Two are better than one, because they have a good return for their labor: If either of them falls down, one can help the other up. But pity anyone who falls and has no one to help them up. Also, if two lie down together, they will keep warm. But how can one keep warm alone? Though one may be overpowered, two can defend themselves. A cord of three strands is not quickly broken.

Ecclesiastes 4:9–12

In the military, we use a common saying, "Two is one, one is none." In aviation, it is most often used when briefing the other crewmember before flight on how aircraft malfunctions will be handled, should they occur. Many of the systems in our aircraft are redundant systems, meaning that if one of them was to break there is a backup system that, generally speaking, allows the aircraft to continue to operate but at a reduced capability. However, to better protect the aircraft and crew, we fly with the "Two is one, one is none," mentality—that two operational systems are the equivalent of one operational system and one operational system is equivalent to none at all. The result of this is that unnecessary risk is mitigated, and there is an overall increase in safety for the flight. In combat, depending on the situation, it may be necessary to continue with the mission, but the vast majority of the time we fly with this mentality.

As believers in Christ, we should approach our faith walk in the same way. We cannot afford to go at it alone without any "backup systems," or other believers in community. We are setting ourselves up for failure if we are alone in our faith walk. The image of God within us specifically possesses a disposition towards relationships and a focus on being in relationships with others. Having friends and mentors in the community of believers around you is essential to ensure that if you fail spiritually, you will have another believer to be your "backup system."

Many of us have friends that do not share in our faith. It is perfectly fine to be friends with them, but that relationship is not a viable substitute for having intimate relationships within the body of Christ. In the Marines, I have incredible bonds with my brothers and sisters in arms who are unbelievers. I place incredible value on these people and the relationships that I have formed with them. However, I have come to learn that there is not a friendship in this world in which I can be more intimate than a friendship formed from shared faith.

For a believer in Jesus Christ, faith is the most intimate part of us; therefore, anyone who does not share the faith could never truly understand who we are as souls bound for heaven. If the joy of our inmost being is Christ Jesus, then having no relationships that share in that same joy means there is no one who truly knows us. The surest way to feel alone in this life is to be unknown. If you have a faith in Jesus Christ, and you have no friends who know everything about you, including the one who saved your soul, then the devil has you right where he wants you. He delights in our isolation, and so we should do everything we can to remain in community.

> And let us consider how we may spur one another on toward love and good deeds, *not giving up meeting together*, as some are in the habit of doing, but encouraging one another—and all the more as you see the Day approaching.
>
> *Hebrews 10:24–25, emphasis added*

Christian community is essential for us to be conformed into the image of God. "As iron sharpens iron, so one person sharpens another" (Proverbs 27:17). Community gives us context as to what genuine Christ-centered relationships should look like. It brings to bear the true power of prayer when many people are gathered together, presenting their requests as a church before God. The Holy Spirit ministers to each of us in community through the other members of the church and the work that God is doing in their lives. Community provides an avenue for confession and repentance without condemnation, but rather grace and mercy, giving us the opportunity to learn and grow as we see the truth of God's Word come alive in our brothers and sisters in Christ.

* * *

Experience Joy, Not Just Happiness

How is it that Paul could be chained to a member of the Roman Praetorian Guard 24/7 while imprisoned, and yet still write so passionately in the book of Philippians about the joy in his heart? I doubt that first-century prisons were nearly as comfortable as those of the modern day, and yet if we found ourselves incarcerated, I would wager "joy" would not be counted among the words used to describe our experience. So why did Paul describe himself as joyful, and what was the root of it? For Paul, "to live is Christ and to die is gain" (Philippians 1:21). He was incredibly grateful that the gospel continued to spread despite his imprisonment, and that gave him true joy. This is not to say that Paul was always happy during his imprisonment.

There is a profound difference between joy and happiness. Happiness is entirely circumstantial. Good circumstances cause us to experience happiness, and bad ones cause sadness. If there is one constant in life, it is that our circumstances are constantly changing. This means that our state of happiness will ebb and flow as well. Joy, however, is different than happiness. Joy—deep pleasure and jubilation that is independent of circumstances—is a fruit of the Spirit that God bestows on his people, and it stems from God's inherent joy within himself (Galatians 5:22–23). It is a constant state for God, and as his followers who constantly have his Spirit within us, it can be the same for us if we allow it. Simply put, in the best of circumstances we can have joy, and in the worst of circumstances we can have the *same* joy.

Paul had incredibly difficult circumstances in his life such as imprisonment, attempts on his life, and even being shipwrecked at sea. Yet, the joy he received from God remained in him despite his circumstances. As the circumstances of our lives change, we need to remember God's ultimate promises and that we must place our hope in them to find the same joy. This does not mean that we will always be happy with our circumstances. Tragedies will occur in life, and we will grieve when they do, but our grief will be with the hope and trust in God's promises and in our overwhelming satisfaction in Christ Jesus.

Take delight in the Lord, and he will give you the desires of your heart.

Psalm 37:4

You will keep in perfect peace those whose minds are steadfast, because they trust in you.

Isaiah 26:3

In his inmost being, God is profoundly joyous. He desires for us to share in this same joy because he made us in his image. Rather than spend our days pursuing happiness in the ever-changing circumstances of the world, we should remain steadfast in the assurance of Christ to make our joy complete (1 John 1:1–4). As we focus our eyes on the author and perfecter of our faith, we must remember that Christ endured the cross to buy this amazing joy for us (Hebrews 12:2).

* * *

Pursue Freedom

A pastor at my church once said a simple phrase that has stuck with me ever since: "Jesus will never be just part of your life, but he will gladly take all of it." This statement is so simple and yet so profound. However simple it may be, do we live like we believe it? Put another way, "Jesus wants *all* parts of your life, not just some of them."

It should be quite clear at this point in this book that the offer that Christ makes for each of us is freedom from our bondage to sin so that we may experience abundant life in him. Nevertheless, freedom from such captivity is not gained by only partially surrendering our lives. We cannot treat Christ as a spiritual vending machine or good luck charm to make our lives better in some areas while clinging to sin in others—he will not have it, and we will not have freedom. Christ makes an all-or-nothing proposition. Therefore, freedom is inextricably tied to complete surrender. There is no freedom from sin apart from complete surrender.

So what does true surrender look like, and what is the cost of attaining it? Surrender to God is placing complete and total control of your life in his hands. A person could let Christ pay for every sin but their pornography addiction, because it is their only worldly refuge when life gets tough. They could let him pay for every sin but their greed in the pursuit of wealth, because they believe financial freedom is necessary to have joy in this life. They could let him take hold of every area of their life but their reliance on their Christian *religion*, because they believe that their works are what makes them acceptable in God's eyes. The reality is, it only took one sin to put Christ on the cross, so it only takes one sin that a person holds onto for them to continue to live in bondage.

Our response as image bearers of the King should be to release every area of our lives to Christ out of reverence for the work that he completed on the cross to buy us complete and perfect freedom. The cost of true surrender is our very life. We must first come to the end of ourselves to be in the perfect position for God to make us a new creation in his image (2 Corinthians 5:17).

In theory, surrendering our entire lives sounds like an easy thing to do. If we have a problem surrendering our lives to Christ, then we just need more faith, right? Wrong. I believe that the reason we struggle so deeply with our sin is because it is so amazingly attractive. On the surface, sin looks much more appealing and life-giving than following God's Word. The deceit of sin is that we will find life when we indulge ourselves in it, but the reality is that it only causes bondage and death. I am not referring to individual, random sins that we commit. These do not preclude us from true surrender—these will continue to happen until Christ returns. It is the repeated patterns of sin that we have indulged ourselves in for a long time that keep us from freedom.

These patterns of sin bind up our souls and are sometimes accompanied by addictive behavior. As difficult as it is, this kind of sin must be recognized and overcome. Habitual sin takes us further than we want to go, it keeps us longer than we want to stay, and it costs us more than we are willing to pay. If we are ever to be free, we must completely rewire the way our brains are programmed, or else we will continually fall right back into the same patterns of sin no matter how hard we try to be free (Romans 12:2). The first step of this hard rewire is surrender to Christ.

We know that the wages of sin is death and that the gift of God is eternal life (Romans 6:23), but how do we move forward in the pursuit of freedom in Christ when some sin patterns in our life seem so insurmountable? What do we do when we feel like we will never be free from some of these burdens? For me, I often wonder how I can have such a deep love for God and the desire to walk upright in his righteousness, and yet in my own weakness, continue to fall short in my struggle with sin like a dog that returns to his vomit (Proverbs 26:11; Romans 7:7–25). After trying to be righteous, I fall back into sin and then find myself crawling back to the cross in search of forgiveness. I pray to God for the strength to overcome when I am next tempted to sin. This cycle of sin and quasi repentance feels like the natural thing to do, and it usually works—for a short time at least. In my initial disgust with my sin, I muster the strength and resolve to walk forward in Christ's forgiveness and grace, only to find myself repeating the same sins shortly thereafter.

What I have learned from reflecting on these patterns is that I was attempting to overcome the power of sin in my life by relying on my own strength. I think to myself that Christ has the power to forgive and cleanse me, but it is I that must have the resolve to overcome my struggles with sin. Everyone knows the cliché coined by Albert Einstein: "Insanity: Doing the same thing over and over again and expecting a different result." Where do we expect to be led when we rely on our own strength to overcome sin? Our powerlessness to overcome sin is the reason Christ died in the first place, right? Do we think that because we have been forgiven, we will no longer be tempted in that way, or that we will no longer have an appetite for that specific sin? This half-hearted, self-reliant type of repentance always fails. Only in Christ can we experience true victory.

No, in all these things we are more than conquerors *through* him who loved us.

Romans 8:37, emphasis added

Experience and God's Word tells me that these patterns are in no way unique to me. Throughout my walk with the Lord, I have fallen back into the same cycle of indulgence in my selfish desires and subsequent purging of sin. The lesson I have learned through this is that the promises of sin are empty and fail to satisfy whatever appetite I sought to fill in the first place.

Why do we expect to find satisfaction in our sin anyway (Micah 6:13–14)? How can we as children of the King be freed from such agony? In this battle, I believe God is trying to teach us a much greater lesson than merely overcoming our sin. Gaining total freedom is a process that results from total surrender, and God will use the circumstances of our sin to produce in us a character more like his Son, Jesus Christ, who was fully surrendered (James 1:2–4).

Second Samuel 12 recounts a familiar story in which the prophet Nathan rebukes King David for his treacherous sin. In this story, King David lusted after Bathsheba, the wife of one of David's top military commanders, Uriah. After sleeping with and impregnating her, David attempted to cover his sin with a plot to have Uriah killed on the front lines in battle. While David's actions are by no means commendable, there is much to be learned from the way in which he dealt with his sins (namely adultery and murder), the bondage he was in, and the freedom he found in God.

The first lesson is that when David was confronted with his sins, he acknowledged and confessed them (2 Samuel 12:13; Psalm 51). He did not hide from his sins, but instead confessed them plainly, without attempting to defend himself or his actions. Complete confession is the first step to freedom (James 5:16). If we have not brought our sins to the light through confession, then we will continue to wallow in darkness.

While God was gracious to forgive David, the child born from the adulterous relationship with Bathsheba still experienced the consequences of sin and died seven days after birth. God forgave David, but still allowed him to experience the painful reality of his sin. Some wonder why the child was punished instead of David. In the story, David understood that his child was covered by the grace of God and would be in heaven to meet him (2 Samuel 12:23). However, would David have changed if God forgave him, but did not allow him to face the consequences of his sin? By taking David's innocent son, God reinforced the truth of the gospel in that an innocent life is the required payment for sin.

In the days leading up to the death of David's son, he spent the entire week in fasting and prayer to God as he pled for mercy on behalf of his son. At the end of the period of fasting and prayer, the child died. David's fervent pleading before God to spare the life of his child did not change God's mind. What God had in mind for David was much different than what David had in mind for himself. David sought to change the present circumstances in his life after falling into sin, but God wanted David to experience freedom from the flawed character that caused him to sin in the first place. This kind of freedom not only changed the circumstances of David's life, but also changed the entire trajectory of it. Gaining this kind of spiritual maturity was something that could only be learned though

272 - J. W. SAUERS, JR.

forgiveness, experiencing consequences of sin, subsequent submission to God, and acceptance.

How often do we become angry with God when his answer is no? David's surprising acceptance to God answering no to his prayers is amazing. Even as David pleaded for mercy, his attitude towards God was rooted in a firm understanding that God is sovereign—the mark of true surrender. We should present every request before God, believing he has the power to grant them (Philippians 4:6), but when God answers our prayers, we must be willing to accept his response. If the sin in our lives gives us spiritual agony and we plead to God to change our circumstances without first changing our hearts, then we have not truly surrendered ourselves to God.

To everyone's amazement, after the death of his son, David cleaned himself up, anointed himself, feasted, and worshiped God despite his terrible circumstances. Why do we often fail to pick ourselves up after receiving consequences from our sin with that kind of acceptance and boldness, never returning to our sin patterns? David never returned to his adulterous ways after this story, and yet in so many areas of our lives we are bound up, repeating the same sins time and time again. If we want freedom from our sin, we must surrender it all to God, like David did, through confession, fervent prayer, and picking ourselves up boldly in acceptance to worship God and subsequently rely on his strength to overcome, not our own.

If we consider ourselves followers of Christ, it is essential to understand that surrender is not giving God only individual parts of our lives to find freedom from our bondage. We are made in the image of God, and so the entirety of our life is what we are called to surrender. Are we willing to surrender everything in our lives during the few decades we have on this earth for an eternity of freedom with him? My hope is that by this point in the book you realize that the call to give the entirety of your being to Christ is radical, but the reward for surrendering it all to him is far more than we could possibly imagine! Additionally, the journey in this earthly life that follows surrender is marked by true life, joy, and freedom!

* * *

The Beginning of Wisdom is the Fear of the Lord

In aviation, there are two types of flight rules that pilots operate under—instrument flight rules (IFR) or visual flight rules (VFR). IFR are designed so that pilots can navigate the skies while flying in the clouds, whereas VFR are designed for pilots to navigate by seeing and avoiding obstacles or other air traffic. When flying in the clouds, pilots must use the instrumentation within their aircraft to navigate and remain oriented because they have no reference to the ground, the horizon, or other visual cues such as optical flow or motion parallax, which give them spatial awareness to inform their basic motor skills.[2] Because of these fundamental limitations when flying in the clouds, the pilot must be aware of the dangers associated with spatial disorientation.

Spatial disorientation is a physical phenomenon in which a person's perceived position and orientation in time and space differ from reality. Vertigo, or "the leans," is a specific type of spatial disorientation that pilots often experience when flying in the clouds. The vestibular system of the human body, which is in the inner parts of our ears, is an important part of what our brain uses to achieve balance and spatial orientation. However, when a person can see, visual cues given by the environment take precedent over the vestibular system—this is why it is harder to keep your balance when your eyes are closed.

When a pilot is flying in the clouds and there is a change to the aircraft attitude (orientation relative to the horizon), the fluid in the inner ear moves and then stabilizes, giving the pilot the "feeling" that the aircraft is in a turn, climb, or descent. If flight control inputs are made too slowly or too rapidly, the inner-ear fluids will significantly lead or lag the aircraft's actual orientation, which means the pilot's body is telling them they are in a steeper or shallower turn, climb, or descent than the aircraft is actually flying. This is a precarious situation because the pilot has no visual cues informing them of their actual orientation relative to the ground—only what their vestibular system is telling them. Sometimes the experience can be so severe that the pilot is physically incapacitated and unable to overcome the disparity between their sensations and what the instrumentation of the aircraft is telling them. They may be right side up according to their instruments, but they feel as if they are upside down. Because of how uncomfortable it is to feel like they are upside down, their senses are telling them to roll the aircraft right side up. Well, if the aircraft is already right side up and the pilot rotates it 180 degrees, now the aircraft is actually upside down.

As a helicopter pilot, I can definitely say that helicopters do not fly well upside down—they tend to violently disintegrate when this happens. How is a pilot taught to combat this extremely dangerous phenomenon that has killed so many people? The pilot must learn to *trust* their instruments. No matter what they feel to be the correct orientation of the aircraft, the instruments in the cockpit are telling the true story of reality to the pilot. From personal flying experience, I can say that vertigo is incredibly difficult to overcome. Nevertheless, choosing to ignore what I am "feeling" and instead trusting my instruments has never failed to save my life.

There is a way that appears to be right, but in the end it leads to death.

Proverbs 14:12

> Trust in the Lord with all your heart and lean not on
> your own understanding; in all your ways submit to
> him, and he will make your paths straight.
>
> *Proverbs 3:5–6*

When flying in the clouds, the feelings that pilots have regarding their spatial orientation is only reliable to the extent that it aligns with what their instruments are telling them. In a similar way, a Christian's perspective on the reality of the world in which we live is often incomplete and misleading if we do not have instrumentation to keep us right side up. We cannot fly through this life operating under visual flight rules, because the image of God is not yet complete in us—we cannot see and avoid everything as pilots do under VFR. Because sin is at work in us and around us, we cannot know the truth apart from God's revealed Word. Our "feelings" of God's will cannot help us comprehend the fullness of God's plan that is working through our lives, and so it is incumbent on us to trust his Word amid our spiritual vertigo as pilots trust their instruments. In doing so, we will live a life that is informed by godly wisdom.

The Bible says that the fear of the Lord is the beginning of wisdom (Proverbs 9:10). We live in a world that offers so much "wisdom" in how we are to go about our everyday lives. The reality is, no one can even come to the starting point of true wisdom until they develop a reverent awe of God's greatness. In understanding who God is, we can understand why life works the way it does, because we are able to understand God's purposes for creation. As God's image bearers we must pursue this wisdom, abiding in God's Word daily. In understanding God's Word, we are better able to understand ourselves made in God's likeness. Faithful application of godly wisdom develops in us a character and experience base that makes us wise, as we take on a greater likeness to Christ.

Adam and Eve chose to believe that they knew better than God and that God was not trustworthy—they did not possess the fear of the Lord. Let's not make the same mistake and define for ourselves what is right and what is wrong. The world does this and fails miserably at it. We, in contrast, are not part of the world. God has already defined true wisdom and has offered to give it to us so long as we earnestly seek to know him (James 1:5). Pursuing wisdom is the most basic call of a Christian. To be a disciple of Jesus Christ means to sit at his feet, learn from him, become overwhelmed by him, and become wise!

QUESTIONS FOR REFLECTION AND DISCUSSION

What does it mean to seek first God's kingdom? What are you seeking first in your kingdom? Is your relationship with God exalted above all else?

Do you seek to better understand the Trinity? What does each member bring to your faith walk? How could you improve your relationship with each member?

What are the spiritual benefits of Christian community? What are the dangers of navigating your faith without such community?

What is the difference between happiness and joy? Which one do you tend to chase more frequently in your life? Why? If joy is not circumstantial, then how does one access it? What is the root of God's joy? Is that also the root of your joy?

What does it mean to have freedom in Christ? What is a common sin that you commit? Do you think you could go the rest of your life without committing that sin? Have you tried? What is the root appetite for this sin? Is Christ enough to satisfy that appetite? If not, what needs to change in your heart for Christ to become enough?

What is the fear of the Lord? Why does the Bible claim that having the fear of the Lord is a prerequisite to wisdom? Why is abiding in God's Word daily a necessity in the pursuit of your ultimate purpose in life in God's image?

Conclusion

For everyone born of God overcomes the world. This is the victory that has overcome the world, even our faith.

1 John 5:5

But we have this treasure in jars of clay to show that this all-surpassing power is from God and not from us. We are hard pressed on every side, but not crushed; perplexed, but not in despair; persecuted, but not abandoned; struck down, but not destroyed. We always carry around in our body the death of Jesus, so that the life of Jesus may also be revealed in our body. For we who are alive are always being given over to death for Jesus' sake, so that his life may also be revealed in our mortal body. So then, death is at work in us, but life is at work in you.

2 Corinthians 4:7–12

As a member of the military, over the past ten years I have met some of the world's finest warriors. The men I am referring to are some tough and intimidating individuals. I have a few friends who are Navy SEALs, and to be honest, I would rather go up against the Cobra gunship that I fly for my job than get in a fight with these dudes. I have always been intrigued by the persona of real warriors. Despite Hollywood's dramatization of war and those who fight them, real warriors are often hard to identify when not in uniform. While some of my Navy SEAL friends are in incredible shape, they look no different than a slightly above-average guy at the local gym. The difference between the Navy SEAL and the guy at the gym is that they have incredible mental toughness and are masters at the basics of modern warfare—teamwork, marksmanship, hand-to-hand combat, innovation, and aggressiveness. It is not what is on the outside that makes a Navy SEAL so lethal, but what is on the inside. These warriors have mastered what is on the inside.

Similarly, in our Christian walks, it is the inner transformation to God's image that we should strive to master. Paul says in 2 Corinthians 10:3–5 that we Christians do not wage war in the way the world does.

> For though we live in the world, we do not wage war as the world does. The weapons we fight with are not the weapons of the world. On the contrary, they have divine power to demolish strongholds. We demolish arguments and every pretension that sets itself up against the knowledge of God, and we take captive every thought to make it obedient to Christ.

Much like the unconventional methods of Navy SEALs, if we want to be effective warriors for Christ, we must learn some new tactics to fight with rather than those used by the world. The old world is passing away; therefore, the old tactics are of no use in the war we fight.

Make no mistake my friends, we are at war with the spiritual forces of evil in this world. If we are to be victorious, we must be strong in the Lord—it is his power that dwells within us. We must put on the full armor of God (Ephesians 6:10–18), which is a metaphorical description of what it means to know God's truth, to trust in that truth, and to walk in that truth daily. If you are a believer in Jesus, take confidence that you are on the side of both truth and victory. God's Word is flawless (Proverbs 30:5; Psalm 12:6) and "sharper than any double-edged sword" (Hebrews 4:12). It is the foundation of our faith, and we must live by its truth in our daily lives to combat the world that wages war against us. As we do this, we are further conformed into the image of God's Son.

The Roman General Vegetius once said, "In times of peace, prepare for war." This sage wisdom should be followed by every believer, because it is inevitable that we will find ourselves in battle. In the same way the military prepares for earthly wars when we are at peace, we must prepare for war as well (2 Chronicles 14). Some of us are fighting spiritual wars right now, while for others it is on the horizon.

What have you done to prepare for this battle? What are you wearing into battle? Are you going into battle with the proper tools that God has given you?

> Therefore put on the full armor of God, so that when the day of evil comes, you may be able to stand your ground, and after you have done everything, to stand. Stand firm then, with the belt of truth buckled around your waist, with the breastplate of righteousness in place, and with your feet fitted with the readiness that comes from the gospel of peace. In addition to all this, take up the shield of faith, with which you can extinguish all the flaming arrows of the evil one. Take the helmet of salvation and the sword of the Spirit, which is the word of God.
>
> *Ephesians 6:13–17*

My fellow brothers and sisters in Christ, as human beings that possess the image of the Almighty God, we were designed to worship him in every aspect of life. Our purpose on this earth is to grow in increasing likeness to Jesus Christ. It is to shed ourselves of the old and become new and perfected beings. In this broken world, God is using the fires of affliction to mold us into mature, perfected beings who will one day leave this temporal state of existence to live in the presence of our Creator. Since the cross, Christ has been undoing in the hearts of believers the decay introduced at the fall of humanity. However, this is not for our glory. God is doing all of this for his glory and our enjoyment.

Amid the spiritual battle that rages around us, I pray that you see yourself as more than a conqueror in Christ Jesus (Romans 8:31–39). God has placed his mark on you, he is at work within you and through you, and he is coming back for you. In the meantime, pursue Christ, stand strong, and put on the armor of God so you may continue to do the good work of making God's kingdom known and display the increasingly perfected image of love within you.

God bless all of you.

Notes

Chapter 1: Soul Searching

1. Koukl, Gregory. *The Story of Reality.* s.l.: Zondervan, 2017.

2. Miracles and supernatural events are often used as opposition to this line of reasoning. However, when discussing the divine, we are by nature discussing something that transcends creation itself. It is reasonable to assume that if such a power exists to create scientific order in the universe, that same power could break or operate outside the laws which they created. In the case of the Christian Scriptures, the all-powerful being that initiates or empowers such events to occur is the divine—the only power that could do such a thing.

3. Strobel, Lee. The Corroborating Evidence: Is There Credible Evidence for Jesus outside His Biographies?," *The Case For Christ* (Grand Rapids: Zondervan, 1998/2016).

4. Jennings, Timothy R. *The God-Shaped Brain.* Downers Grove: InterVarsity Press, 2017.Hebb, Donald. *The Organization of Behavior: A Neurophsycological Theory.* s.l.: Psychology Press, 1949. 978-=0805843002.

5. "H7307 – ruwach." *Strong's Exhaustive Concordance.* Blue Letter

Bible. https://www.blueletterbible.org/lang/lexicon/lexicon.cfm?t=kjv&strongs=H7307.

6. "H5315 – nephesh." *Strong's Exhaustive Concordance.* Blue Letter Bible. https://www.blueletterbible.org/lang/lexicon/lexicon.cfm?t=nkjv&strongs=h5315.

7. Collins, Jon and Mackie, Tim. *The Bible Project.* [Online] November 13, 2017. https://thebibleproject.com/podcast/you-are-soul/.

8. Alcorn, Randy. *Heaven.* Carol Stream: Tyndale House Publishers, Inc, 2004. 978-0-8423-7942-7.

Chapter 2: Imago Dei

1. Ratzinger, Joseph. In the Beginning: A Catholic Understanding of the Story of Creation and the Fall. Grand Rapids, MI: Eerdmans, 1995, pp. 44–45, 47.

2. Jennings, Timothy R. *The God-Shaped Brain.* Downers Grove: InterVarsity Press, 2017.

3. Erickson, J. Millard. *Christian Theology Second Edition.* Grand Rapids: Baker Books, 1998.

4. Ibid.

5. "H6754 – tselem." *Strong's Exhaustive Concordance.* Blue Letter Bible. https://www.blueletterbibile.org/lang/lexicon/lexicon.cfm?t=kjv&strongs=h6754&ss=0.

6. Erickson. *Christian Theology.*

7. Smith, Joseph P. *Proof of the Apostolic Preaching.* New York: Paulist Press, 1952.

8. Weinandy, Thomas G. *St. Irenaeus and the Imago Dei.* Logos, 2003.

9. Erickson. *Christian Theology.*

10. Barth, Karl. "No!". [book auth.] Emil Brunner and Karl Barth. [trans.] Peter Fraenkel. *Natural Theology.* London: Geoffrey Bles: The Centenary Press, 1946, pp. 87-90.

11. Erickson. *Christian Theology.*

12. Keller, Timothy. *Prayer.* New York: Penguin Books, 2016.

13. Erickson, J. Millard. *Christian Theology Second Edition.* Grand Rapids: Baker Books, 1998.

14. Lapin, Daniel. *Thou Shall Prosper.* Hoboken: John Wiley & Sons, Inc, 2010.

15. "Evangelical." *Merriam-Webster Dictionary.* [Online] https://www.merriam-webster.com/dictionary/evangelical.

16. Lewis, C. S. *Mere Christianity.* New York: Harper Collins, 1980.

17. "Tselem." *Strong's.*

18. "H1823 – demuwth." *Strong's Exhaustive Concordance.* Blue Letter Bible. https://blueletterbible.org/lang/lexicon/lexicon.cfm?t=kjv&strongs=h1823.

19. Grudem, Wayne. *Systematic Theology.* Grand Rapids: Zondervan, 1994.

Chapter 3: The Image of the Triune God

1. Erickson. *Christian Theology*.

2. "Ontology." *Merriam-Webster Dictionary*. [Online] https://www.merriam-webster.com/dictionary/ontology.

3. Augustine. *De Trinitate*. p. 8–10.

4. Ryken, Philip and LeFebvre, Michael. *Our Triune God*. Wheaton: Crossway, 2011.

5. United States Census Bureau. America's Families and Living Arrangements:2018. *Census*. [Online] 2018. https://census.gov/data/tables/2018/demo/families/cps-2018.html.

6. Stoner, Peter and Newman, R.C. *Science Speaks: an evaluation of certain Christian evidences*. Chicago: Moody Press, 1952.

7. Piper, John. "Is God for Us or for Himself?" *Desiring God*. [Online] October 23, 1984. https://www.desiringgod.org/messages/is-god-for-us-or-for-himself--2.

8. Shorter Catechism of the Assembly of Divines. *A Puritan's Mind*. [Online] https://www.apuritansmind.com/westminster-standards/shorter-catechism/.

Chapter 4: The Attributes of God's Image

1. Koukl, Gregory. *Tactics*. Grand Rapids: Zondervan, 2009.

2. See explanation of God's relationship with time in the following subsection of this chapter for understanding on the use of quotations with the word "time" here.

3. As finite beings, time is a necessary component of our existence both now and in heaven. We will experience what is traditionally call *eternity* in heaven to the degree that time will never again be interrupted by death. However, the attribute of eternity is reserved for God alone as the only being with no *beginning.* Anything that has begun to exist, meaning everything but God, is subject to time and therefore not truly eternal. These Scriptures reference the state of human existence in heaven that prove we will continue to exist as beings bound to time—our lives will continue to occur in the chronological rhythm of time, one moment after the next.

4. For a further discussion of humanity's free will and how it is that consequential choice in the lives of human beings has not been negated by God's experience with time, see chapter 8.

5. Lewis. *Mere Christianity.*

6. Chapman, Gary and Green, Jocelyn. *The 5 Love Languages Military Edition: The Secret to Love That Lasts.* Chicago: Moody Publishers, 2013.

7. Hematohidrosis is the rare medical condition in which the capillaries that feed the sweat glands of the face rupture under extreme physical or emotional distress. This causes the sweating of blood as described in Luke 22:44.

8. Edwards, W.D., Gabel, W.J and Hosmer, F.E. *On the Physical Death of Jesus Christ.* 1986, JAMA, pp. 1455-1463.

9. A "check ride" is a term used in aviation for a formal evaluation of skills to certify a pilot under instruction to safely exe-

cute the skills being examined by themselves, or "solo" in the aircraft.

10. Lewis, C. S. *The Abolition of Man.* New York: HarperCollins, 1944. pp. 63–66.

11. For example, in light of the ubiquity of media devices and an annual pornography industry revenue of $13.33 billion (twice the size of the NFL), the rise in medical conditions such as erectile dysfunction in adolescent males from prolonged exposure to pornography is staggering. (See 1 Corinthians 6:18 for Biblical proof of this.)

12. Weiss, Douglas. *Clean.* Nashville: Thoman Nelson, 2013. (33)

13. Lapin, Daniel. You Must Provide for Yourself First, so That You Can Help Others Later. *Thou Shall Prosper.* Hoboken: John Wiley & Sons, Inc, 2010, pp. 153–154.

14. Rich, Tracy R. Havdalah Home Ritual. *Judaism 101.* [Online] 1999-2020. https://www.jewfaq.org/havdalahref.htm.

15. Stewart, Don. Why Is the Bible Divided into Chapters and Verses? *Blue Letter Bible.* [Online] https://www.blueletter-bible.org/Comm/stewart_don/faq/bible-special/question8-why-is-the-bible-divided-into-chapters-and-verses.cfm.

16. Ramsey, Dave. Giving Until It Hurts. *The Legacy Journey.* Brentwood: Ramsey Press, The Lampo Group, Inc., 2014, pp. 48–52.

17. Singer, Peter L. "Federally Supported Innovations: 22 Examples of Major Technology Advances That Stem From Federal

Research Support." Information Technology & Innovation Foundation, February 2014. http://www2.itif.org/2014-federally-supported-innovations.pdf.

18. Jennings, Timothy R. *The God-Shaped Brain.* Downers Grove: InterVarsity Press, 2017.

Chapter 5: What About Satan?

1. Lewis, C. S. Letter 8. *The Screwtape Letters.* Las Vegas: FAB, 2016, pp. 25–26.

2. There are different interpretations for this portion of Scripture. Some interpret this prophecy to refer to the fall of the actual king of Babylon, possibly Nebuchadnezzar, while others believe it be a reference to Satan himself. It is my belief that both are true. While the prophecies in Isaiah held to be true about the fall of Babylon, Babylon itself is used in reference to all people who oppose God (Revelation 17;18). While most of chapters 13 and 14 of Isaiah fit the view of Babylon's fall, the strength of the language cited in Isaiah 14:12–15 fits a depiction of the fall of the king of all people who oppose God—Satan.

3. Alcorn, Randy. Jesus, Venus, and the Morning Star. *Eternal Perspective Ministries.* [Online] March 29, 2010. https://www.epm.org/resources/2010/mar/29/jesus-venus-and-morning-star/.

4. Piper, John. Should I hate Satan? *Desiring God.* [Online] December 15, 2015. https://www.desiringgod.org/interviews/should-i-hate-satan.

5. Tryptophan is an essential amino acid that relaxes the brain as the body uses it when producing the hormone serotonin, which is known to cause drowsiness. It is not unique to turkey, as many would believe, but common to most meats.

6. For this this lie not be taken out of context, one must have a proper understanding of what it means to fully "believe." See chapter 6 for an explanation of *demon faith* in comparison to *saving faith*—they are extraordinarily different.

Chapter 6: Falling Short of Our God-Given Image

1. Lewis. *Mere Christianity*.

2. Schorn, Daniel. Transcript: Tom Brady, Part 3. *CBS News*. [Online] November 4, 2005. https://www.cbsnews.com/news/transcript-tom-brady-part-3/.

3. Horymski, Chris. U.S. Consumer Debt Statistics for 2019. *Lending Tree*. [Online] April 24, 2019. https://www.lendingtree.com/debt-consolidation/consumer-debt-statistics-2019/.

4. Horymski. U.S. Consumer Debt Statistics for 2019.

5. A mortal sin is a sin that is considered to be of such gravity that it completely severs one's relationship with God. The Catholic Church believes that if a person who has committed a mortal sin was to not seek reconciliation with God, they would face eternal damnation.

6. A venial sin is a sin that is considered to not severe but weaken one's relationship with God.

7. Spurgeon, Charles. *All of Grace.* San Antonio: Bibliotech Press, 2019.

8. Chan, Francis, and Danae Yankoski. *Crazy Love: Overwhelmed by a Relentless God.* Colorado Springs, CO: David C. Cook, 2013.

Chapter 7: The Image of God Manifested: Jesus the Christ

1. Grudem. *Systematic Theology.*

Chapter 8: A Reason for the Fall of Humanity

1. It is beyond the scope of human understanding to accurately surmise the reality of God's perfect justice in hell. It is my belief that however God determines hell to operate will be in accordance with his good purposes and there will be righteous justification for its intricate design or lack thereof.

2. Staff, USMR. How Much Gold Is In the World? Less Than You May Think. *U.S. Money Reserve.* [Online] July 26, 2017. https://www.usmoneyreserve.com/blog/how-much-gold-is-in-the-world/.

Chapter 9: Soul-Sending

1. United States Department of Labor. Bureau of Labor Statistics. *American Time Use Survey* . [Online] https://www.bls.gov/tus/.

2. *Optical flow* is the apparent visual motion that you experience relative to other objects or surfaces in a particular visual scene. A great example of your body experiencing optical flow are those times that you sit at a stop light and the car next

to you begins moving forward, giving you the "feeling" that you are drifting backwards. *Motion parallax* is the phenomenon that occurs when objects at a constant speed seem to be moving faster or slower based on the distance they are from the observer. An example of this is riding in a sports car versus a truck. If both the sports car and the truck are moving at 70 miles per hour, the person in the sports car feels as if they are moving much faster because of how low they are relative to what is moving quickly from their perception (the ground).